Evaluating Research

Second Edition

For Linda

Sara Miller McCune founded SAGE Publishing in 1965 to support the dissemination of usable knowledge and educate a global community. SAGE publishes more than 1000 journals and over 800 new books each year, spanning a wide range of subject areas. Our growing selection of library products includes archives, data, case studies and video. SAGE remains majority owned by our founder and after her lifetime will become owned by a charitable trust that secures the company's continued independence.

Los Angeles | London | New Delhi | Singapore | Washington DC | Melbourne

Evaluating Research

Methodology for People Who Need to Read Research

Second Edition

Francis C. Dane

Jefferson College of Health Sciences

Los Angeles | London | New Delhi
Singapore | Washington DC | Melbourne

FOR INFORMATION:

SAGE Publications, Inc.
2455 Teller Road
Thousand Oaks, California 91320
E-mail: order@sagepub.com

SAGE Publications Ltd.
1 Oliver's Yard
55 City Road
London EC1Y 1SP
United Kingdom

SAGE Publications India Pvt. Ltd.
B 1/I 1 Mohan Cooperative Industrial Area
Mathura Road, New Delhi 110 044
India

SAGE Publications Asia-Pacific Pte. Ltd.
3 Church Street
#10-04 Samsung Hub
Singapore 049483

Acquisitions Editor: Leah Fargotstein
Editorial Assistant: Yvonne McDuffee
Production Editor: Kelly DeRosa
Copy Editor: Erin Livingston
Typesetter: C&M Digitals (P) Ltd.
Proofreader: Jeff Bryant
Indexer: Naomi Linzer
Cover Designer: Anupama Krishnan
Marketing Manager: Susannah Goldes

Printed in the United States of America

Library of Congress Cataloging-in-Publication Data

Names: Dane, Francis C., 1952-

Title: Evaluating research : methodology for people who need to read research / Francis C. Dane, Jefferson College of Health Sciences.

Description: Second edition. | Los Angeles : Sage, [2018] | Includes bibliographical references and index.

Identifiers: LCCN 2017002662 | ISBN 9781483373348 (pbk. : alk. paper)

Subjects: LCSH: Research—Evaluation. | Research—Methodology.

Classification: LCC Q180.55.E9 D355 2018 | DDC 001.4—dc23
LC record available at https://lccn.loc.gov/2017002662

This book is printed on acid-free paper.

18 19 20 21 10 9 8 7 6 5 4 3

Brief Contents

Detailed Contents

Preface

Welcome to the world of research. Having taught research methods in one form or another many times over many years, I know that you probably are taking this course because it is required and not because you have an intrinsic interest in understanding and using research. Whether you do or do not have an intrinsic interest in research, I have written this text with you, the student, foremost in mind. My goal is to enable you to have the knowledge required to evaluate research and critically use empirical results as you attempt to engage in evidence-based practice in your profession.

I have tried to present the material with a style designed to pique your interest. I thoroughly enjoy research, the methods employed to produce it, and the application of research results to practice and policy, and I have tried to convey that enjoyment throughout this manuscript. I admit to a straightforward attempt to help you achieve that same level of enjoyment. For those who are thrilled about this course, welcome to the family; for those not so thrilled, I hope to welcome you to the family by the time you finish reading this book. Either way, I want you to develop a greater appreciation for the ways in which consuming research can add to our understanding of the way the world works and how we can enhance our efforts to improve the world, which is basically what practice should be—a way to improve the world.

Trying to convey my enjoyment of research is not the only aspect designed to make your mastery of the material more efficient. The running glossary is one example. The first time a new term is introduced, it appears in **boldface** type. Definitions appear in the text in *italics*, so you don't have to interrupt reading to find the term in the back of the book. Just in case you can't remember a definition and can't remember where in the text the definition is, there is also an end glossary.

This second edition has many updated examples of research that span a wide range of research topics and disciplines. Every chapter has been reworked to focus more intently on how to use research to engage in evidence-based practice. There is a new chapter on qualitative research and a heavily updated chapter on conceptual statistics as well as a slightly different order of the chapters to bring them more in line with the order in which you will encounter information in a research article.

Finally, I encourage you to contact me with your reactions to the book. I would appreciate any comments, good or bad, that you have about this book. Send an e-mail to me; my address is fcdane@jchs.edu. If you prefer to send anonymous comments, my postal address is Jefferson College of Health Sciences, 101 Elm Avenue, Roanoke, VA, 24014, USA. Compliments are always delightful, but complaints are the source of improvement. If you don't like something, let me know. I'll try to change it in the next edition. In the meantime, I hope you enjoy your sojourn into research. It really is exciting.

Frank Dane
Roanoke, VA

Acknowledgments

Although the author line contains only my name, this book was not written without considerable input from many different people. There are too many to list everyone, but some deserve specific mention. I am grateful to Vicki Knight, SAGE acquisitions editor, for seeing the realized promise in the first edition and suggesting a second, and to Leah Fargostein, SAGE acquisitions editor, who saw me through to the completion of the revision oh so very patiently. Everyone else at SAGE who was involved in the project also deserves a great deal of gratitude. They made the process of revising one of the smoothest, least trying, and most efficient in my experience with publishing. Please pay attention to the names listed on the copyright page and thank them if you ever run into them, for they, too, made this book possible.

The reviewers who provided careful, informed commentary on the draft also deserve thanks, for they improved the content more than I could have done on my own. They include

Pamela K. Barnes, Baker University
Macall Gordon, Antioch University, Seattle
Heather D. Hussey, Northcentral University
Sally Kuykendall, Saint Joseph's University
Janet Witucki Brown, South College School of Nursing

I am grateful to Dr. Lisa Allison-Jones, dean of academic affairs at Jefferson College, for her support during the completion of the revision, and to all of the faculty and staff in arts and sciences for their forbearance as time was diverted from their interests to this revision.

I have lost count of the number of people who piqued my interest in, provided information about, and generally enhanced my knowledge about, skills in, and experience with conducting research as well as my passion for communicating about research. There are too many to list, but I do have to mention Jackie Dane Fussell, partly because it was she who first taught me the value and thrill of satisfying curiosity, and partly because, even though she is no longer with us, I still can imagine her saying, "What, you wrote a book and didn't mention your mother?"

Finally, the greatest acknowledgment, gratitude, and thanks are reserved for Linda Dane. Her companionship, love, trust, encouragement, confidence, and all things valuable are without limit.

1

Introduction

*How can our intellectual life and institutions be arranged so as to expose
our beliefs, conjectures, policies, positions, sources of ideas, traditions,
and the like—whether or not they are justifiable—to maximum criticism,
in order to counteract and eliminate as much intellectual error as possible?*

—W. W. Bartley III (1962, pp. 139–140)

OVERVIEW

This chapter is an introduction to research. Like most introductions, it is a broad overview of what is to come. Admittedly, it is also an attempt to pique your interest. You
will learn what research is (and is not) and what the goals of research are. You will also
learn about a number of different research projects, projects that illustrate that no single research method is necessarily better than any other. Part of this process is learning about a general framework for understanding and evaluating research conducted
by others so that you may inform your own plans and decisions about professional
activity, programs, traditions, and the other aspects of life to which Bartley referred in
the opening quote. You will learn how the remainder of this book fits into the overall
approach toward learning about research and becoming an informed, critical consumer of research. Finally, you will learn how to begin searching for research articles.

INTRODUCTION

You may have a song (or two) to which you have attached so much meaning that you want
to stop everything when you hear it and concentrate on listening and conjuring memories
associated with the song. For me, that song is "Who'll Stop the Rain?" (Fogerty, 1970)

performed by Credence Clearwater Revival. For those of you who have not heard the tune, the rain is a metaphor for the confusions and mysteries of life. Somewhere behind all those rain clouds is the sun, answers to the mysteries of life. Although everyone has been looking for the sun, the singer continues to wonder who'll stop the rain. As you read this, you may be wondering the same about research, the course you are taking, and this book. What you need now is some sun, but all you see is rain. I'll try to provide some sun, although I don't promise to clarify the mysteries of life.

I need not point out how important getting things right in healthcare has been, is, and will be in our lives. I also need not point out that programs, therapies, treatments, and other things don't always work out the way they should; they often involve unintended consequences, are sometimes more costly than necessary, and occasionally don't do much of anything. In Fogerty's words, they can become "five year plans and new deals, wrapped in golden chains." Like noted methodologist Donald Campbell (1969, 1971), I believe understanding research methods will help you to learn enough to remove some of those golden chains. In our complex and rapidly changing world, we cannot afford to be armchair theorists trying "whatever" in hopes that it works nor can we depend upon others' opinions, however well considered, as we search for understanding and try to make the world a better place. We need to use research to sort what we already have as well as to point the way to more useful treatments and programs. But incorporating research into our everyday, professional behavior must involve more than accepting on faith what "the experts" write. The plethora of dissemination outlets for research reports enables just about anyone to claim to have published a scientific report, often without any review, so we can no longer count on the experts to be, well, experts. We need to become experts ourselves, not in conducting research but in critically evaluating research done by others so that we can determine whether or not that research is good enough to apply to and incorporate in to our professional activities. Without the ability to read research critically, we cannot truly engage in evidence-based practice (APA Presidential Task Force on Evidence-Based Practice, 2006; Sackett, Straus, Richardson, Rosenberg, & Haynes, 2000).

Therefore, this book is about research: what it is, how to evaluate it, how to tell people about it, and how to use it. It is about trying to find an answer to the question posed by Bartley, and it is about stopping Fogerty's rain. As you read further, you will come to realize that research is one of the means by which people avoid making intellectual errors. That is, research is a part of life, a particularly exciting part of life that involves trying to discover the whys and wherefores of the world in which we live. As you learn about research, I hope you will also have some fun and maybe, just maybe, you might even find the sun.

Definitions

It is always best to start at the beginning when attempting to learn a new topic, and for research, that beginning is a definition of research. Unfortunately, it is not easy to arrive at a single definition of research. The online edition of the Oxford English Dictionary (http://www.OED.com) includes the definition "systematic investigation or inquiry aimed at contributing to knowledge of a theory, topic, etc., by careful consideration, observation, or study of a subject." I have always liked Kerlinger's (1973) definition: "systematic, controlled, empirical, and critical investigation of hypothetical propositions about the presumed relationships among natural phenomena" (p. 11). Both of these definitions, however, are a little too restrictive for me, because research is not always systematic and it is not always careful and controlled. The more systematic and controlled research is, the better it is, but even poor research is still research.

When it comes down to what is important, the definition of research is rather simple. **Research** is *a critical process for asking and attempting to answer questions about the world.* Sometimes asking and attempting to answer questions involves a questionnaire, sometimes an interview, sometimes an experiment, and sometimes an entirely different method. Simple definitions, however, can be misleading. There is more to research than its definition, or this would be the last page of the book.

Research, as a critical process, is one of the tools we use to achieve Bartley's state of maximum criticism. We do so not by pointing out only negative qualities of a particular topic but by examining all of its qualities—good, bad, or indifferent. Regardless of the condition(s) to which our practice is brought to bear, the ultimate subject of our criticism is human behavior, something about which all of us already know a great deal. That knowledge, however, can sometimes get in our way. If, for example, we fail to examine critically some aspect of human behavior because "everyone knows it is true," then we have fallen short of the goal of evidence-based practice. We should, instead, be like a little child who continually asks "Why?" Of course, we are more sophisticated than little children, but we need to return to research to evaluate the answers we obtain to our questions. As critical questioners, we need not believe every answer we obtain. For that matter, research enables us to ascertain whether or not we have even asked the appropriate question.

One of the appropriate questions we must ask is, simply, "Why pay any attention to research?" To answer this, we must make a brief foray into **epistemology**, *the study of the nature of knowledge, of how we know what we know.* In the late 19th century, Charles Peirce (1877) codified the four primary methods we use to decide how we know what we know: (1) a priori method, (2) authority, (3) tradition, and (4) science. As we consider each of the four methods, keep in mind that there are questions that are more amenable to one of these methods than another; no method of knowing is best for all questions.

Also known as logic, intuition, and sometimes faith, the **a priori method** *defines knowledge as anything that appears to make sense, to be reasonable.* There are some advantages to the a priori method, not the least of which is the ease with which we can develop certainty or relieve ourselves of doubt. Thus, Descartes (1637/1993) employed the a priori method to arrive at his famous decision about how he could be certain that he was real, that he (and the rest of us) existed: *cogito ergo sum.* As you might suspect, developing certainty is also the chief disadvantage of the a priori method; it is all too easy to close enquiry prematurely because we hit upon a reasonable answer. Thus, many people are certain that most medieval people believed the earth was flat (Russell, 1991), some are certain that aliens from outer space have abducted people (Carroll, 2005), and others are certain that the best way to prevent teen pregnancy is by teaching abstinence (O'Donnell et al., 2007). Like all of the other methods of inquiry, the a priori method does not guarantee that the knowledge developed will be useful knowledge. The quality of knowledge derived in this way is a function of the quality of the reasoning employed by the individual producing the knowledge.

In the context of epistemology, **authority** involves *believing something because the source of the knowledge is accepted as inherently truthful*. As children, for example, we believed our parents. Sometimes the belief was correctly placed—stove burners can be hot—and sometimes not—tooth fairies do not exchange our baby teeth for money or prizes. As adults, we rely on authority as an epistemological method when we accept an expert's conclusion simply because the person is an expert. This can lead to positive outcomes, such as a much-needed prescription for hypertension medication, or it can lead to negative outcomes, such as sterilizing people because they are "mentally defective" (Gejman & Weilbaecher, 2002). When we rely on authority for knowledge, the quality of the knowledge rests upon the quality of the authority.

Tradition involves *believing something because of historical precedent or because it has always been believed*. For example, we tend to eat oysters only in months that include an "r" in the name. The reasoning is sound; warmer weather makes safe storage and transportation more difficult, and bacteria are more plentiful in warmer water (Miliotis & Watkins, 2005), but rapid refrigeration at harvest makes the tradition less important now than it was before such techniques were developed. A very different tradition, shaking hands when meeting someone, may have its roots in demonstrating that one is not capable of holding or reaching for a weapon (Morris, 1971). Such concerns are not as relevant as they once were, but the tradition continues with a very different rationale. We now believe we can determine someone's personality from his or her handshake, and we use that belief to project a desired impression of ourselves (Chaplin, Phillips, Brown, Cianton, & Stein, 2000). We continue to engage in the behavior because "we've always done it that way" and to believe knowledge is produced from the tradition, even when the original reasons no longer make sense. Thus, what we know from tradition may be useful but only as long as the reasons for the tradition are valid.

Science, *the process of using systematic, empirical observation to improve theories about phenomena based on a set of rules that defines what is acceptable knowledge*, enables us to develop knowledge by testing our explanations of the world against what we can observe in the world. For example, we know that training nurses in advanced cardiac life support techniques (ACLS) increases the success of in-hospital cardiopulmonary resuscitation about fourfold (Dane, Russell-Lindgren, Parish, Durham, & Brown, 2000). The researchers systematically compared the resuscitation outcomes of people who were discovered to be in distress by an ACLS-trained nurse with the outcomes of people who

TABLE 1.1   A Summary of Epistemological Methods

Method	Process for Establishing Knowledge, Deciding What Is Truthful
A priori	Accepting information because it makes sense or is reasonable through the application either of intuition or deductive logic
Authority	Accepting information because the source is believed to be inherently truthful or knowledgeable
Tradition	Accepting information because it has always been accepted; historical precedent in one's family, government, society, culture, or other socialization unit
Science	Accepting information because it was obtained through systematic, empirical observation

were discovered by a nurse not yet trained in ACLS. Prior to that study, many people believed ACLS training for nurses would benefit patients who required resuscitation, but that explanation was not tested. Unlike other ways of knowing, however, science includes continual testing of explanations. As you will learn in the next chapter, no theory is ever accepted as true, never again to be examined. Similarly, science continues to develop new questions based on obtained answers. For example, other researchers have demonstrated that nurses trained in ACLS are as capable of leading a resuscitation attempt as are physicians (Gilligan et al., 2005). Thus, while the knowledge we obtain from science is only as good as the data generated from research, the continual generation of data serves to produce an accumulation of knowledge in which misinterpretations of data are corrected instead of perpetuated.

In summary, the four different ways of knowing are equally useful, depending upon the questions being asked and the knowledge desired. (See Table 1.1 for a summary of epistemological methods.) Science cannot, for example, determine how we can know we are real, and a priori reasoning cannot determine whether ACLS training for nurses prolongs lives. Science cannot explain why we began to shake hands, but tradition cannot determine whether or not we can learn something about a person's personality by shaking his or her hand. Science is best used to gain knowledge about empirically testable ideas or explanations. That covers an extremely large number of phenomena but does not cover all phenomena. I hope to convince you that science, through empirical research, is an effective way to make decisions about the utility of what we do as professionals.

GOALS OF RESEARCH

The ultimate goals of research are to formulate questions about testable phenomena and to find answers to those questions. Nestled within these are other goals toward which researchers strive. No one can ask all of the questions and no one can find all of the answers to even a single question, so researchers need to find some way to organize what we attempt to do. The immediate goals of research—exploration, description, prediction, explanation, and action—provide us with an organization for how to evaluate research.

Exploration

Exploratory research *involves an attempt to determine whether or not a phenomenon exists.* It is used to answer questions of the general form, "Does X happen?" Exploratory research may be very simple, such as noting whether men or women (or boys or girls) are more likely to sit toward the front of a classroom. If one or the other gender does sit in front more often, then we may have discovered a social phenomenon that merits further investigation (Okpala, 1996). More recently, Elmer et al. (2015) used a registry of intensive-care patients who had to be reintubated during the course of their treatment to investigate whether or not complications were different and/or more numerous for the first compared to the last intubation. They did find that complications were more frequent with the last intubation. Their discussion section contains some material regarding potential reasons for this difference, but they and other researchers will have to conduct considerably more research as they follow up on this finding.

Exploratory research may also be very complex, and sometimes the object of exploratory research is the research process itself. For example, building upon Durkheim's (1951/1897) and many other researchers' work on suicide, Jacobs (1967) noted that researchers were generally failing to consider an important source of information about suicide—the notes left behind by those who committed the act. His analysis of the content of such notes revealed that many people valued some degree of uncertainty in their lives. Specifically, people who wrote the notes appeared to prefer the uncertainty of death to the certainty that life would continue to become worse.

Regardless of the topic of exploratory research, the basic question addressed by the researchers involves whether or not something exists or is happening. A myriad of questions usually follow the initial finding, but those additional questions do not detract from the finding per se. Even though they, and we, cannot yet explain why last intubations tend to involve more complications than first intubations, Elmer et al.'s (2015) finding, like those of all exploratory research, needs to be somehow incorporated into the understanding and practice of those who may deal with patients who need to be reintubated.

Description

Descriptive research *involves examining a phenomenon to characterize it more fully or to differentiate it from other phenomena.* Munsterberg (1913), for example, began his inquiries into the consistency and accuracy of eyewitness testimony after wondering about his own perceptions following a burglary at his home. He wondered why he thought, and testified, that the burglars had broken through a basement window when they had actually forced open a door. Since he first questioned his own perceptions and began conducting systematic research on the topic, a number of researchers have been investigating eyewitness accuracy and applying their results to courtrooms and other settings (Strauss & Smith, 2009). Empirical attempts to describe more comprehensively the limits of eyewitness accuracy have been conducted from the time of Munsterberg's first musings to the present (Rounding, Jacobson, & Lindsay, 2014), and they are likely to continue well into the future. Indeed, even the most recent studies on eyewitnesses have some basis in the research Munsterberg conducted at the beginning of the previous century.

Perhaps the most extensive descriptive research is that conducted by the U.S. Bureau of the Census. The goal is to count and describe the characteristics of the entire U.S. population, and the impact of this research is extensive. Billions of dollars in federal, state, and municipal aid shift with the changing population. Congressional districts appear and disappear, and hundreds of researchers rely on these data to assess the representativeness of their own research samples (e.g., DiBennardo & Gates, 2014).

Descriptive research captures the flavor of an object or event at the time the data are collected, but that flavor may change over time. The U.S. Census Bureau, for example, repeats its very costly research every 10 years, engages in interim data collection every year, and updates results regularly (Salvo & Lobo, 2013). Other research results may change even more rapidly. Research on unemployment is conducted monthly, and public opinion polls about certain issues may be conducted as often as every day.

Research results are not timeless, simply because change is one of the complexities inherent in our world. Descriptive research should be evaluated the way one might evaluate a photograph; it captures a moment in time but should not be compared to a video.

Prediction

Sometimes the goal of research is **prediction**, *identifying relationships that enable us to speculate about one thing by knowing about some other thing.* While this may seem complicated, it really is not. We all conduct and use the concept of **predictive research** every day. Predictive research *involves any study in which the purpose is to determine whether a relationship between variables exists such that one can use one of the variables in place of another.* We know, for example, about the relationship between hours on a clock and the probability of a certain business being open. Or we understand the relationship between a thermometer reading and the necessity of a coat when going outside. Or we know about the relationship between the scores on entrance exams and performance in the first year of college (Camara & Kimmel, 2005) or graduate school (Kuncel, Hezlett, & Ones, 2001).

Predictive research also gives clues about whether or not one variable is the cause of another. We can learn from the research of Angela Lee Duckworth and her colleagues, for example, that the personality variable known as *grit* may be an important component of success. There are studies in which grit is related to success in spelling bees (Duckworth, Kirby, Tsukayama, Berstein, & Ericsson, 2010), to performance in elite colleges (Duckworth, Peterson, Matthews, & Kelly, 2007), to performance as a teacher (Duckworth, Quinn, & Seligman, 2009), and even to success in Army Special Operations Forces training (Eskreis-Winkler, Shulman, Beal, & Duckworth, 2014). Note the careful wording of the first sentence in this paragraph—"clues about" causes. Because Duckworth and her colleagues were not able to create different levels of grit among their participants—they could not control grit—they were not able to test grit directly as a cause of success.

Explanation

Explanatory research *involves examining a cause–effect relationship between two or more phenomena.* It is used to determine whether or not an explanation (cause–effect relationship) is valid or to determine which of two or more competing explanations is more valid. Explanatory research usually involves creating two or more groups of participants by manipulating some aspect of the situation and assigning participants to the groups that were created.

Oermann, Kardong-Edgren, and Odom-Maryon (2011), for example, conducted an experiment to test whether or not brief periods of practice were sufficient to maintain nursing students' cardiopulmonary resuscitation (CPR) skills for a year. To do this, they assigned some of the students to complete six minutes of practice per month, while the other students were not assigned any practice time. Every three months, some students from both groups were tested on hand placement, compression rate, compression depth, ventilation rate, and ventilation volume. While both groups were able to maintain proper rates, students in the brief-practice group were better able to maintain proper compression depth (push hard enough to get enough blood flowing) and proper ventilation volume (get enough air into the lungs). From this study, we learn that practice is a cause of performance for some CPR skills. Oermann et al. did not test specific explanations for the practice effect, however, so we don't know why practice helps to maintain skills, but we do know that practice causes better performance of CPR skills.

Action

Research can also be used to attempt to do something about a particular phenomenon. **Action research** *refers to research conducted to solve a social problem* (Lewin, 1946). Action research can involve any of the previously mentioned goals but adds the requirement of finding a solution, of doing something to improve conditions, of generally making the world a better place beyond adding new knowledge. For example, Becker and Seligman (1978) noted that many people continue to run their air conditioners even though the outside temperature is lower than the temperature inside their house. To address this problem, Becker and Seligman conducted an experiment to test potential solutions to this instance of wasted energy. They created four different groups by providing some people with a chart showing them how much energy they were using, other people with a light that flashed whenever the outside temperature was lower than the inside temperature, still other people with both chart and light, and still others with neither chart nor light. They measured the amount of electricity used by each of the four groups and discovered that the charts did not alter people's energy efficiency. The signaling device, however, decreased electricity consumptions by about 16%. Through their action research, they provided a solution to the problem of wasted electricity: a simple signaling device.

Action research, in general, is an extremely important aspect of science, for it is through action research that we are able to test applications of other research results. We might all want to make the world a better place, but the complexity of the world requires that we test proposed solutions to problems before applying them on a large scale.

Research goals affect the ways in which we attempt to evaluate and eventually apply research. It would not be appropriate to reject research because it did not meet goals it was not designed to meet. We should not, for example, devalue Becker and Seligman's research because they did not explain why flashing lights created more efficient use of energy. Explaining why was not part of their project. We do need to understand the initial goals of every research project, but understanding the goals is only the beginning of evaluating research. The five goals of research are described in Table 1.2.

TABLE 1.2   The Five Goals of Research Expressed as Abstract and as Concrete Questions

Abstract Questions	Concrete Questions
Exploration: Does it exist?	Do suicide notes contain any information about people's motivations concerning suicide?
Description: What are its characteristics?	How accurate are eyewitnesses?
Prediction: To what is it related?	Is grit related to success in life?
Explanation: What causes it?	Does practice maintain CPR skills?
Action: Can this be used to solve a problem?	Can feedback about outside temperature be used to help people to conserve energy?

EVALUATION OF RESEARCH

Before we apply research results, we have to accept them as reasonable, which means we need to be able to know the extent to which they are worthwhile. Evidence-based practice involves much more than simply paying attention to the latest research. We need to evaluate research results and the methods used to produce them, and we need to do so critically. Critical evaluation involves noting both positive and negative aspects, the good and the bad. Critical evaluation also involves noting the indifferent and irrelevant, the things to which research is not related. As consumers of research, we need to be able to determine which research project is relevant and which is not. To construct a systematic framework for evaluating research, I have borrowed some familiar questions from journalism: who, what, where, when, why, and how. These questions will be used throughout the remainder of the text, which also allows me to provide a preview of what is to come in subsequent chapters.

Who

The *who* of a research project involves three different questions: Who are the researchers? Who are the participants? Who are the consumers? The answers, of course, vary from project to project, and all have something to do with how one evaluates the project.

We learn from the first page of a research article the names of the authors, but asking about the researchers involves more than simply discovering their names. What we really want to know is something about the characteristics of the researchers, their competence, and their biases. We presume researchers are competent until we learn otherwise, but once we learn otherwise, we should be unwilling to consider their research seriously. For example, I know of no one willing to place a great deal of faith in research conducted by Sir Cyril Burt in light of his fraudulent research on intelligence (Hearnshaw, 1979). It may sound cruel, but my recommendation is to discount all research by someone for whom a research article is retracted on the grounds of misrepresentation.

Beyond outright fraud, one rarely has specific information about a researcher's reputation at the outset of a career in evaluating research. As you read critically, however, you will develop opinions about specific researchers as you read their work. Some write better than others, some include more detail than others, and some make you think more than others. As an evaluator of research, it is important to avoid letting judgments about the researcher weigh too heavily in our judgments about their research. Science is about the data, not about who collected them. When we allow ourselves to become over- or underimpressed by someone's writing or institution, then we are no longer engaged in science, we are engaging in authority or another of Peirce's (1877) ways of knowing.

In the abstract and method sections of an article, we learn about the participants in a research project. They, too, are an important consideration in the evaluation of research. Should you read Oermann et al. (2011), for example, you would learn that their participants included nursing students from 10 different programs throughout the United States and included different types of nursing programs: diploma, associate degree, and baccalaureate. The comprehensive source of their participants means that their results should be given different weight than results obtained from students in a single institution or a particular type of nursing program.

The intended consumers of research also play a role in one's ability to evaluate a project. Researchers tend to write their reports for other researchers as opposed to the general public. They often use jargon that they expect readers to understand. At this point, the phrase *a 2 × 2 factorial design* probably doesn't mean much to you, but it denotes a specific research design. The design carries with it a variety of assumptions, implications, and techniques, all of which would be very time consuming, not to mention boring, to describe every time someone wrote about it. Inability to understand jargon makes it difficult to evaluate research, which is one of the reasons for the glossary in this text. At the completion of this course, you will be evaluating research quite differently from the way you evaluate it now.

What

We learn about the *what* of research primarily from the introduction, in which researchers explain the topic as well as the theory on which the research is based. It should be obvious that different research topics require different methods. Attempting to interview people who have committed suicide is ridiculous, not to mention macabre. On the other hand, an interview or survey is entirely appropriate for a project dealing with energy use. What may not be so obvious is that different questions about the same research topic may require different methods. If researchers are interested in perceptions about electricity use, interviews may be just what they need to use. But if they are interested in actual electricity use, then they might do as Becker and Seligman (1978) did and read meters instead of asking people how much electricity they used.

Through the theory they use as they derive their research questions, researchers also affect the manner in which they conduct the research. Sales (1972), for example, specifically tested Marxist theory, so he included economic conditions (one of the major components of Marxist theory) as one of his research measures. If instead he was interested in theories about psychological depression, he probably would have used some sort of depression scale and ignored economic indicators. Both economics and depression may be related to membership in a religious organization (Jenkins, 2003), but which variable gets included in a single research project is determined by the theory from which the research question is derived. The evaluation of research involves assessing whether or not what is included in research is appropriate to the theory on which it is based.

Beyond the level of theory, **worldview**, *the basic set of untestable assumptions underlying all theory and research*, also plays an important role in research. Kamin (1974), for example, pointed out that researchers were willing to accept the notion that men and women did not differ in intelligence, and so those developing intelligence tests generally excluded from intelligence tests items that produced gender differences. They were not, however, so willing to accept the notion that racial and ethnic minorities were as intelligent as themselves. Thus, early measures of intelligence did not exhibit a gender bias but did exhibit a number of racial and ethnic biases. Political beliefs may also affect the topic one selects for research (Frank, 1981). Understanding a particular researcher's worldview is generally not something one obtains from a single article, however. Worldview is something we come to know from a collection of someone's articles, including responses to commentary about the research.

Where

Also from the method section, we learn about the *where* of research, which includes the physical and social environment in which the research was conducted. Certain conditions are possible in one setting but not in another, and some settings do not allow certain types of research to be conducted at all. We cannot, for example, legally study jury deliberations in any systematic fashion by recording what occurs in the deliberation room, although some researchers have been able to do so under extraordinary circumstances (Devine, Clayton, Dunford, Seying, & Pryce, 2001; Ellison & Buckhout, 1981; Simon, 1975). Similarly, we cannot ethically examine reactions to an emergency by shouting "Fire!" in a theater. On the other hand, we can study simulations of juries (Cox, Clark, Edens, Smith, & Magyar, 2013) as well as simulations of emergencies (Helton, Funke, & Knott, 2014; Kaplan, Connor, Ferranti, Holmes, & Spencer, 2012). Bringing trials or emergencies into a research laboratory may introduce an element of artificiality, but artificiality alone is not grounds for devaluing a research project. Just as it is with other evaluation questions, it is necessary to engage in critical assessment of the relationship between the physical setting and the research goals.

The influence of the social environment may include very general aspects of the society as well as cultural biases. Someone doing research in a country without a jury system—Japan, for example—might never decide to use a jury simulation to study group decision making. Similarly, the belief in the United States and Canada that beauty was in the eye of the beholder kept social scientists from systematically studying the effects of physical attractiveness until the 1960s. The first few studies about physical attractiveness, however, blew that belief right out of the water. After decades of research and its attendant publicity, few of us have any trouble responding to a question that begins with "On a scale from 1 to 10, how attractive is . . . ?" and even fewer of us doubt our rating will agree with those of many others (Adams, 1977; Rhodes, Halberstadt, Jeffery, & Palermo, 2005).

When

From the year of publication, we learn the time frame of a particular study. Time frame may, of course, alter its utility, but it can also be the major purpose of the study. Science operates on the basis of cumulative knowledge most of the time (see, e.g., Fleck, 1979). Each bit of information adds to what is already known. In 1990, for example, it was concluded that a daily, low-dose aspirin was useful for preventing cardiovascular disease (Ewy, 2014). As daily use became prevalent, the relationship between daily aspirin and other diseases could be studied (Illingworth & Parmet, 2015), including cancer

(Orenstein & Yang, 2015), and eventually to very specific genotypes (Rupp, 2011). During that same time period, there were occasional reports of complications concerning aspirin (e.g., Patel et al., 2015), but such reports did not negate the earlier research. Someone paying attention only to the latest research might well have felt as though they were the ball in a ping-pong match—take it, don't take it, take it, don't take it, take it—but research should not be consumed one study at a time in a vacuum, so to speak. Knowing when research was conducted allows us to place it in the context of existing information about the research topic.

Changes in conditions over time may themselves be the focus of research, and such information comes from the method section of the research article. Oermann et al. (2011), for example, found no differences between the brief-practice and no-practice groups in terms of adequacy of CPR compression depth in the first 3 to 9 months of their study. By 12 months, however, the differences were considerable, and those differences remained even after a refresher course.

Why

We have already dealt with the general reasons why research is done: exploration, description, prediction, explanation, and action. From the introduction of the article, we also learn more specific reasons. We learn, for example, what the authors think about how the research results fit into the existing knowledge about the topic.

Our critical consumption of the introduction gives us contextual information about the research. Because we want to know about all of the research relevant to a specific topic, we use the introduction to learn of the existence of additional research to include in the evidence relevant to our professional practice. Oermann et al. (2011), for example, cited 12 different studies about the decline in CPR skills that occur over time and another eight studies about the utility of practice to reduce or prevent such declines. If we are reading Oermann et al. to learn about preventing the decline of CPR skills and did not already know about all 20 studies, then we have additional information to incorporate into our body of evidence. Reading critically about research, however, means that we have to get and read the additional articles. We should not merely accept what Oermann et al. wrote about the other research; that would be using Oermann et al. as authority (Peirce, 1877) instead of engaging in science.

How

The goals of research affect how it is done (its methods), and so we turn to some of those methods as a way to preview the remainder of this text. The design and procedures are likely to be the most critically evaluated aspects of research and so deserve the greatest amount of attention.

The *hows* of research range from the manner in which one obtains an idea to the ways in which one writes about the research results, and understanding each of these is useful in our attempts to consume research conducted by others. Nestled between these two activities are issues concerning measurement, design, data analyses, and interpretations. In addition, there are many aspects of research that may or may not be relevant to a particular research project. Scale construction and obtaining large, representative samples are just two examples of such aspects.

Like most of life, research can be extremely boring if you only read about it with no particular purpose in mind. Although you may not be able to apply everything discussed in this text, you can think about the relevancy of various topics to your professional interests throughout the text. As you continue to read, think about how you might use the information you are reading in your current or your intended profession. Imagination cannot replace activity, but imagination is better than nothing. At some point, and I hope it is soon, you may be in a position to prepare a research-based manuscript, even if it's only a memo suggesting a change in process in your workplace. If you have thought about it ahead of time, you'll be able to take advantage of the opportunity.

INITIATING A RESEARCH REVIEW

Research results are always placed in context, and our professional interests provide a framework for new ideas about what to research. There is no official starting point in this relationship, but I have chosen to begin the discussion of how to review research with choosing a topic.

Choosing a Topic

The first step in conducting a research review is to choose a topic. There are no rules for this step, but there are some general guidelines. Topics for literature reviews are infinite, for anything may stimulate an interest in empirical research. Indeed, anyone can come up with any number of questions that could be answered empirically, but the trick to conducting a research review is to develop a good question, one that is likely to have been addressed by researchers. Recognizing and formulating a researchable, empirical question takes a little practice and requires some understanding of research methods, but one does not have to be an expert in research methodology to begin the process. Perhaps the most important suggestion that can be made about deciding upon a question upon which to base your review is to limit your questions to topics that are particularly interesting to you. I can think of no more boring task than reviewing research on a topic in which I have no interest.

You may be assigned a topic for review by a supervisor who wants empirical information on a specific policy, process, or program. Barring such an assignment, however, you need to consider various sources for information about potential review topics. Perhaps the most important source is your involvement in your profession. What do you want to know more about? Is there a particular procedure or process that comes to mind? Is there a particular type of client about which you'd like to learn more? Another good source for review topics is a research journal. Choose a journal relevant to your discipline or scope of activities and scan the table of contents until you find a topic of particular interest. Read the article to find out what issues and questions are being addressed. Think about questions you would like to ask the author if you had the opportunity. Also, take the time to ask coworkers or supervisors about their own questions. They may be interested in aspects of the profession that didn't occur to you but sound interesting once you learn of them.

Once you have developed a question, regardless of its source, you have begun the research review process. The next step is to become familiar with your topic. This point may seem too obvious to bother making, but more than a few reviewers have begun amassing sources only to discover that they were woefully unprepared to interpret those sources. If your interests involve a formal theory, read about the theory and its related research. If your interests involve a specific process or procedure, read about that. Remember, for critical consumption of research, you need a context into which you can place the research.

Operationalization

As you read about your topic of interest, pay attention to the range of **operational definitions**—*concrete representations of abstract theoretical concepts*—that could be related to your interests. Heat is a theoretical concept, for example, and the number of units on a thermometer is one operational definition of it. How researchers operationally define the concepts they include in their research has an impact on the results they obtain. Oermann et al. (2011), for example, included five different operational definitions of "follow-up time": 3 months, 6 months, 9 months, and 12 months as well as 12 months with the refresher basic life support course. Their definitions included two different versions of 12 months, which means that they could (and did) change as a function of which measure of *12 months* was being used. One of the ways in which Duckworth, Weir, Tsukayama, and Kwok (2012, p. 3) measured *success* was in terms of lifetime income, which was operationalized "using the average indexed monthly earnings in Social Security-linked records and adjusted to constant dollars of 2006 using the same wage index." Clearly, this is a different operational definition than asking people to report their lifetime income, but both definitions would be reported as *lifetime income* in a research article.

It is important to keep in mind that the operational definition of a concept is not the same as the concept itself, but it does represent the concept. A score on an intelligence test, for example, is not the same thing as intelligence, nor is lifetime income the same as success. Campbell (1969) coined the term **definitional operationism** to refer to the *failure to recognize the difference between a theoretical concept and its operational definition*. Years later, Leahey (1980) used the phrase *myth of operationism* to label the same problem. Theoretical concepts must have operational definitions before anyone can do research related to the concepts, and as consumers, we need to maintain the distinction between a concept and its operationalization. You will need to consider the variety of different ways in which the concepts of interest to you can be operationalized, or made concrete, through research. You do not have to know all of the possible operational definitions of concepts in which you are interested, but it helps to consider some of them before beginning your research review. Operational definitions can be extremely useful as key words in a search.

An operational definition of a concept is also called a **variable**—*a measurable entity that exhibits more than one level or value.* A thermometer reading is a variable, for it is measurable and it exhibits more than one level. Similarly, we are all too familiar with how variable lifetime income is. Other examples of variables include a score on an intelligence test, a rating of 1 to 10 on a scale of physical attractiveness, and survival (yes or no) after cardiopulmonary resuscitation. Variables need not be numeric, but they must vary; there must be more than one level (at least the presence or absence) of some quality.

Once you have some operational definitions for the theoretical concepts of interest, you also need to understand how those variables are used to form **hypotheses**—*statements that describe a relationship between variables.* A hypothesis is a concrete statement analogous to an abstract relationship described in a theory. Dane et al. (2000) tested the hypothesis that ACLS training (yes or no) for nurses was related to survival after CPR in a hospital. They measured the variables—ACLS training and survival—and applied statistical analyses to examine the relations. There was no formal theory in their research, but the suspected link between ACLS training and survival was a hypothesis.

For any particular theory, the number of ways in which a concept may be operationalized is limited only by the imagination of the researcher. We cannot, however, evaluate variables solely on the basis of creativity. You probably would not want your instructor to be creative when operationalizing your knowledge of research methods in terms of your body temperature and award the highest grades to the most feverish students. This may be a creative approach, but it is not valid. **Validity**, in general, refers to *the extent to which a claim or conclusion is based on sound logic.* There are many specific kinds of validity in research and we will eventually discuss all of them, but the relevant validity here is **construct validity,** *the extent to which a measure represents concepts it should represent and does not represent concepts it should not represent.* Validity, including construct validity, is assessed through consensus.

If you agree with Dane et al. (2000) that being discharged alive from a hospital is survival and dying while in the hospital is not survival, then you consider their measure of survival to be valid. Similarly, if you agree with Oermann et al. (2011) that 12 months without a refresher course is different from 12 months with a refresher course, then you consider their measurement of follow-up time to be valid. The consensus of science, however, is not merely popularity—it is based on logic derived from the theory—but it is agreement. Sometimes, however, the popularity of a particular variable leads to its misuse as an operational definition. The mere existence of a valid operational definition is not sufficient reason to use it in a review of research; whatever research variables you include in your review should be based on a logical analysis of the concept(s) or issue(s) to be addressed in your research question.

By the time you have an interesting research question; have found an applicable theory, policy, or program for your question; and have (at least temporarily) decided upon some operational definitions, you have become intimately involved in the cyclical practice of science (see Figure 1.1).

FIGURE 1.1   The Cyclical Nature of the Practice of Science

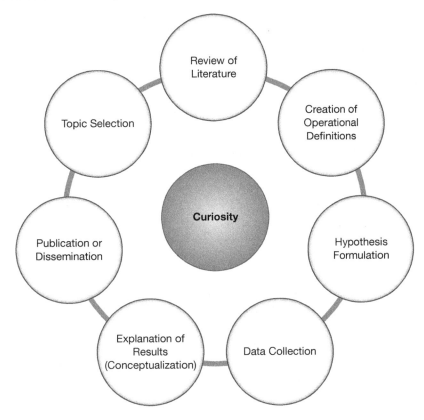

FINDING RESEARCH

Before one can use research as part of evidence-based practice, one has to be able to find research reports, what researchers refer to as *the literature*. Despite use of the definite article, there is no one, single literature; instead **literature** is *the generic term used to refer to the collection of articles, chapters, and books that contain research results relevant to a particular topic.* Knowing that *the literature* is out there, somewhere, is a beginning, but is not much help if one doesn't know where to look to find it. In this section, we will examine how to find sources.

Published Sources

Some of the best, as well as some of the most overlooked, sources for literature are textbooks. They contain a great deal of information, some of which you may have forgotten since you took the course, and the good ones have many pages of references. Granted, the information is usually discussed at a superficial level (reading the textbook will not be sufficient), but there is usually enough information to decide whether or not the research is related to your interests. Once you have identified relevant information, you can use the reference section to determine where to find the original article, chapter, or book.

Other good sources for published material are research journals in your interest area. These journals include material on a variety of research topics, so not every article will be relevant to your interests, but if you scan their tables of contents online, then you are likely to find a fair amount of information related to your interests. You can also peruse journals in other disciplines that are aligned with your interests. Your library maintains a list of the periodicals it holds, and it can usually be searched online by subject or title. The list will provide the call numbers that enable you to locate current and back issues of the journal in the library or URLs for online access.

Journals are not the only sources for relevant literature, although they are likely to be the major sources. Every year, Annual Review, Inc. publishes a series of volumes titled *Annual Review of* . . . for most of the major disciplines dealing with human behavior. Other review series, often titled *Advances in* . . . , can be found by perusing the library's electronic card catalog by title.

Skimming through textbooks, issues of journals, or annual series is one way to develop your research idea and to find information related to it. Indeed, you have probably taken enough courses to have a good idea about which journals or series are likely prospects for perusal. Let us move on, then, to some very specific tactics for tracking down information you have decided you need.

Key Topics

One of the best tactics for locating relevant literature is searching for specific topics. When you know some of the key topics relevant to your research idea, there are even faster methods for locating related literature. You are probably familiar with a few indexing or abstracting services available through your library's search databases, such as ProQuest, MedLine, EBSCO, Google Scholar, OVID, PsychNet, and others. Each of these resources contains a compilation of empirical journals and other publications, all of which can be searched via one or more keywords.

Which databases are available through your library will depend upon the extent of the subscription services. It is not possible for me to describe or even list all of the available indexes nor would it do much good for me to try to guess which, in print or in digital format, your library might have. The easiest way to find out what is available to you is to talk to one of the reference librarians.

I have not provided very many details about how to use any of the indexes or abstracts because it is much better to find out from a person rather than a textbook. Local options vary so much on most computerized indexes, even if it is officially the same index, that my telling you about how my library's index works could be a waste of time. It is worth your effort to get the information from your local reference librarian. I have been assured that most reference librarians really do enjoy showing people how to use the services they offer. One reference librarian likened it to showing off one's favorite toys. Another said that reference librarians enjoy talking about their reference services almost as much as professors enjoy talking about their research—now that's enjoyment.

Key Authors

In almost all but the newest areas of research, there are likely to be key researchers—people whose names are known and who have written much on a particular topic. If you have exhausted your key topics, cannot think of any key topics, or just want to expand your search opportunities, then one way to continue your literature search is by examining the work of key authors. You may discover key authors from perusing textbooks or general journals or by reading whatever material you were able to discover through a key topic search.

Chances are, however, that the research of key authors will be dated, but that is not a problem. There is nothing inherently wrong with old research. Indeed, older articles will provide the background you need to understand more recent research. Most database resources enable you to search for articles in which a particular, older article has been cited, so you can use the old research as a key study.

Key Studies

Sooner or later in your search, you will find an article that seems perfectly related to your interests—a key article. Once you have found them, key articles are one of the most effective bases for a comprehensive literature search. The reference section of the key study will list relevant research reports that were published before the key study was published. Consulting those references provides the means for discovering related research in the relative past.

Key articles are a great find, but I can imagine you asking "What if my key article is ten years old?" No matter how old your key article may be, you can use the key terms listed for that article to discover additional articles related to the same key terms. This helps you to overcome the problem associated with any differences between the specific key terms used by the database organizers and the key terms you think they should have used when organizing the database. As noted earlier, you can also search for more recent articles in which the authors included the key article among the references.

Unpublished Studies

Not all of the empirical and theoretical work related to your policy issue idea can be found in published sources. Some of the references you obtain in your search will be found in either *Dissertation Abstracts International* or *Masters Abstracts International*. These publications contain abstracts of doctoral dissertations and master's theses, respectively, and have indexes through which you can find dissertations and theses related to various topics. In both publications, however, the abstracts are very short, about 300 words, and you will have to access ProQuest, usually through your library, to get a copy of the entire research report. Finally, let me add a caution about using general, online search engines (e.g., Google, Bing). Using these will certainly produce many hits for almost all key words, and some of these may actually be research articles, but the majority of the material is likely to be more opinion than research. You might be able to find good background information, but you are likely to find more information than you are able to peruse efficiently. Critical consumption of all sources is important, but it is particularly important when the material has not been peer reviewed.

Enough reading for now; go develop a topic of interest and search for some research articles.

SUMMARY

- Research can be defined in many ways, the most general of which is a process through which questions are asked and answered systematically. As a form of criticism, research can include the question of whether or not we are asking the right question.

- The ultimate goal of research is to be able to answer the questions asked. However, exploration, description, prediction, explanation, and action are different ways to ask the same question.

- Exploration involves attempting to determine whether or not a particular phenomenon exists.

- Description involves attempting to define a phenomenon more carefully, including distinguishing between it and other phenomena.

- Prediction involves examining the relationship between two things so as to be able to make educated guesses about one by knowing something about the other.

- Explanation also involves examining the relationship between two things but specifically involves trying to determine whether or not one causes the other.

- Action involves using research to attempt to solve a social problem. Action research may involve any of the other goals of research, but it includes a specific application.

- Evaluating research involves the questions *who*, *what*, *where*, *when*, *how*, and *why*. Researchers, participants, and consumers of research may all affect the outcome of the research as well as the manner in which the outcome is interpreted.

- The topic, theory, and worldview on which research is based are also involved in evaluating research critically, as are the physical location of the research and the social climate in which it is conducted.

- Research results are not timeless, mainly because the world itself is dynamic. Changes in research results, however, can themselves become the focus of research.

- Searching for research reports is best done through search engines designed for scholarly publications. Using key terms, key authors, and key articles, as well as textbooks, should provide you with a comprehensive set of reports, the literature related to the policy or program in which you are interested.

EXERCISES

1. Obtain a popular-press report (newspaper, magazine, blog, etc.) about an issue of interest and determine whether the information in the report is based on a priori reasoning, appeal to authority, tradition, or scientific content. (Note: There may be a mixture of types of epistemological methods represented in any given report.)

2. Obtain a popular-press report containing reference to scientific research. Decide what kind of purpose is attributed to the research. (Ideally, choose a report that contains enough information about the research so that you can later track down the article[s] on which the report is based.)

3. Using a new popular-press report or one you used in the other exercises, answer as many of the who/what/where/when/how/why questions as possible.

4. Identify an issue or concept in which you are interested and use the resources in your library to track down at least two empirical (research) articles that are relevant to that concept or issue.

2

The Scientific Approach

> It [science] is not perfect. It is only a tool. But it is by far the best tool we have, self-correcting, ongoing, [and] applicable to everything. It has two rules. First: there are no sacred truths; all assumptions must be critically examined; arguments from authority are worthless. Second: whatever is inconsistent with the facts must be discarded or revised.
>
> —Carl Sagan (1980, p. 333)

OVERVIEW

This chapter contains a description of the scientific approach as it applies to the theory and practice of research. You will learn why science, despite being the best approach to research, is not subject to proof from outside its own logical system. Scientific knowledge and its growth are a function of agreement, and you will learn how agreement is facilitated by the use of inductive reasoning. You will also learn about distinctions between scientific and nonscientific research, various misconceptions about science, and the importance of theory in the research process. You will learn how to use theory and other resources to facilitate your understanding, critical evaluation, and application of research. Finally, you will learn about the ethics of consuming research.

INTRODUCTION

Many people think of scientific research as something done by intelligent-but-absent-minded people wearing white coats while surrounded by strange-looking equipment with blinking lights. Some may think of scientists as despoilers of a simple, nontechnical lifestyle.

Others may think of scientists as the harbingers of an idyllic age. None of these views is correct; one of the goals of this chapter is to dispel these and other myths about science. Science is not something one does; rather, it is an approach toward doing things, and one of the most important things scientists do is research. Scientists certainly do not all wear white laboratory coats nor do we all use strange equipment, with or without blinking lights. Some scientists may be extremely intelligent or absent minded, but these qualities do not make a person a scientist; neither does adopting a scientific approach necessarily make someone intelligent or absent minded.

I noted in Chapter 1 that everyone, not just scientists, does research. What distinguishes scientific from other kinds of research is not the activity itself but the approach to the activity. Scientific research is, among other things, systematic. There are other guidelines about what is and what is not scientific research as well as guidelines about what to do with scientific research once we have it, including ethical guidelines. Scientists know what these guidelines are, agree about them, and attempt to adhere to them. Nonscientists either do not know them or do not consistently use them. It is not research that distinguishes scientists from nonscientists; it is the approach one takes toward research. As we learned in Chapter 1, science is a systematic approach to the discovery of knowledge based on a set of rules that defines what is acceptable knowledge. Just as there are rules for such things as tennis or international diplomacy, there are rules for science. And just like tennis or international diplomacy, not everyone necessarily operates according to the same set of rules.

A PHILOSOPHY OF SCIENCE

Years ago, I was discussing religion with a friend. We disagreed about a lot of things, but we were calmly discussing the relative merits of our personal beliefs. At one point, I asked my friend to explain why she believes what she does. She replied very simply, "I believe it because I know it's true." Then I asked how she knew it was true, and she said, "I know in my heart it's true." She could not explain why she believes what she believes any more than I could explain why I believe what I do about religion. We both thought we were correct, but neither of us could logically prove we were correct in any absolute sense. At best, we could point out we were not alone in our beliefs. Of course, most people accept the notion that there is no absolute proof when the topic is religious beliefs. What many people do not understand is that the same is true about science.

Any set of rules that defines what is acceptable, empirical knowledge may be called a **philosophy of science**. Among philosophers of science and among scientists, however, there is more than one accepted philosophy. This is partly because philosophers, like members of any other discipline, are developing, changing, and assessing new ideas and formulations in an attempt to improve upon what we know. Whatever their differences, however, all philosophers of science need to address the same four basic questions: (1) When is something true? (2) If we have more than one explanation, how can we tell which one is better? (3) How can we put what we know into practice? and (4) Why do we do it the way we do it?

In this chapter, we will concentrate on a particular philosophy of science called *nonjustificationism* (Strauss & Smith, 2009; Weimer, 1979). The name of this viewpoint is derived from the position that a scientific approach cannot be justified—proven valid—except through unproven assumptions; **nonjustificationism** is a *philosophy of science for which the major premise is that we cannot logically prove that the way we go about doing research is correct in any absolute sense*. While this conclusion may seem outlandish right now, the remaining discussion should help you understand why this outlandish conclusion is quite logical and not at all inconsistent with a scientific approach to understanding the world.

When Is Something True?

This first question to be answered through any philosophy of science is usually called the question of **rational inference**—*a philosophical problem concerning the difficulty inherent in supporting any claim about the existence of a universal truth*. Just as when my friend and I were discussing religious beliefs and there was more than one truth, there is more than one solution to the problem of rational inference. In order to be scientific, whatever we accept as our answer to the question of when something is true (i.e., our interim solution to the rational inference problem) must be based on **facts**—*objectively verifiable phenomena or characteristics available to anyone who knows how to observe them*. Recall Sagan's (1980) second rule of science: Whatever does not agree with the facts is wrong and must be changed or rejected completely. Although the statement is simple, deciding how to go about the process is a little more complex.

Behavioral scientists, for example, are interested in understanding how people interact with each other at a variety of different levels. We want to understand as much about people and human phenomena as possible. No matter how many facts we have, however, we cannot understand them until we have a way to summarize those facts. Summarizing facts—making them comprehensible—is what theories are all about.

But anyone can make up a theory about human behavior. Given enough time, just about everyone in the world can articulate some sort of theory for any given phenomenon. Thus, we have the equivalent of a very large warehouse that is full of theories. This imaginary warehouse contains as many different theories about people as there are people in the world, multiplied by the number of different theories each of those individuals has for each of the various phenomena that make up human behavior. Clearly, we need to imagine a very large (and probably quite disorganized) warehouse. Of course, each discipline has its own warehouse of theories, so deciding what to do with all of the theories in all of the sciences can be somewhat daunting, but it is not impossible.

At a very simple level, all we have to do is compare each theory in the warehouse to the facts: If the theory does not fit the facts, we change it or throw it out of the warehouse.

This process may sound good, but it just does not work that way. Theories are made up of **concepts**—*abstract words that are used to represent concrete phenomena*. We can point to concrete examples of concepts, but the concepts themselves are abstract. For example, conflict, as a theoretical concept, is not the same thing as a family argument or a revolution. Family argument and revolution are, of course, concrete examples of conflict, but they are only examples and not complete definitions. No matter how compellingly practical a concept may be, it is only an approximation of reality, and any given concrete phenomenon is only an approximation of a concept (Wartofsky, 1968). Theories symbolize, represent, or summarize the real world in which we live and behave, but the concepts within the theories are not the same thing as the real world. Because concepts are abstract and the facts we rely on to test them are concrete, deciding whether or not a theory fits the facts is rather difficult.

This difficulty arises because we must rely on inductive reasoning when connecting facts to a theory. **Inductive reasoning** is *a process of generalization; it involves applying specific information to a general situation or future events.* That is, we are generalizing from a concrete fact to an abstract theory. Let me illustrate with a story about a college instructor of mine who consistently arrived 10 minutes late for class. About three weeks into the semester, I came to the conclusion that he would continue to do so, which meant I could sleep an extra 10 minutes on those days and still arrive "on time" for class. This conclusion was a generalization, an inductive inference. Based on the instructor's specific behavior—arriving late during the first three weeks—I attributed to him a general or abstract quality—tardiness—and used that abstract concept to predict his behavior in the future. Unfortunately, it never occurred to me he would show up on time for the midterm exam, and I developed cramps in my hand trying to write fast enough to make up for the time I lost by arriving late. It was a rather painful way to learn that inductive reasoning does not necessarily lead to absolute truth.

Despite the inability of inductive reasoning to lead us to absolute truth, we must rely on it in any scientific approach to research. We simply cannot let all those theories pile up in the warehouse until we have all of the facts nor can we wait for all the facts before we begin to construct theories to put in the warehouse. Instead, we simply accept the notion that inductive reasoning is the best process of generalization we have until something better comes along.

Had I waited until after the midterm exam before attributing tardiness to my instructor, I could have saved myself some writing cramps (and perhaps gotten a better grade on the exam). But even then, I could not have been sure that he would be on time for the final exam nor could I be certain that he would not begin arriving on time after the midterm. Of course, I could have just arrived on time myself every day, but that would have meant missing out on hours of extra sleep accumulated across the entire semester. I weighed the alternatives and constructed my theory about his behavior. After he showed up late the first day after the midterm, I reverted to sleeping an extra 10 minutes, but I showed up on time for the final exam. I adjusted my initial theory to fit the new facts, but I did not wait until I had all of the facts before constructing my new theory.

I have simplified the arguments involved in this issue, but the basic point of the rational inference problem is rather simple: Inductive inferences cannot be proved true. Nevertheless, we need to use them to construct theories until we have evidence to the contrary. If we have enough contrary evidence, we can throw a theory out of our warehouse, but that does not mean that any of the theories remaining in the warehouse are true. We are left with no choice but to provide support for a theory by trying to show that alternative, competing theories are not true. If we make a prediction from a theory and test the prediction and if the prediction fits the facts, then we have *not* proved the theory to be true; instead, we have failed to prove that the theory is false. It is difficult to think in terms of double negatives—Theory X is not not-true—but that is the logic forced on us by the rational inference problem. Thus, research in which we test between two competing theories is more efficient than research in which we test only one theory because comparing theories is one way to deal with the rational inference problem.

How Can We Tell Which Theory Is Better?

The absence of absolute truth does not limit what we can learn in a scientific approach, but we are faced with a particular path in our quest to learn about behavior and other real-world phenomena. We can, as I mentioned above, test between two different theories and decide which one is better. Testing between theories is like a grand tournament in which every theory is pitted against every other theory; the theory with the best win–loss record at the end of the tournament is the winner. That does not mean that the winning theory is true—only that it is the best theory we have until another, better theory is entered in the tournament. Like all tournaments, the tournament of scientific theories has some rules about which theories are entered and how many times a theory has to lose in order to be eliminated.

The rules of the grand tournament of science bring us to the problem called **criteria for growth**—finding *standards that can be used to decide whether one explanation is better than another.* We all know, for example, that as an explanation of the apparent movement of the sun across the sky, current theories of astronomy are more accurate (but less poetic) than the myth of Helios, the sun god, waking every morning and driving his fiery chariot across the sky. We would scoff at anyone who seriously believed the Helios explanation, just as any ancient Greek would have scoffed at our current theories. How we came to decide that astronomy is better than mythology involves our criteria for growth: paradigms and facts.

Theories, whether in or out of our imaginary warehouse, do not exist in a vacuum. Every theory is related to at least one other theory through shared concepts or propositions. Kuhn (1962) was the first to use the term *paradigm* (pronounced "pair-a-dime") to describe such groups of related theories. A **paradigm** is *a logical system that* *encompasses theories, concepts, models, procedures, and techniques.* The earth-centered solar system, for example, was once a paradigm in physics, just as instinct was once a paradigm in psychology (McDougall, 1908). At the time McDougall was theorizing about human behavior, the predominant explanations included some notion about instinctual processes; there was an instinct for survival, one for aggression, and so on. New observations about behavior were interpreted in terms of existing instincts, and if new observations did not fit, then new instincts were invented to account for the observations.

During a period of time in which a particular paradigm is accepted, which Kuhn referred to as a period of *normal science*, research is directed toward solving problems related to matching current theories with observations. At such times, research tends to be directed toward refining theories, toward trying to make them better, such as inventing new instincts to fit research observations. New research and the refinements of theories add to the strength of the paradigm, which in turn leads to the perception that the paradigm, including its associated theories and procedures, is the best way to explain what goes on in the world.

Eventually, however, problems with the paradigm emerge as more and more information cannot be fit into the existing theories. I note "eventually" because no matter how reasonable or useful a paradigm may be, it, too, is based on inductive reasoning and thus cannot be considered to be universal truth. When enough problems emerge and an alternative paradigm, complete with its own theories and procedures, arises that fits the observations better, then the old paradigm gives way to a new one during what Kuhn calls a *scientific revolution*. Thus Galileo started a scientific revolution with his notion of a sun-centered solar system, although it took years before the followers of the earth-centered paradigm accepted the new paradigm. Then the new paradigm becomes *the* paradigm and the field returns again to normal science until the next paradigm shift occurs.

Underlying all of normal and revolutionary science is reliance on facts. Observations are considered to be facts when people can point to concrete examples of the observation. Although it may seem tautological to require facts to be observable, that very requirement is one of the reasons McDougall's instinct theories eventually gave way to modern explanations of behavior; there was no way to observe—to be able to point to concrete examples of—the processes by which instincts influence behavior. Today, of course, we have some evidence for instinctual processes as one of several possible explanations for some behaviors (see, for example, Lea & Webley, 2006; Snyder, 1987), but we do not use instinct as the primary explanatory concept for all behavior.

In addition to being observable, facts must also be objective. Within a scientific approach, **objectivity** means *that an observation can be replicated, observed by more than one person under a variety of different conditions.* If I am the only researcher who can demonstrate a particular effect, it is not objective. If, however, several others note the same effect under different conditions, then we have a fact, an objective observation that needs to be incorporated into existing theories.

Thus, during normal science, theories are compared on the basis of their fit into the existing paradigm as well as our ability to use them to account for the existing facts. During revolutionary science, comparisons occur between old and new paradigms, but the basis for such comparisons remains the existing facts. Then, upon return to normal science, theories within the current paradigm are again evaluated in terms of their fit with the facts. It is important to note, however, that because a new paradigm may redefine what is an acceptable fact, the facts may change from time to time (Fleck, 1979).

How Can We Put What We Know Into Practice?

By now, you may be having some serious doubts about how a scientific approach can be a path to anything except confusion. There are no absolute truths, and sometimes what were once considered to be facts are no longer considered to be so. We have arrived at the problem of **pragmatic action**—*determining how we should go about putting a scientific approach into practice*. Essentially, those who adopt a scientific approach must get together and decide how they are going to use that approach. The solution to the problem of pragmatic action, the answer to the question of how we put what we know into practice, lies in agreement.

Just as legal theorists assume that a decision made by 12 jurors is better than a decision made by 1 juror, scientists agree that evidence obtained by a number of different researchers is better than evidence obtained by one researcher; that is, objective data—repeatable observations—are agreed to be better than subjective data. The greater the number of researchers who produce the same research results, the more we consider those results to be facts to which we must fit our theories; notice that the theories must fit the facts, not the other way around (we don't change facts to fit the theory; we change the theory to fit the facts). A variety of reasonable arguments support this agreement about objectivity, but no one can prove, in any absolute sense, that the consensus is correct. As Sagan (1980) suggested, it is not perfect, but it is the best we have.

One of the problems inherent in the use of objectivity is the variety of different research methods available to study any particular phenomenon (see, for example, Gone, 2015; Watson, 1967). When researchers use different methods to study the same phenomena, they often come up with different observations. Consensus, then, must extend into agreement about which research methods are appropriate for which research questions as well as agreement about whether or not a particular method was used properly. Essentially, that is what this book and the course you are taking are all about. You cannot rely solely on the assumption that the experts have used the correct research method to answer their question; you must be able to determine yourself whether the methods used by the researchers fit the way in which you want to use the research results.

For example, in the early years of research about differences between men and women, one of the more common methods was to select a group of men and a group of women, have both groups do something (such as solve math problems), and then compare the performances of the two groups. If the performances of the groups were different, then the researchers concluded that the results reflected basic differences between the two sexes. Deaux and Major (1987), however, presented convincing, empirical arguments that such things as the context of the situation, self-presentation strategies, researchers' and participants' beliefs about whether or not the sexes ought to be different, and a variety of other factors can change the results obtained from such methods. Therefore, the potential influence of such factors must be considered before we conclude that gender differences reflect basic differences between men and women.

We now know that simply comparing a group of men to a group of women is not an effective way to examine gender differences. Then again, everyone "knew" back in the old days that such simple comparisons were the best way to study gender differences. Even though we rely on consensus for such purposes as fitting theories to facts and even for deciding what is a fact, we must keep in mind that a new consensus might emerge after we have obtained more information. Still, there can be no scientific approach without consensus.

Why Do We Do It the Way We Do?

Every time I discuss consensus as the basis for a scientific approach, I can hear my mother saying, "Would you jump off a cliff just because everyone else is doing it?" That was her response, for example, to my wanting to stay out late because my friends' parents allowed them to stay out late; I am sure you have heard the same response when you have tried to use similar reasoning or you have provided the same response when your children used that reasoning. What we have come to, then, is the problem of **intellectual honesty**—*the individual scientist's ability to justify the use of science itself*. If we can never prove that theories are true, if paradigms are only temporary, and if facts and methods for gathering them may change, then why would we ever accept a scientific approach as a valid way to learn anything?

Consider a simple survey of students' attitudes about current grading practices. In order to understand and apply that study, we must rely on a great deal of background information. We must accept research about students' reading levels when examining the questionnaire, accept research that suggests that a survey is a reasonable way to measure attitudes, accept research concerning the best way to format the questions on the survey, accept research about which statistics are appropriate to analyze the data, and so on. All of that research comes from within a scientific approach, and we are using that information to add more facts to the same scientific approach. Where does it all end?

The solution to the intellectual honesty problem—the answer to why we do it the way we do—can again be found in Sagan's quote at the beginning of this chapter: It is "by far the best tool we have." We do it the way we do it because we have not found a better way. Very simply, we adopt a scientific approach because we have a certain amount of faith in it because it works or, as my grandfather used to say, "If it ain't broke, don't fix it." Note, however, that the faith is placed in the approach itself, not in any particular theory

TABLE 2.1   Justificationist and Nonjustificationist Approaches to the Four Basic Questions Inherent in Any Philosophy of Science

The Questions	Justificationist Approach to Science	Nonjustificationist Approach to Science
The rational inference problem: When is something true?	Facts produce a single, correct theory	Facts are summarized by many incorrect theories
Criteria for growth: How can we tell which theory is better?	Better fit with paradigm and facts	Better fit with paradigm and facts
Pragmatic action: How can we put what we know into practice?	Consensus produces the correct paradigm	Consensus enables a better, but not correct, paradigm
Intellectual honesty: Why do we do science the way we do?	Science produces absolute truth	Science is the best way to obtain knowledge

that comes from the approach. Table 2.1 describes both justificationist and nonjustificationist approaches to the four basic question inherent in any philosophy of science.

SCIENCE AND NONSCIENCE COMPARED

I keep bringing up the notion that we all conduct research all of the time. We are all, in one way or another, gathering new information to increase our knowledge about our world. Such everyday research is not necessarily scientific, but it does provide us with a way to satisfy our curiosity. In addition to the points noted above, the differences between scientific and nonscientific research generally revolve around avoiding mistakes. Mistakes can occur when we make observations, when we interpret observations, or when we accept various misconceptions about what is included in a scientific approach toward research.

Observation

Whenever we observe something, we make errors—period, no exceptions, ever. The errors, which researchers generally call *bias*, come from selecting what to observe and interpreting what we observe as well as from the act of observation itself. We cannot avoid bias entirely, but we can attempt to reduce error to a minimum and be aware of error that we have not been able to eliminate.

For example, what we decide to observe creates a form of bias because it prevents us from making other observations at the same time. This is an error of omission that results simply because we cannot be in two places at the same time. That does not mean that what we do observe is wrong or incorrect but rather that it is incomplete. Essentially, we need to keep in mind that what we have been observing is not all that could be observed. Duckworth, Peterson, Matthews, and Kelly (2007), for example, noted that individuals were discussing concepts very much like grit as far back as the late 1800s, but no one had gotten around to measuring it until more than century later; everyone was busy observing other "stuff."

Of course, objectivity is another way to reduce, but not eliminate, the bias inherent in observation. When more people observe the same thing, under the same or different conditions, then the collection of observations becomes more accurate (less biased, more complete). Different observers, different situations, different locations, and different definitions of what to observe all contribute to the objectivity of data and all reduce observation error. Realizing that all observation contains some amount of error or bias is an important part of a scientific approach to research, for it prevents anyone from saying, "Your results are wrong and mine are correct." If we accept the notion that everyone's data are at least a little bit wrong (contain some error, some bias), then we can concentrate on trying to figure out why our observations do not agree; that is, we can begin to refine our theories so that they more closely fit the existing facts.

Logical Analysis

The quality of observations is one distinction between scientific and nonscientific research, but it is far from being the only one. Once observations are made, we must interpret them and draw conclusions about them. We have already discussed the scientific reliance on inductive reasoning, so it should come as little surprise that induction plays an important role in data **interpretation** (*the process whereby recorded observations are used to describe events, generate hypotheses, or test hypotheses*).

Suppose I look out my window and observe 90° displayed on the scale of a thermometer. I could, of course, reasonably conclude that the temperature outside my office is 90°, assuming I had reason to believe that my thermometer was accurate. Anyone else could also look out the same window and note the same reading, and they would probably come to the same conclusion. Inductive reasoning enters the interpretation process when we attempt to move our conclusions beyond the immediate area outside my window, beyond the immediate confines of the data collection environment. Beyond my window is the remainder of the neighborhood, the city, the county, the state, the country, and so on. How far beyond our immediate observations we can reasonably interpret those observations is both a matter of inductive reasoning and yet another distinction between scientific and nonscientific research.

Given our general knowledge about meteorology, we could reasonably conclude that the temperature around the neighborhood and city is about 90°. I would be reluctant to speculate about temperature across the state, as would most people. The same reluctance applies to interpreting data collected in a research project: how far we

generalize, *relate findings gathered from the research situation to other situations*, is limited by common sense and background information about the research topic. I would feel comfortable, for example, generalizing the results of a study of nursing students' cardiopulmonary resuscitation (CPR) performance (Oermann, Kardong-Edgren, & Odom-Maryon, 2011) to actual nurses by claiming actual nurses use the same physical skills that the students used. However, I would not feel comfortable claiming that actual nurses would make the same *decisions* that the students did. The way in which students and nurses conduct CPR may be the same, but the decisions about when to use CPR may be quite different because they may pay attention to different information (have different biases) and may have different life experiences with which to interpret the information they receive. **Overgeneralization**—*drawing conclusions too far beyond the scope of immediate observation*—brings scientific research into the realm of nonscientific research.

Research Reports

From time to time, you may find yourself reading a research article in which it appears as though the researchers designed their study to test a theory, collected data, and supported the theory discussed in the introduction of the article. You should know, and the researchers should know, that logic does not enable us to support a theory. Yet they write such phrases as "research supports the theory of . . ." or "the theory of X has received a great deal of empirical support." In such cases, the language of scientific research appears to conflict with scientific philosophy.

Keep in mind that the reason that research cannot support a theory is that support for a theory comes not from finding results consistent with a theory but from failing to find results that do not fit the theory. Remember the double negative logic of science: Failing to disconfirm a theory is the only empirical way to provide support for a theory. But support for a theory does not mean the same thing as proof that a theory is correct. It is a little too verbose to write "a number of researchers have attempted to disconfirm Theory X and have failed to do so" continually, and so we sometimes write "Theory X has received empirical support."

Most authors of research articles create the impression that the researchers knew, from the start, exactly how the major results of the study would come out. Instead, research is often conducted with extremely little certainty about how the results will turn out. The researchers are not trying to hide their inability to predict the results accurately; rather, they are succinctly providing a theoretical context for their results. No matter how unexpected the results of research may be, they cannot contribute to what we already know unless they can be placed into a theoretical context. Placing results in context, however, is not the same as making up a theory to fit the results one obtained. Kerr (1998) refers to such writing as HARKing (Hypothesizing After the Results are Known) and notes that there are costs associated with such writing (see also Rupp, 2011).

Definitive Studies

Although any study may satisfy someone's curiosity about a particular issue, no study ever satisfies all scientific interest in an issue. That is, despite the fact that one often hears the phrase used in one or another context, there is no such thing as a **definitive study**—*a research project that completely answers a question.* Because any particular phenomenon is extremely complex, someone will always ask, "But what if . . . ?" Such questions point out the need for additional research. Proposing that a definitive study can exist produces premature closure of activity; as Yogi Berra is supposed to have said about a baseball game, "It ain't over 'til it's over." It is, of course, difficult to argue with such logic. Within a scientific approach to research, it is not over until it is no longer possible to ask "What if?"

Although definitive studies may not exist, there are highly influential studies that set an entire research program, or series of programs, in motion. These studies have a great deal of **heuristic value**—they *stimulate a great deal of additional research activity.* Milgram's (1963) research on obedience is one example of a study with high heuristic value. It not only generated a great deal of controversy concerning research ethics, it also stimulated extensive research on compliance of individuals and groups. Munsterberg's (1913) studies of the accuracy of eyewitnesses' recollections, many of which were demonstrations conducted in the classroom, were also highly heuristic. Many examples of current research on eyewitnesses can be traced to one or another of his demonstrations.

As a research consumer, you should neither look for nor believe you have found a study that conclusively proves whether or not a program is effective; you won't find such a study because they simply don't exist. You will, however, find many claims that others have found such a study. I recently searched for the phrase "science proves" on Google and turned up about 378,000 sites, not all of which were quack sites, which merely demonstrates that there are many individuals who don't understand the limitations of science. In case you are interested, another search for the phrase "research proves" resulted in about 410,000 sites; a quick scan of some of those sites convinced me that many writers confuse *prove* with *demonstrate,* a confusion that could lead to erroneous conclusions about the value of a program or policy.

Determinism

Perhaps the most misunderstood concept in a scientific approach to research is **determinism,** *the philosophical assumption that every event has at least one discoverable cause.* As defined here, determinism means nothing more than "events do not happen by themselves." We assume that there is always a causal agent and that the agent can be discovered through a scientific approach to research. If you think about it at all, you will realize that there could not be science without determinism. The purpose of psychology, for example, is to understand the causes of human behavior; if we did not assume that every human behavior had at least one cause, then there would be no point to trying to understand the causes of human behavior.

Many people, however, incorrectly mistake determinism for **predestination,** *the philosophical assumption that events are unalterable and that, once initiated, events cannot be changed.* The two assumptions clearly are not at all similar. Indeed, there is some notion in determinism that once we are able to discover the cause of an event, we can alter the cause and thereby alter the event. There may, of course, be theories that include the assumption of predestination, and some of those theories may be tested through scientific research, but predestination is an aspect of a specific theory and not an assumption inherent in science.

Table 2.2 contains a summary of the differences between what is and what is not included in a scientific approach to research. Although there may be many other comparisons that could be drawn, you should have enough background in philosophy of science to begin putting it into practice.

TABLE 2.2   Comparisons Between Science and Nonscience

Science Is	Science Is Not
A way to obtain new information	An activity per se
Described by a philosophy	Defined by only one philosophy
Generalizing from facts	A way to prove theories true
Grounded in paradigms	Blind acceptance of tradition
Based on consensus	Relying on personal authority
A matter of faith	Uncritical faith
Deterministic	Predestination
The best approach we have	Refusing to search for a better approach

ETHICS OF CONSUMING RESEARCH

I continue to be amazed that codes of ethics for researchers, particularly those who do research on human beings, did not emerge until the middle of the 20th century. To that point, the public, including researchers, assumed that scientists had sufficient integrity so as to make formal guidelines and regulations unnecessary, but the torture and other inhumane treatment of concentration camp inmates by the Nazis during World War II convinced the world community that guidelines were necessary, and the Nuremberg Code was enacted (Nuremberg Military Tribunal, 1949). The code emphasized the importance of **informed consent**, *the process by which potential research participants are provided* *with all of the information necessary to allow them to make a reasonable decision con-cerning their participation*, and a balance of risks and benefits such that the latter out-weighed the former (Gorman & Dane, 1994). Expansion of the code for physicians and other medical researchers resulted in the Declaration of Helsinki (World Medical Association, 1964), which further clarified the relationship between research and treatment.

In the United States, breaches of research ethics, again primarily in biomedical research (see, e.g., Jones, 1993), led to the passage of the 1974 National Research Act. The act included the creation of the National Commission for the Protection of Human Subjects of Biomedical and Behavioral Research (National Commission for the Protection of Human Subjects of Biomedical and Behavioral Research, 1979; Seiler & Murtha, 1981), the purpose of which was to recommend an overall policy for research with human partic-ipants. The commission provided a report that led to a number of changes in the ways in which biomedical and behavioral research is conducted. Eventually, a formal set of regu-lations was adopted in the United States ("Final regulations amending basic HHS policy for the protection of human research subjects," 1981; "Protection of Human Subjects," 2005) that included the establishment of institutional review boards (IRB) to conduct prior review and continuing oversight of all human subjects research conducted within the purview of any institution or organization that received federal funds. Similar devel-opments in other countries have led to a nearly global adoption of some form of guidelines or regulations concerning the conduct of human subjects research (Office for Human Research Protections, 2007).

The existing regulations and guidelines provide considerable direction as research-ers attempt to balance the mutual obligations of developing new knowledge (Cook, 1981; Mindick, 1982) and treating individuals involved in our research with proper consider-ation (Dane, 1990). If you find yourself in a position to conduct research, or direct others to conduct research, you should become familiar with these guidelines and regulations. For the purpose of consuming research, however, it is more important to understand the principles that are used to guide the development of such regulations and to recognize the ways in which these principles apply to research consumption.

Ethical Principles of Research

In the Belmont Report, the National Commission for the Protection of Human Subjects of Biomedical and Behavioral Research (1979) established three principles by which all research should be guided—respect for persons, beneficence, and justice—and to these have been added trust and scientific integrity (Dane, 2006, 2007b; Dane & Parish, 2006). These five principles will form the basis of our discussion of the ethics of research consumption.

Respect for Persons

Respect for persons is a principle derived from the ethical theory proposed by Immanuel Kant (1788/1997), from which we obtain the admonition never to use another human being merely as a means to an end; that is, this principle involves maintaining others' **autonomy**, *the ability to direct oneself, particularly through the exercise of independent processing of information.* We see this implemented, among other ways, in the presumption of informed consent for research participants. In the context of research consumption, respect for persons involves giving researchers proper credit, representing others' work accurately, and providing comprehensive information to those who will benefit from our consumption of research.

At this point in your academic experience, you are well familiar with the requirement to use quotation marks or other, similar conventions whenever you use someone else's words; to do otherwise is plagiarism. The purpose of this convention is to ensure that the individual who wrote the words receives credit for having done so and to prevent readers from thinking that the words are ours instead of the original author's. Similarly, whenever we obtain information from another source or use an idea obtained from someone else's work, we give credit by citing the source from which we obtained the information or idea; again, this prevents readers from thinking that the information or idea is original to us. Giving researchers proper credit, however, involves going beyond the usual conventions to avoid plagiarism; we also do so through the manner in which we write about the research. Thus, we should refer to the authors, not to unnamed researchers or "research" (see, e.g., American Psychological Association, 2010). For example, when describing the research mentioned in Chapter 1, we should write "Oermann et al. (2011) demonstrated that brief practice periods maintained CPR skills" instead of writing "Research has demonstrated that brief practice periods maintained CPR skills (Oermann et al., 2011)." While both sentences provide credit to Oermann et al. for the information, the former makes it clear that Oermann et al. conducted the research; the latter refers only to Oermann et al. as the source of the information and could mean that anyone conducted the research about which we learned from reading Oermann et al.

Just as we respect others by giving them proper credit as the sources of the information we use, we also respect others by representing their work accurately. Obviously, we want to convey correctly information we obtain from others, but accuracy goes beyond getting it right in the sense that we must avoid oversimplifying research results. Rector (2002), for example, reported that an evaluation of the Not Me, Not Now abstinence-only advertising campaign (Doniger, Riley, Utter, & Adams, 2001) included a reduction in pregnancy rates among 15-year-old teens but did not report that Doniger et al. also found no change in pregnancy rates among women aged 17. The failure to report the additional results oversimplifies the results and could mislead those reading the report, leaving them to think that the change in pregnancy rates was longer lasting than it actually was. Conveying the complications sometimes demonstrated in research can be difficult, but our ethical obligation to respect individuals, those who reported the research and those who will read our review of that research, requires that we overcome such difficulty. Accurately reporting results also involves making sure that our readers understand what was measured in the research we review. The Union of Concerned Scientists (2006), for example, reported numerous examples in which government reports concerning abstinence-only sex-education programs labeled various programs as effective without noting that *effective* was defined in terms of attendance or changes in attitudes about sexual behavior; actual sexual behavior was not measured in the research included in these reports. There is, of course, nothing wrong with considering attitude change to be a desired outcome, but it is inaccurate, and therefore undermines autonomy, when one implies that changes in attitudes toward sexual activity are synonymous with changes in sexual behavior per se.

Finally, we demonstrate respect for persons when our reports about research are comprehensive, when they include all relevant research and not just those studies that conform to our preferences or those of our intended audience. Imagine your reaction upon reading about a researcher who reported only part of the data, only those data that were consistent with a conclusion drawn by the researcher even before data were collected. I hope your reaction would include outrage and a general conclusion akin to "That's not right" or "That's dishonest." Indeed, such behavior would be evidence of a lack of respect for one's audience through undermining autonomy by misleading the readers; it would be dishonest. A failure to present all relevant studies in a review of research, too, would be similarly dishonest.

In summary, respect for persons, in the context of consuming research, involves giving credit where it is due, accurately reporting research procedures and results, and comprehensively reporting the available, relevant research. To do anything less undermines the autonomy of our audience; it reduces the accuracy or amount of information for decision making available to our audience members.

Beneficence

While researchers have an ethical obligation to generate new knowledge (Cook, 1981; Mindick, 1982), they also have an ethical obligation to do so in a manner that promotes the public good (National Commission for the Protection of Human Subjects of Biomedical and Behavioral Research, 1979). The notion that knowledge is beneficial in and of itself has a long tradition in Western thought (see, e.g., Plato, 2005), and so, to some extent, researchers satisfy both ethical obligations simply by producing new knowledge. As research consumers, as we engage in evidence-based practice, we also have an ethical obligation to promote the public good, to engage in beneficence (Illingworth & Parmet, 2015; Orenstein & Yang, 2015). We, too, partially fulfill that obligation simply by producing new knowledge.

It may seem strange to think that a reviewer of others' work produces new knowledge—after all, the information already exists in the original research reports we review—but a good review goes beyond simply noting what others have found in their research. Yet even simply noting what others have done can be beneficent in the sense that a list and description of sources in a single document makes information available in a more convenient format. Nevertheless, a good review involves using the information in existing sources to make a particular point, to draw a conclusion that would not have been obvious from reading only one or two of the original sources.

Of course, one can argue that engaging in evidence-based practice is itself another way in which to promote beneficence. As noted long ago by Mead (1969), increases in knowledge often precipitate fear about how that knowledge will be used. A careful review of research knowledge before putting it into practice can be used to reduce such fear. Reviews can be used to identify ways to improve practice, as opposed to recommend only "yes" or "no," in much the same way that research is used to improve scientific theories. The absence (or insufficiency) of empirical research can be used to promote additional research on a specific practice, process, program, or problem in general. Many people also tend to be afraid of research as a result of experience or hearsay regarding misuse of such efforts (see, e.g., Posavac, 1994), but a careful, comprehensive review of research can be used to allay such fears. Thus, the ethical obligation of beneficence (promoting the public good) is relevant to reviewing research; indeed, the obligation can be met by ensuring widespread dissemination of research reviews.

Justice

In the context of conducting research, the ethical obligation for justice refers generally to ensuring that risks and benefits associated with research are distributed equally throughout the population (National Commission for the Protection of Human Subjects of Biomedical and Behavioral Research, 1979). For example, toward the end of the 20th century, a great deal of attention was focused on the underrepresentation of women included as subjects in biomedical research (Mastroianni, Faden, & Federman, 1999). This meant that men were much more likely to benefit from the results of such research and that too little attention was paid to women's health issues, which eventually came to be perceived as patently unfair or unjust. More recently, we see that the risks associated with stem cell research are being inequitably borne by those governmental regions that allow such research (Dane, 2007a).

It may seem puzzling to think in terms of risks associated with reviewing existing research: After all, how likely is it that someone could be harmed by your writing about research that has already been done? But reviews can have considerable impact, particularly when they are used to influence practice. Consider, for example, the American Heart Association (2006) review of research that produced the compression-only guidelines for CPR. That produced a major change in the way almost everyone learned (or relearned) CPR, which affected millions of people. The change to compression-only CPR continues to receive empirical support (Ewy, 2014).

Again, we return to the notion that careful writing is important, but meeting one's ethical obligation of justice involves going beyond careful writing. You have already read about the difficulties inherent in generalizing from research results, and this becomes particularly relevant when reviewing research for evidence-based practice. It becomes quite important to consider the range of research subjects included in the relevant research and compare that range to the diversity of individuals who will be affected by the practice.

Trust

As we learned earlier, the enterprise of science relies heavily on trust. Although a scientific approach is self-correcting, scientists have to rely on each other and trust each other because it is logistically impossible to double-check everything, to look over each scientist's shoulders to ensure that he or she is doing exactly what was presented in a research report. Thus, those reading about our research on the effects of training nurses in advanced cardiac life support (Dane, Russell-Lindgren, Parish, Durham, & Brown, 2000) have to trust that we correctly identified which nurses were trained and which were not, that we correctly identified which patients survived a resuscitation attempt and which did not, that we actually conducted the statistical analyses that we wrote about, and so on. The self-correcting nature of science will determine whether or not the sample we used was unique—if no one else can replicate the results we obtained, then our sample was unique—but ultimately, the entire scientific community must trust that we did the research the way we described doing the research.

So, too, those reading our reviews of research must trust that we actually read and understand the research reports we include in our reviews; they must trust that we made a good-faith effort to identify all relevant research reports, and so on. Our willingness to enter the scientific community as consumers of research creates an ethical obligation to be as trustworthy as those who produced the research. Beyond simple honesty, those who will read our reports and those who will be otherwise affected by the content of our reports are owed a high degree of competency in the construction of those reports.

Regardless of the discipline in which evidence-based practice is engaged, all those who are affected must place a considerable amount of trust in those who develop, analyze, and implement the practice (Gille, Smith, & Mays, 2015; Svara, 2007; Yarborough, 2014). As with other ethical obligations, honest, comprehensive, careful, and expert review and application of research brings us quite far along the path of fulfilling the obligation of trust. Independently evaluating the quality of the research, for example, meets this obligation much better than merely accepting researchers' conclusions because they're the experts. We know that the self-correcting nature of research means that, indeed, errors are made; thus, we become part of the self-correcting process by examining critically all research we review. Even though we may have biases about what conclusions we would like to include in our review, we have an obligation to set aside those biases and ensure that our conclusions are based on sound, methodological principles rather than on personal preferences.

Scientific Integrity

   The ethical obligation for scientific integrity involves having respect for the scientific process itself and acting accordingly. For researchers, this involves, quite simply, "doing good research" in all that the phrase entails (Committee on Assessing Integrity in Research Environments, 2002). For consumers of research, this involves adopting a scientific approach to reading, understanding, and reporting on others' research, even if one is not actually a scientist. Thus, it involves behaving like a scientist when using science as the basis for commenting on programs or policies.

   In addition to intellectual honesty, accuracy, fairness, and respect for those involved directly and indirectly, scientific integrity involves giving careful consideration to actual and potential conflicts and, if relevant, explicitly declaring those conflicts and comprehensively trying to overcome such conflicts. Just as in Chapter 1, where we learned that one important part of critically reviewing research involves assessing the *who* of research, an important part of reviewing research ethically involves making potential readers aware of who we, the reviewers, are and what biases might have influenced our review. Although it is best to avoid conflicts of interest, it is probably not possible to do so entirely (Adams, 2007; Kimmelman, 2007; Pachter, Fox, Zimbardo, & Antonuccio, 2007). A program or practice you are reviewing may be the *raison d'être* for your department and an unfavorable review may put your position in jeopardy, or the program or practice may be a favorite of influential policy makers. In such circumstances, even the best attempt to be objective may not be fully successful. In a very well-known study, for example, Rosenthal and Fode (1963) demonstrated that merely telling undergraduate researchers that research rats were "bright" as opposed to "dull" resulted in "bright" rats performing better in a discrimination task. Similarly, Rosenthal and Jacobson (1966) demonstrated that, compared to a **control group** (*the group in a study composed of individuals who received the original treatment or no treatment at all; the group to which the treatment group is compared*), randomly assigned first- and second-grade students gained 10 to 15 intelligence quotient (IQ) points after their teachers were falsely informed that the students had scored highly on a "test for intellectual blooming" (p. 115). (The effect was not obtained among students in Grades 3–8.) In neither study was there any evidence of cheating (such as falsely reported scores) among the researchers or teachers; Rosenthal and Jacobson believed the effect was much more subtly produced, probably without the researchers' or teachers' intentional efforts or awareness. In healthcare, the placebo effect is well known (Kisaalita, Staud, Hurley, & Robinson, 2014).

   Given that we cannot avoid conflicts of interest entirely and that we cannot avoid bias entirely when we have a conflict of interest, you may be tempted to think that there is nothing to be done, that we simply cannot meet the ethical obligation for scientific integrity, but you would be mistaken in that conclusion. There are tactics we can employ to overcome bias in a conflicted-interest situation. Perhaps the most important of these is becoming aware of the conflict (Cain, Loewenstein, & Moore, 2005). In the Rosenthal et al. studies (Rosenthal & Fode, 1963; Rosenthal & Jacobson, 1966), for example, neither the student researchers nor the teachers were aware that the information presented by the experimenters could bias them; you are in a much better position because you are now aware that even seemingly innocuous information can produce bias. Knowledge of potential bias is necessary but not sufficient; we also need to consider carefully and objectively how the bias could affect our decisions about the research we are reviewing. In other words, we need to think critically about our own thought processes and make our reasoning explicit (Moore & Loewenstein, 2004). Cooper (1998) refers to this as the "*60 Minutes* Test," as in thinking about how we would explain our decision if we were facing one of the interviewers on the CBS television show. Thus, while we make notes about one or another research project, we should keep asking ourselves questions such as these: Is this note correct? Would the project researchers agree with my characterization of their research? Could someone else argue with my notation? The text in our review must also match the notes we have taken.

In general, then, the ethical obligations with respect to consuming research are somewhat different than those for conducting research, despite the obligations having been based on the same five principles: respect for persons, beneficence, justice, trust, and scientific integrity. With the exception of scientific integrity, as opposed to integrity in general, you probably noticed that the obligations are very much the same as those included in the code of ethics, guidelines for responsible conduct, or other requirements established by the professional organizations of which you are a member. When we are functioning as experts, we must pay considerable attention to the actual and potential impacts we have on nonexperts. Similarly, when we function as research experts, we must pay attention to the actual and potential effects of our actions.

SUMMARY

- Science is not an activity but rather an approach to activities that share the goal of discovering knowledge. One of these activities is research.

- Like any approach, a scientific approach has limitations. These limitations include rational inference, criteria for growth, pragmatic action, and intellectual honesty.

- Rational inference is a limitation on the extent to which we can propose universal truths. Because we must rely on inductive reasoning for such proposals, we cannot prove their accuracy. Thus, we accept theories as temporarily correct while always assuming that another, better theory is likely to come along.

- Criteria for growth is a limitation on the standards by which to judge the relative merits of explanations. Although such judgments are based on objective observations, we must be aware that the objectivity and relevance of observations are limited to the paradigm on which their relevance and objectivity are based.

- Pragmatic action is a limitation on the practice of research concerning methodological issues. Consensus, based on sound reasoning, is the way we decide how best to practice research.

- Intellectual honesty is a limitation on our willingness to accept a scientific approach. Placing one's faith in the scientific approach, however, does not involve believing in one or another particular theory.

- It is axiomatic that all observations contain some degree of error. Objectivity—the extent to which more than one observer can make the same measurement—decreases measurement error but does not eliminate it.

- Although research reports are written so as to place research results in a theoretical context, it is often the case that the theoretical context was logically derived after the research was conducted. This is a shortcoming when the author suggests that the hypothesis was derived prior to data collection.

- Despite the fact that a scientific approach includes the goal of comprehensively testing theories, there is no such thing as a definitive study. No study produces the final answer to a research question, in part because there is always the possibility that another theoretical context raises additional questions.

- One of the basic assumptions of a scientific approach to research is determinism—the assumption that every phenomenon has at least one discoverable cause. Although people often confuse determinism with predestination, the two concepts are entirely different. Predestination refers to the belief that events cannot be altered.

- Regardless of the point at which one begins a research project, the project is always related to one theory or another. Variables—logically derived, concrete representations of theoretical concepts—are used to form hypotheses; it is hypotheses that are directly tested in a research project.

- Construct validity refers to the extent to which a variable represents a theoretical concept. Consensus is necessary for validity, but it is possible to misuse a variable on which consensus has been achieved. Avoiding the belief that a variable is the same as the concept it represents prevents such misuse.

- Ethics for scientific research were not formally codified until the second half of the 20th century. The first of these, the Nuremberg Code, was in response to the Nazi atrocities.

- There are five primary principles that guide ethical research: respect for persons, beneficence, justice, trust, and scientific integrity. These same principles can be used to guide ethical consumption of research.

- Respect for persons involves giving researchers proper credit, representing others' work accurately, and providing comprehensive information to those who will benefit from our consumption of research.

- Beneficence involves promoting the public good.

- Justice refers generally to ensuring that risks and benefits associated with research, including the consumption of research, are distributed equally throughout the population.

- Trust involves much more than honesty; those who will read our reports and those who will be otherwise affected by the content of our reports are owed a high degree of competency in the construction of those reports.

- Scientific integrity involves intellectual honesty, accuracy, fairness, and giving careful consideration to and, if relevant, explicit declaration of conflicts of interest and a comprehensive effort to overcome such conflicts.

EXERCISES

1. Find examples in which people have written or said things that indicate they do or do not understand the rational inference problem in science.

2. Find examples in which people have written or said things consistent with the notion of comparing one theory against another. (Note: This may be somewhat difficult because most popular-press reports usually mention only one theory, if any.)

3. Find examples of reports in which the author(s) claim(s) to be reporting a consensus about scientific conclusions. Can you determine the source of the reported consensus?

4. Find an example of what you think is biased reporting of research. Explain why you think it is biased. Can you think of any conflicts of interest you might have with the report?

3

Reading a
Research Report

*People don't usually do research the way people who write
books about research say that people do research.*

—A. J. Bachrach (1981)

OVERVIEW

The purpose of this chapter is to provide you with an overview of how to read a
research report. You will learn about a technique to enhance your critical-reading
skills. You may not have enough knowledge about methodology and statistics to
understand everything in a research report, but you will learn about general style as
well as the difference between what is typically included, what is sometimes included,
and what is generally not included in a research report. You will also learn about the
traditional organization of a research report. Finally, you will learn about a general
rubric for evaluating research articles and incorporating research information into your
evidence-based practice.

INTRODUCTION

Good critical reading requires practice, thought, and awareness. The more critical reading
you do, the more your reading will improve. The more you think about what you are reading and the more you pay attention to what others have written about what they read—
good or bad—the more your reading will improve. To become a better reader, read more

and write about what you read. Beyond reading more, however, there are specific techniques that can be used to improve your critical-reading skills. One of these is the **SQ3R** method—*survey, query, read, recite, and review—a technique designed to enhance understanding while reading*.

The SQ3R method of reading (Robinson, 1970; Vacca & Vacca, 1999), slightly adapted for higher-level materials (and readers), will help you to organize what you are reading. It takes a little practice and seems somewhat awkward at first, but I find it to be well worth the effort. The method works well for incorporating technical material into one's existing knowledge about an area (Carlston, 2011; Feldt & Hensley, 2009; Huber, 2004) and is particularly well suited to the highly structured nature of research reports.

The *survey* part of the technique represents obtaining an overview of the material to be read. For research reports, this can be accomplished by reading the title and abstract; you also should examine any tables and figures contained in the article. The overview you obtain from an abstract serves as the foundation for organizing the information contained in the report. As you survey (by reading the abstract), *question* why the author(s) decided upon this particular research question, why this particular method was used, why the results turned out the way they did, and why the author(s) reached this particular conclusion. As well, skim through the report and ask as many questions as possible about any included tables and figures. You don't need to try to understand tables and figures at this point; ask yourself questions about what you think you need to learn from them. It may feel awkward to ask questions before you actually read the report— Why not just start reading?—but the questions enable you to think about your existing knowledge about the topic, which in turn enables you to begin to incorporate the new information into that existing knowledge. The more questions you ask, the more focused your reading will be.

The first of the three *R*s stands for *read*, which is an obvious component of reading a research report, but in this case, the reading should be done actively. Don't just allow the words to pass in front of your eyes; try to answer the questions you asked during the survey phase of the process. As you encounter something you do not understand, stop to figure it out, search online for information, and use other techniques to ensure that you understand what you are reading before continuing. I find that *read* works best when I do it one paragraph at a time; I make sure that I understand each paragraph before attempting to read the next paragraph.

The second *R* represents *recite*, which stands for articulating in your own words what you just read in the paragraph. I prefer to *recite* using an open document on my computer; I write, in my own words, the point that was made in the paragraph I read. Whether you actually recite or write, the purpose of this *R* is to test your knowledge of what you have read. Note that using a highlighter to mark passages you think are important is not sufficient; highlighting only marks the author's words. Instead, you should express the author's idea in your own words; either say or write what you think the paragraph means or what you learned from the paragraph. If you can express the point in your own words, then you are more likely to understand the material. *Reciting* forms an outline of what you have read, and the notes are very convenient for the final *R*, *review*. Before you decide that you have read and understood a research article, review the notes you have made to make sure that those notes still make sense in the context of the entire article. You may discover, for example, that some of your earlier notes can be improved as a result of your more comprehensive understanding of the entire article. Among other things, think about whether or not your reading answered all of your questions from the initial survey.

An alternative to SQ3R is SOAR: selection, organization, association, regulation (Jairam & Kiewra, 2009; Jairam, Kiewra, Rogers-Kasson, Patterson-Hazley, & Marxhausen, 2014; Kiewra, 2005). *Selection* refers to taking notes efficiently while reading material. *Organization* involves rearranging the information into a structure that makes sense to you, that helps you understand the information better. As you learn how to evaluate each component of a research report, we will address organization of learned material. *Association* involves relating parts of a research report with each other as well as relating new information into your existing knowledge about the topic. Finally, *regulation* involves self-testing, asking yourself about your understanding of the information in the research report. Can you remember, for example, the age range of the research participants? Similarly, can you remember which group scored higher and how much higher?

That is about all I can include in this chapter about how to improve your reading, for to comment any more would require a one-on-one, in-person session. Instead, the remainder of this chapter deals with why and how to read a research report. There are some general (and a few specific) conventions adopted by those who write reports about research, and we will examine these conventions in this chapter. Obviously, I cannot provide comments about specific reports you may read nor does it make much sense to predict the kinds of reports you will read. Instead, I will discuss the content of the three articles that have served previously as examples: Dane, Russell-Lindgren, Parish, Durham, and Brown (2000); Eskreis-Winkler, Shulman, Beal, and Duckworth (2014); Oermann, Kardong-Edgren, and Odom-Maryon (2011).

RESEARCH REPORT ORGANIZATION

The general purpose of a research report is simple: to inform others about the research the investigators conducted. The audience for which most researchers write is other researchers, which means authors of research reports focus on the things that they believe other researchers want to know: the theoretical and empirical background of the research, the method and procedures used to collect the data, the results of the data analyses, and how those results add to the existing literature. As you read research reports, you will encounter a fair amount of jargon. (You need to be familiar with such jargon in order to understand the article, so it may help to ensure that you have access to the Internet when you read to look up words and phrases that are unfamiliar.) One reason for the jargon is that the report is written for other researchers, "insiders" who know what the jargon means. Another reason for the jargon is that research writing in general is quite succinct, much denser than, say, a novel or even an advanced textbook. Therefore, you should be prepared for reading much more slowly and much more carefully than you have previously done.

The organization of a report of empirical research is fairly standard among behavioral and social sciences—indeed, most sciences. In psychology, the standard is comprehensively described in the *Publication Manual of the American Psychological Association* (American Psychological Association, 2010). Slightly different formats may be used to present the organized material, but every research report is likely to contain an introduction and sections for method and/or procedures, results, discussion, and references as well as a summary or abstract of the report.

The major sections—introduction, method, results, and discussion—are often described as analogous to an hourglass of information through which the author guides the reader. As depicted in Figure 3.1, the report begins with one or more general statements that place the research in context, followed by increasingly more specific statements until the reader is informed of the intentions and hypotheses of the research. The method section includes information about how the data were collected, the results section contains what was found, and the discussion is used to bring the reader back to the general context. As the center of the hourglass, the results are the focus of the research report. For this reason, you cannot consider your understanding of the research to be more than a tentative idea until you understand the results.

Not every aspect depicted in Figure 3.1 appears in every research report. Dane et al. (2000) and Oermann et al. (2011), for example, include more empirical and historical context in their reports and not much theoretical context. Similarly, Dane et al. (2000) do not include nearly as much information about data-collection procedures in their report as are included in other reports because their data came from a previously documented data registry. Readers who want details about the data-collection process were referred to a different report containing those details. Eskreis-Winkler et al. (2014) included four research projects in their report, so the hourglass is somewhat distorted by their inclusion of a specific discussion for each project and a general discussion of the implications of all four projects. Despite such differences, the general structure depicted in Figure 3.1 is present in almost every research report.

Introduction

To explain the purpose of the research, most researchers include an introduction, which enables you to learn how the particular project described in the report fits into the general scheme of inquiry. The introduction also provides you with the opportunity to find out about other, related research reports that you may want to read to ensure that your knowledge of the literature is as comprehensive as possible. As the authors put

FIGURE 3.1   The Hourglass Analogy of the Research Report

The introduction begins leading the reader from very general issues to successively more specific issues until the results, the center point of the article, are presented. Then, the reader is led back from the very specific results to the most general implications of the results.

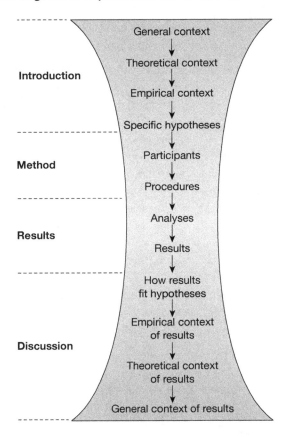

their research into the context of the literature, you may discover previously unknown publications that are relevant to the topic of your practice issue.

General Context

Most research reports begin with reference to a general context for the project, a context described in terms of society rather than research per se. Using quotations from Woody Allen, Eskreis-Winkler et al. (2014) make the point that it is logical to consider goal commitment ("showing up") an important part of success. In their second paragraph, they make multiple references to persistence rates in different contexts as a way to introduce the personality concept *grit*, which they connect to passion and perseverance ("showing up"). In only two paragraphs, they present the general area into which their research fits (success) and introduce the specific aspect on which they will concentrate (grit). There are, of course, other aspects of success than grit, but their connection between grit and showing up give us a context from which to understand why they did the research they are reporting.

Literature Review

After presenting the general context of the research, we next learn about other research that is relevant to the specific project described in the report. Understanding the empirical and theoretical context is important to understanding and interpreting the results of someone's research project. It is from the literature review that we gain clues about why the researchers chose the measures they chose, why the researchers compared different groups, even why the researchers chose the research participants. Without such background information, it is much more difficult to judge the relative importance of the results for our purposes.

In one relatively brief paragraph (the second of the introduction), Oermann et al. (2011) cite nine different research reports as they summarize the existing research on practice and maintenance of cardiopulmonary resuscitation (CPR) skills. In the next paragraph, they note that few of those studies included brief practice sessions, and none of the studies included nursing students as research participants. From those 19 lines of text, we learn why it is that they set up their study the way they did. If we are interested in the effects of practice in general, as opposed only to brief practice, we also learned about nine other research studies we may need to read.

Hypothesis Statement

At some point, usually toward the end of the introduction, we learn about the specific hypothesis to be tested in the project, which amounts to the specific purpose of the study. The statement does not always include the word *hypothesis*. Dane et al. (2000, p. 84) write about "purpose of the present study," while Oermann et al. (2011, p. 1) refer to "primary aim" and "secondary aim." Eskreis-Winkler et al. (2014) describe the hypothesis they wished to test on page 1 and later describe their purpose more specifically as examining "the predictive validity of grit for retention" (p. 2). In keeping with the opening quote from Bachrach (1981), the hypothesis statement is almost always in the introduction, but it may not be placed exactly as depicted in Figure 3.1.

The Method Section

The method section of the report is where we learn how the researchers collected their data, which in turn enables us to judge both the extent to which the research is relevant to our practice issue and the quality of the method and procedures used. If, for example, you care about success but are not now interested in grit as a measure of persistence, then you probably are not going to consider Eskreis-Winkler et al. (2014) relevant to your present concerns. (If you did not read the method section, however, you would not find out that they included personality measures other than grit in their research.) Alternately, if you are not interested in any of the six arrhythmias included in Dane et al. (2000), then you may not consider at least some of their results relevant to your practice.

Participants

The first subsection of the method section is usually a description of the participants. It contains information about who they were, how they were selected, and other pertinent information. From Oermann et al. (2011), for example, we find out that their participants were nursing students from a variety of degree programs, while from Dane et al. (2000), who do not label subsections in their method section, we learn that their participants were hospital nurses who called a resuscitation code. Because Eskreis-Winkler et al. (2014) included four different studies in their article, they have a different participants subsection for each study.

Sampling

Sometimes included in the participants subsection, and sometimes elsewhere, is information about how the sample was obtained (the sampling process). In their first study, Eskreis-Winkler et al. (2014) recruited participants among soldiers who qualified to enter the Army Special Operations Forces selection course. Oermann et al. (2011) recruited participants from 10 different nursing schools (although we learn that from information presented before the participants subsection), and from Dane et al. (2000), we learn that recruitment occurred in a different research project, as was the case in Study 4 for Eskreis-Winkler et al. (2014). When we are directed to another source for sampling information, it is a good idea to obtain that other source to make sure that we understand how it is that the participants were included in the project.

As you will learn in Chapter 4, understanding the sampling process is important because it determines, in part, the extent to which you may generalize the results of the project. Most researchers employ a form of **convenience sampling**, which is a *type of sampling based on the availability of participants or ease of inclusion* and is not meant to enable the participants to represent any population. The 120 nurses included by Dane et al. (2000), for example, were included because they were willing to be interviewed about their experience and do not represent all nurses or even all nurses in that hospital.

In addition to the sampling process, there also should be information about the extent to which the sample the researchers obtained is different from the sample they were trying to obtain. (This information is often presented in the results section instead of the method section.) In their first study, Eskreis-Winkler et al. (2014) note that the included soldiers differed from non-included soldiers only in terms of years of education (included soldiers had fewer) and note that their sample is otherwise similar to soldiers who were selected for the special-operations course in previous years. This information also helps us decide the extent to which the results of the project are relevant to our practice interests.

Materials and Measures

The materials and/or measures subsections are included if the researcher used any special equipment or materials in the study. Oermann et al. (2011) tell us the type of equipment they used to measure depth and rate of chest compressions and other variables. It may seem to be useless detail unless we want to replicate their research, but how researchers measure their variables affects their results. If other researchers obtain different results concerning chest compressions, for example, one consideration for understanding the difference may be the equipment used in the measurement process. In three of their four studies, Eskreis-Winkler et al. (2014) used the eight-item short version of the grit scale, which we should note in case their results differ from results obtained using the longer, 12-item version of the scale (e.g., Duckworth, Peterson, Matthews, & Kelly, 2007). In Study 3, only four of the eight short-version grit items were included, which produces yet another, slightly different measure of grit.

How many materials and measures subsections may comprise the method section depends upon the type of research completed, but there should always be some information about measurement included. Other sources may be cited, and we should read and understand those other sources when such citations are used. As you will learn in Chapter 5, understanding the measures used in research is a critical component of evidence-based practice. If we don't know and understand what was measured, then we can't really know how the results are relevant to our interests.

Research Design

The design subsection includes information about the arrangement of groups in the project. Oermann et al. (2011), for example, included two groups in their study: One received monthly brief-practice sessions, the other did not receive those sessions. The researchers determined who received those practice sessions and who did not, and the researchers determined what those practice sessions involved, including the length of the session, the equipment on which the participants practiced, and so on. We also learn that participants were randomly assigned to those groups, which enables us to draw different conclusions about the project than if the participants had not been randomly assigned. (You will learn about those differences throughout the book, but especially in Chapters 6 and 7.) In contrast, Dane et al. (2000) relied on preexisting groups. They compared nurses who were certified in advanced cardiac life support (ACLS) with those who were not but did not make becoming certified part of the research procedures. Similarly, Eskreis-Winkler et al. (2014) relied on naturally occurring groups in their studies: soldiers who completed special-forces training versus those who did not, continuing versus non-continuing sales personnel, graduated versus non-graduated high school students, and adults who remained married versus those who separated or divorced. Most of the rest of this book is about research design because, even though results are what we want to know from a research report, our knowledge of design is what enables us to consume those results critically.

Manipulations

When researchers use experimental **manipulations** or **interventions**, they are *creating differences between groups of participants or changing participants over time*, usually to find out what effects those changes have on the participants. When used, manipulations are described in a subsection of the method section, such as the paragraph used by Oermann et al. (2011) to provide detail about the practice sessions they used to create differences between their two groups of nursing students.

Data Analyses

Particularly in research concerning healthcare, the method section may include a subsection in which the researchers describe the type of statistical analyses that were used to obtain results. Oermann et al. (2011), for example, provide considerable information about how they dealt with missing data and how they summarized different variables as well as the specific statistical procedures performed on the data. Eskreis-Winkler et al. (2014) do the same for each of their four studies. Dane et al. (2000), instead, include information about statistical analyses in the first paragraph of their results section.

Before leaving the method section, it is a good idea to form some sort of record of what was measured in the study. Because you will want to add columns as you continue to read the report, I recommend that you use software to create a digital table or spreadsheet (see Table 3.1). Creating a summary table ensures that you are actively and critically reading the method section. Creating a summary table also provides a convenient set of notes that will be useful when you are trying to write about the project or are otherwise trying to remember procedures and results. It is best to include as much information as possible because details may not become important until long after you have finished reading the report. In Table 3.1, for example, I included the note about not knowing how Eskreis-Winkler et al. (2014) measured age: They might have obtained it from official Army records, asked the soldiers to report it on a questionnaire, or gathered the information some other way. Months or years later, perhaps when I read a report about grit and age in which different results were obtained, it might help to know, or know that I don't know, how age was measured.

TABLE 3.1   Measurement Table for Study 1 From Eskreis-Winkler et al. (2014)

Study 1	Eskreis-Winkler et al. (2014) "The Grit Effect: Predicting Retention in the Military, the Workplace, School and Marriage"	
Concept	**Measurement**	**Type of Variable**
Retention	Completion (yes/no) of special-ops course	Outcome
Grit	Eight-item short form	Predictor
General Intelligence	Armed Services Vocational Control Aptitude Battery—General Technical	Control
Physical Fitness	Army Physical Fitness Test	Control
Education	Self-report number of years of formal education	Control
Background	Age: measurement procedure not reported	Control

The Results Section

As is implied by the name, the results section is where we find the results, the outcomes of the study. Results, however, are not always numerical; it depends upon the method used to obtain them. In qualitative research, for example, results might be topics that were mentioned in an interview or photographs of outcomes. Whether numeric or not, results sections are written with the assumption that readers know all they need to know about statistics and other processes to understand the results. If you are unsure of your understanding of the statistics and/or processes described in a results section, take time out to review them.

The results section also contains more information than the overall outcome of the project. Just like the method section, the results section may contain several different subsections.

Preliminary Results

Depending on the procedures, there may be any number of things that are described at the beginning of the results section before the authors present the main results. Typically, results concerning demographic and other variables of interest will be presented first, as will any preexisting differences between groups produced by manipulations. Oermann et al. (2011) present results about differences between their brief practice and no-practice groups in terms of age and previous training as well as differences between those who persisted and those who opted out of the study after starting. Eskreis-Winkler et al. (2014) begin each of their four results sections with a statement of the percentage of participants who were successful at each of the activities they studied.

Although not presented in any of the exemplar articles, the preliminary results subsection may include results that enable us to determine the extent to which a manipulation or intervention was implemented as described. Oermann et al. (2011), for example, could have reported how many (if any) of the participants assigned to the brief-practice group skipped a practice session during the 12 months of the study.

Main Results

The main results of the study usually include the most central or most important results first, followed by clarifying results. For each set of results, what question the result is supposed to answer is usually presented, although not necessarily stated in the exactly the same way as in the introduction.

In Eskreis-Winkler et al. (2014), for example, we read that grit, general intelligence, and physical fitness were each related to completing the special-ops course. From their Table 1A, we also learned that grit is not related to the other two variables, and then we learned about grit's independent prediction of completion through a report of more complicated, follow-up results.

Active, critical reading of the results is just as important as in other sections of the report. You may have already guessed that I recommend adding notes about results to the summary table you created from the method section, as is depicted in Table 3.2. Note that I included information about the analyses as well as the results. Months or years from now, I will not remember how the data were analyzed, but I won't have to remember so long as the information is in the summary table. Note also that I included all of the results about grit and retention. As I develop my review of the research concerning grit, knowledge about how grit is correlated with other predictors of retention should be useful. I completed Table 3.2 based on my existing knowledge of the literature and understanding of statistics, so the entries are quite brief. Until you develop more knowledge about research, you may want to make more extensive, more explanatory entries in your summary tables. You might, for example, include a note about what *bivariate logistic regression* is or spell out in words what ΔR^2 means. Eventually, you will develop your own form of abbreviations, but I recommend that you only use abbreviations after you understand fully what the long version means. The summary table will not serve as a memory aid if you do not understand what you have written in the summary table.

The Discussion Section

We find out about the authors' conclusions in the discussion section of the report, in which authors begin to expand the hourglass (see Figure 3.1), beginning with a restatement of the main result(s). After a brief restatement of the research question, for example, we read in Oermann et al. (2011, p. 5), "By practicing only 6 min a month . . . students maintained their ability to compress with an adequate depth throughout the entire 12 months." In some respects, the discussion section is the reverse of the introduction: Instead of learning why the research was done, we learn how the authors think the results contribute to the existing literature. Through active, critical reading, we obtain

TABLE 3.2   Results Table for Study 1 From Eskreis-Winkler et al. (2014)

Study 1	Eskreis-Winkler et al. (2014) "The Grit Effect: Predicting Retention in the Military, the Workplace, School and Marriage"			
Concept	**Measurement**	**Type of Variable**	**Main Result**	**Secondary Result**
Retention	Completion (yes/no) of special-ops course	Outcome	58% completion	
Grit	Eight-item short form	Predictor	Predicts retention: bivariate logistic regression OR = 1.28	Independent of control variables: $\Delta R^2 = 1.84\%$; hierarchical regression significant; not correlated with intelligence ($r = -0.07$), fitness ($r = 0.06$), or education ($r = 0.00$), but is correlated with age ($r = 0.12$, $p < .01$)
General Intelligence	Armed Services Vocational Control Aptitude Battery—General Technical	Control	Predicts retention: bivariate logistic regression OR = 1.60	Independent $\Delta R^2 = 2.76\%$
Physical Fitness	Army Physical Fitness Test	Control	Predicts retention: bivariate logistic regression OR = 1.79	Independent $\Delta R^2 = 7.28\%$
Education	Self-report number of years of formal education	Control	Predicts retention: bivariate logistic regression OR = 1.53	Independent $\Delta R^2 = 1.19\%$
Background	Age: measurement procedure not reported	Control	Did not predict retention: bivariate logistic regression OR = 0.94	Independent $\Delta R^2 = 0.09\%$

a summary of the results and how those results add to what is already known about the issue of interest.

Toward the end of the discussion section, we often read suggestions for future research. Oermann et al. (2011) suggested that others investigate the frequency of practice. Even if we do not plan to engage in any research, these suggestions help us to understand what is still not well-enough known about the issue.

It is a good idea to have the summary table handy when reading the discussion so that you can make sure that the conclusions are well represented in the summary table. Nothing we read in the discussion should be a surprise, but we do want to ensure that our notes are comprehensive as well as accurate. If something we read in the discussion does not seem consistent with our summary table, we should resolve the inconsistency before moving on to the next research report.

Other Sections

The introduction, method, results, and discussion sections constitute the bulk of the research report. There are, however, a few other sections that may appear in a research report. Even though they may not be included in the limelight, they are equally import-ant in terms of the information an active reader can glean from them. They include the abstract and the references. Again, the American Psychological Association's (2010) publication manual is an excellent source for additional information.

Abstract

Most reports will contain a summary, usually called an *abstract*. This will likely be the same brief description of the report that was provided by the search engine you used to find the report. In addition to deciding whether or not to read the entire report, I like to use the abstract as a final review or regulation of my understanding of the article. After reading the report and creating the summary table, I reread the abstract sentence by sentence, check-ing to make sure that I agree that the sentence reflects my memory of the report.

References

Any published material to which the researcher refers in the report will be referenced in what is called, straightforwardly enough, the references section. Styles for references vary from journal to journal, but the predominant style in the behavioral and social sci-ences is that recommended by the American Psychological Association (2010) in its pub-lication manual. Whatever the style, the reference entry will contain enough information for you to track down a copy of the original report (usually by asking your reference librar-ian). The references are an excellent source of additional material to read as you prepare your research review.

Enough. The only way to improve your reading skills is to read some research articles. So, go and read a research report (but first read the summary).

SUMMARY

- Good reading requires practice, thought, and critical thinking. The more you do of any of these things, the more your reading skills will improve and the more efficiently you will be able to read research reports.

- The purpose of reading a research report is to find out about the results the researcher obtained. The results are the focal point of any research report.

- Research reports are organized in an hourglass fashion. Presented first is information about the general phenomenon, then more specific issues related to the phenomenon, the details about the research procedures, then the results, and finally, interpretations that typically end as generally as the introduction began.

- Because scientific writing is succinct, active reading is required to obtain as much information from the article as the researcher put into it. Passive voice, third person writing, and past tense make it difficult to read a research report quickly. The SQ3R or SOAR methods of reading will help you read more efficiently.

- The introduction contains information about why the research was conducted and usually ends with the specific hypotheses of the study.

- The method section includes information about how the data were collected, including the specific measures that were used in the study.

- The results section includes the outcomes of the project.

- The discussion contains information about how the results add to the existing literature.

- The abstract includes the main points of the complete report and is useful for deciding whether or not to read the entire report, as well as a final check of our understanding of the report.

- References may be useful in identifying and obtaining additional material relevant to your practice/interest as well as background about the information contained in the research report.

- Building a summary table for every research report you read ensures that you have read critically and actively and serves as a convenient memory aid in the future.

- Stop reading this book now, and go read a research report.

EXERCISES

1. If you have not already done so, practice the SQ3R or SOAR method while reading this chapter.

2. Find a research report relevant to your interests (or use one you already have) and identify the paragraph(s) corresponding to Figure 3.1.

3. Using an interesting research report, identify parts that you do not understand. Make a list of the things you need to know in order to understand this article. Do the authors provide references that you can read for additional clarification?

4. Create a summary table for the report you have read.

5. Find a popular-press report of one of the research articles you have found and compare the popular-press version to the research article.

4

Sampling

I don't like turnips, and I don't like liver. Call it prejudice if you wish,
but I have no intention of ever trying either again just to
make sure I don't like them. I am sure.

—Andy Rooney (1982, p. ix)

OVERVIEW

In this chapter, you will learn about the principles and procedures researchers use to select the people or things from which they obtained data. You will learn about terminology used to describe sampling as well as the theory and importance of sampling distributions. You will also learn about the difference between the two major types of sampling procedures: probability and nonprobability sampling. In addition to learning about the various procedures, you will learn about the advantages and disadvantages of each. Finally, you will learn that understanding the limitations on applying results that stem from the sampling choices made by researchers is an important part of consuming research and applying it to policies and programs.

INTRODUCTION

Like columnist and *60 Minutes* commentator Andy Rooney, most people have an aversion to one or another type of food. They've tried it, didn't like it, and insist there is no need to try again. When I was in college, I hated coconut. I tried it several times and disliked it each time I tried it. You would have had to pay me a semester's worth of tuition to get me to eat anything with coconut in it. One night, eating at the home of a friend, I agreed to a second piece of cake. My friend was very surprised. She knew I didn't like coconut, and she knew that her mother had included coconut in the cake. She thought I was eating the first piece just to be polite. When she told me, I was equally surprised as well as curious. Had my tastes changed? What was going on?

No, my tastes had not changed. Instead, I had become a victim of sampling error. Until I ate that cake, all I had ever sampled was processed coconut, which I continue to dislike. Eventually, I learned that fresh coconut had been used in the cake. I had generalized from my limited experience with processed coconut to all coconut; I had stereotyped all coconut on the basis of my experience with only processed coconut.

Generalizing from a sample is something that every one of us does every day. We may be attempting to answer a question about people without including all people in our sample. We may see one episode of a television program and decide never to watch the program again or watch one of a director's movies and decide to see more of them when we get the opportunity. And so it is with research. Because all research is based on a sample, we need to know how to avoid incorrect generalizations of the research we read, which is what this chapter is all about. Before learning how to avoid sampling error, however, we have to learn a little of the jargon associated with sampling.

When discussing **sampling**—*the process of selecting participants for a research project*—scientists tend to use a great deal of jargon. One reason for all the jargon is that we need to be able to communicate very specific notions about sampling to those who will read our research reports, and very specific notions often require jargon. You need to understand the jargon to be able to read others' reports.

Sampling unit and **sampling element** are both used to refer to *a single thing selected for inclusion in a research project*. If the researcher samples people, then a person is the unit or **element** (*a single thing selected for inclusion in a research project*). If television shows are sampled, then a single program is the unit, and so on. *All possible units or elements that theoretically could be included* make up the **population**. A population is an abstract concept, something that cannot be seen or measured, even though it consists of concrete units. The population of the United States, for example, can be estimated but it cannot be accurately counted because one can never be sure one has counted everyone; someone could be hiding, for example, or a new person could be born after the researcher has already counted everyone in a particular location.

Instead, research is done on a **sample**—*a portion of the elements in a population*. Any part of a population is considered a sample, and any given sample can be a part of more than one population. You and two of your classmates, for example, are simultaneously a sample of your class, a sample of university students, a sample of students in general, a sample of the people living in whatever country in which you may reside, and so on. A sample, then, is a concrete portion of a population, probably of more than one population.

Although a sample is a portion of a population, technically the sample is not selected from the population. Instead, samples are selected from a **sampling frame**—*a concrete* *listing of the elements in a population.* Again using you and your classmates as examples, I could select you from the registrar's list of all students at your campus, which would then be the sampling frame, but I could never be sure that the registrar's list included the entire population. Some students may be left off the list, some may be included on the list even though they are no longer students, and so forth. Essentially, the sampling frame is the largest possible sample of a population; it is everything that can be selected.

A **parameter** is *a value associated with a population.* It is an abstract value simply because we cannot calculate, for example, the mean of a population if we don't know how many units are in the population and cannot measure the entire population. Instead of calculating parameters, we have to estimate them from **statistics**—*any numerical value calculated from a sample.* Most people think *statistic* refers to statistical analyses, such as correlations, but the term applies to any value calculated from a sample. Because a sample is always concrete, we can calculate statistics. When we use statistics to estimate parameters, the statistics are inferential statistics. However, because they are estimates, inferential statistics always contain some amount of error, usually error resulting from the sampling process.

Sampling error is the term applied to *the extent to which a sample statistic incorrectly estimates a population parameter.* Consider, for example, the taste I had associated with coconut. Because I had sampled only processed coconut, that test contained some sampling error. I used that taste, however, to make inferences about all coconut (the population of coconut), just as a sample statistic is used to make an inference about an entire population. The more error involved in the sampling process, such as my ignoring raw coconut, the greater the sampling error of an inferential statistic.

If you had asked me how confident I was about my reaction to coconut before I ate that piece of cake, I, like Andy Rooney, would have told you I was 100% certain. That would have been a statement about a **confidence level**—*the probability associated with the accuracy of an inferential statistic.* I might have said the probability of my disliking any coconut you gave me was 1.00, a probability we now know was an overestimate. Indeed, a confidence level of 1.00 is always an overestimate, for no statistic can be 100% accurate. There is always going to be some sampling error, a confidence level less than 1.00, simply because we can never be sure exactly what is and is not included in any given population.

Enough jargon. You now know that units and elements are things and that they make up populations and samples. Populations are abstract collections of everything, whereas samples are only a portion of things in the population. A sampling frame is the largest sample that can be obtained from a population; it is almost every thing in the population. Further, statistics are sample values, which are often used to estimate population parameters (values). Any statistic contains some amount of error, which can be determined by calculating the confidence level associated with the statistic. Whenever a sample is taken from a population, there is always some sampling error. Fortunately, under certain conditions, we can estimate sampling error, which is what we turn our attention to next.

SAMPLING DISTRIBUTIONS

In this section, we will deal with the basis for estimating sampling error and confidence limits. If you have had a course in statistics, you've probably seen this material before. But if you are like most of us, you can always use a review. Whether or not this is a review, knowledge of sampling distributions is necessary to understand the limitations of the sampling procedures you will encounter as you read research reports.

The basis for all statistics dealing with sampling distributions is sampling theory. We will use a running example in which we are interested in discovering the mean grade point average (GPA) of the students in a fictitious methods class. We will have to assume that everyone in the methods class constitutes a population and will use fictitious numbers, including the fiction that there are 35 students in the class. The data are reflected in Figure 4.1.

The simplest way to discover the mean GPA in the class is to ask everyone to report his or her GPA. But not everyone may be willing to report his or her GPA, or some may be absent on the day the data are collected. Suppose a researcher, who is also a member of the class, asks four people in the class to report their GPAs: the people sitting in front, behind, to the left, and to the right of the researcher. They report GPAs of 3.5, 2.0, 2.2, and 1.9, and the researcher adds her own GPA of 3.2. We now have a sample of five students and can calculate the sample mean:

$$(3.5 + 2.0 + 2.2 + 1.9 + 3.2) / 5 = 2.56$$

The question is whether 2.56 is a reasonable estimate of the mean for the entire class. The answer is that we have no way of knowing: The researcher might have asked four other people and obtained a different sample mean. To explain why we have no way of knowing, we will have to learn a little more about sampling theory.

FIGURE 4.1   The Population of 35 Grade Point Averages Obtained From a Fictitious Class of Students

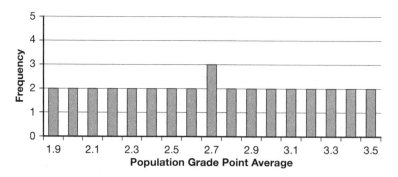

Population Versus Sample

Suppose that the distribution of GPAs in the entire class is the distribution illustrated in Figure 4.1; the distribution of the sample of five students is shown in Figure 4.2. The mean of the population is 2.70, which is not exactly the same as the sample mean of 2.56. Clearly, the sample statistic is not an accurate estimate of the population parameter, but you should already know that statistics are never perfectly accurate. To estimate how accurate a sample is requires that the sample be a random sample.

FIGURE 4.2   A Sample of Five Scores Obtained From the Population
Depicted in Figure 4.1

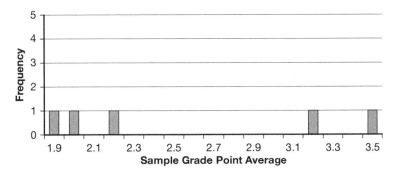

Random Selection

The key to being able to use a sample statistic to estimate a population parameter is the manner in which the sample is selected. **Random selection** or **random sampling** includes *any technique that provides each population element an equal probability of being included in the sample*. Please note that this definition of *random* is very different from the everyday use of the word. In everyday language, we might say that the four people sitting closest to the researcher are just some random people, but not everyone in the class an equal chance of being included in the sample (because the people sitting further away never had a chance), and so the sample of five people is not a random sample. If, instead, the researcher put the names of everyone in class into a hat and drew out five names, she would have obtained a random sample. Later in the chapter, you will learn about the variety of ways in which a random sample can be obtained, but they are all basically derivations of this "everyone's name in a hat" procedure.

Standard Error

When the sample is a random sample, it is possible to estimate the amount of error in the sample by taking advantage of certain properties of sampling distributions.

FIGURE 4.3   The Sampling Distribution of Means Obtained From 200 Randomly Selected Samples of Five Grade Point Averages From the Population Depicted in Figure 4.1

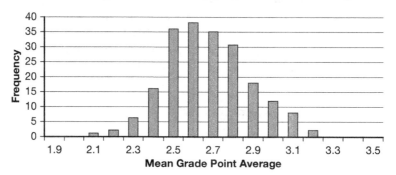

A **sampling distribution** is *a distribution of statistics theoretically created by repeatedly selecting random samples from a population.* Assume that instead of the four people around her, the researcher randomly selected five students from her class. If she calculated the mean GPA of that sample and then repeated the same procedure another 199 times, she might obtain the sampling distribution presented in Figure 4.3.

Compare Figures 4.3 and 4.1. Although the two distributions have almost identical means, their shapes are very different. The population distribution in Figure 4.1 is very flat, whereas the sampling distribution in Figure 4.3 is peaked and considerably less spread out. Even though there are more scores in the sampling distribution—200 compared to 35 in the population—the variability of the sampling distribution is smaller. The **standard deviation** (*the square root of the value produced by dividing the sum of squared deviation from the mean by one less than the sample size*) of the population is 0.48, whereas that for the sampling distribution is 0.21—less than half than that of the population. This is always the case; sampling distributions exhibit less variability than do population distributions.

Once again, however, we must come back to the real world of research. It is fine to run around generating sampling distributions, but that requires a great deal of time and effort as well as more information about the population than is usually available. But when a sample has been randomly selected, the researcher doesn't need to generate sampling distributions. Let me demonstrate with the first random sample I selected in order to create the sampling distribution in Figure 4.3. That sample consisted of GPA values of 1.9, 3.3, 2.7, 2.6, and 3.4.

The mean of this random sample is 2.78 and its standard deviation is 0.61. As sample statistics, they are supposed to be estimates of the population parameters and, forgetting about the fact that we actually know what those parameters are, we can estimate the population mean and standard deviation to also be 2.78 and 0.61, respectively. In order to calculate *the standard deviation of the sampling distribution of means*—the **standard error** of the mean—all we have to do is apply the formula below:

$$S_{\bar{x}} = \frac{S}{\sqrt{n}}$$

Where $S_{\bar{x}}$ is the standard error of the mean, S is the standard deviation of the sample, and n is the size of the sample. In the case of our random sample of five students, $S_{\bar{x}} = 0.27$.

Confidence Intervals

To estimate the amount of sampling error in a random sample, we use **confidence interval**—*the inclusive, probabilistic range of values around any calculated statistic.* Remember that at the beginning of this exercise, we wanted to estimate the mean GPA of everyone in the fictitious methods class (that is, the population mean). Our sample mean, 2.78, is an estimate of the population mean, but we also know that it is an imperfect estimate. The population mean may or may not be 2.78, but it certainly ought to be close to 2.78. The question, then, is how close? What is the range of values around the sample mean that could reasonably include the population mean—that is, what is the confidence interval of our statistic?

We could, of course, simply say the population mean is somewhere between 0.0 and 4.0 and we would be absolutely correct. But that would be uninformative; we knew that before we collected any data from the sample. But the more restricted we make the range of values, the less sure we can be about whether that range contains the population mean. What we must decide, then, is how sure we want to be. Or put another way, what are we willing to accept as the probability that the range we select is wrong? In most sciences, the rule of thumb for being wrong is a probability of .05—five chances in 100 of being wrong.

We can take advantage of the central limit theorem in order to create our confidence interval. We know from that theorem that about 95% of all scores in a normal distribution fall within about two standard deviations of the mean (technically, within 1.96 standard deviations). Because a sampling distribution is composed of an infinite number of randomly selected samples, any sampling distribution is normally distributed. Therefore, we can infer that 95% of our sample means should fall within plus or minus two standard errors of the mean. Our estimate of the population mean is 2.78, and our estimate of the standard error is 0.27. Thus, we can be 95% certain that the true population mean is somewhere between [2.78 − 2(0.27)] and [2.78 + 2(0.27)] or somewhere between 2.24 and 3.32. The probability that we are wrong is .05. By starting with a sample of five students, we have estimated that the mean of the population is between 2.24 and 3.32. In doing so, we made use of sampling theory and the central limit theory, and we had to calculate a sample mean, a sample standard deviation, and the standard error of the sample mean.

Sample Size

Look again at the formula used to calculate the standard error of the mean:

$$S_x = \frac{S}{\sqrt{n}}$$

Notice that the square root of the sample size is in the denominator of the formula. What this means is that the larger the sample size, the smaller the standard error of the mean. A smaller standard error of the mean results in a smaller confidence interval. To get a smaller confidence interval, a more precise estimate of the population, researchers often select a larger sample.

You can see the relationship between sample size and standard error by examining Figure 4.4, which was created by assuming, for illustration purposes, that the standard deviation of the sample was 10. The size of the sample, indicated on the **abscissa** (*X* axis; *the horizontal axis of a graph*), varies from 10 to 1,000, but the standard deviation of the sample remains at 10. As the sample size increases, the size of the standard error decreases. The change, however, is not linear. When the sample size changes from 10 to 50, the change in the standard error is considerable. Beyond samples of 50, however, increasing the sample size does not dramatically affect the standard error. Keep in mind, however, that larger samples make the estimate of the population more precise, but do

FIGURE 4.4   The Relationship Between Standard Error of the Mean and Sample Size. All samples have a standard deviation of 10.

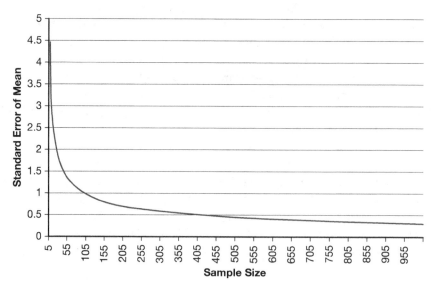

not necessarily make the sample more accurate. A large nonrandom sample can be just as far off the mark as a small nonrandom sample.

PROBABILITY SAMPLING

The foregoing discussion of sampling distributions relied entirely on samples resulting from a random sampling procedure. To create the distributions in the various figures, I used a computer to generate 200 random samples from a population that contained 35 GPAs. As mentioned before, whenever one can obtain a random sample, one can rely on the central limit theorem and the properties of the normal distribution to determine the amount of sampling error in a sample. In general, **probability sampling** is *any technique that ensures a random sample*—that is, a technique that ensures that every element in the sampling frame has an equal chance of being included in the sample. There are a number of variations on the names-in-the-hat example discussed before, and we turn our attention now to describing those variations.

Simple Random Sampling

Names selected from a collection of name tags in a hat and a list of random numbers generated by a computer program are both examples of **simple random sampling**—*techniques that involve an unsystematic random selection process*. Basically, simple random sampling involves identifying every element in the sampling frame and choosing among them using any process that ensures that every element has an equal opportunity of being selected. When sampling frames are too large for slips of paper in a hat or some similar procedure, a random number generator, contained in software such as Microsoft Excel, SPSS, SAS, and so on, is usually used. The importance of a random number generator is that the software is written so that each number is independent of every other number, which is exactly what is required to ensure that each entry has an equal probability of being selected for the sample.

Systematic Random Sampling

Simple random sampling can be a rather inefficient way to select a sample. With a very large sampling frame and a large sample, one could spend a long time generating random numbers. **Systematic random sampling** is accomplished by *choosing elements from a randomly arranged sampling frame according to ordered criteria*. Frequently, systematic random sampling is accomplished by choosing every 10th, 15th, or some other nth element in the sampling frame.

Systematic random sampling produces the same result as simple random sampling: a random sample. Both procedures require a list of the sampling frame, but systematic random sampling requires that the list be in random order. As research consumers, however, we have to accept that the researchers used systematic sampling correctly.

Stratified Random Sampling

Both simple and systematic random sampling procedures require a list of the sampling frame and that the elements in the sampling frame are relatively homogeneous. If a sampling frame is not homogeneous but instead contains subgroups, such as seniors, juniors, and so forth in a listing of university students, then the researcher may need to represent those subgroups in the sample. Whenever subgroups of a population are necessary for research purposes, stratified random sampling results in less sampling error than occurs in either simple or systematic random sampling.

Stratified random sampling is accomplished by *employing random selection separately for each subgroup in the sampling frame.* Stratified random sampling for a sampling frame of university students would involve either simple or systematic sampling within the senior class, the same procedure within the junior class, and so on until all classes are represented in the sample. The subgroups within the sampling frame are treated as though they were separate sampling frames themselves.

Researchers use stratified random sampling to ensure that a sample will contain equal or some other proportionate numbers of males and females, people with ages above and below 30, or any other subgroups that are desirable. If a researcher wants to select a specific number of each subgroup's members, the technique is called *probability sampling with quotas.* In that case, one establishes a quota for each subgroup—say, 20 men and 50 women to oversample women for some purpose—and then randomly samples members of that subgroup until the quota is met. Whether you read about stratified random sampling or probability sampling with quotas, the key point to remember is that the sample is a random sample.

Cluster Sampling

Simple, systematic, and stratified random sampling procedures are all variants of the basic name-in-a-hat process described earlier. Essentially, the entire sampling frame is listed and elements are randomly selected from it. Sometimes, however, researchers do not have a list of the sampling frame and cannot obtain one. One would not, for example, be likely to be able to find or generate a sampling frame list for all college students in the United States. When sampling frame lists are unavailable, researchers use **cluster sampling**—*randomly selecting hierarchical groups from the sampling frame.* The groups included in the sampling frame are called *clusters,* and one samples finer and finer gradations of clusters until one is at a level at which one can obtain a list of elements. To select a random sample of 500 college students in the United States, for example, a researcher could first create a sampling frame consisting of a list of colleges and universities and then randomly select, say, five colleges from this list. Then, from those clusters, the researcher could randomly select 100 students from each college to obtain a random sample of 500 college students residing in the United States. Figure 4.5 illustrates this sampling procedure.

Figure 4.5 A Two-Stage Cluster Sampling Procedure for Obtaining a Random Sample of 500 College Students in the United States

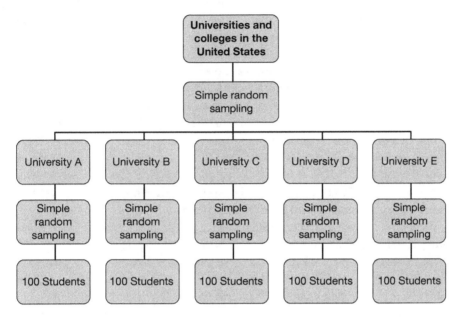

Combining different probability sampling procedures is not uncommon, and it is acceptable to combine any two or more probability sampling procedures. So long as researchers used random selection procedures, any combination will still have produced a random sample. What is not acceptable, however, is combining probability with nonprobability sampling procedures.

NONPROBABILITY SAMPLING

Unlike probability sampling, **nonprobability sampling** refers to *any procedure in which elements have unequal chances for being included in the sample.* If one chooses elements on the basis of how they look, where they live, where they sit in a classroom, or some other criteria, then the researcher limits the chances of those who do not meet the criteria. There are several different types of nonprobability sampling procedures, but they all have one thing in common: When a nonprobability sample is obtained, one cannot estimate sampling error. Because nonprobability samples are not random samples, it is usually impossible to determine the appropriate sampling distribution, which is required for estimating sampling error.

Convenience Sampling

The most common procedure for obtaining a nonprobability sample is **convenience sampling**—*selection based on availability or ease of inclusion*. As you might guess, the person-on-the-street interviews often shown during local newscasts are examples of convenience sampling. The interviewer selects whoever is willing to talk in front of the camera. Convenience sampling is also called *availability sampling*, but it is sometimes mislabeled as random by those who are using the vernacular meaning of random instead of the scientific meaning of random.

It is relatively easy to recognize a convenience sample when reading a method section because the key word *random* is missing from the sampling description. Dane, Russell-Lindgren, Parish, Durham, and Brown (2000); Goodman (1961); Eskreis-Winkler, Shulman, Beal, and Duckworth (2014); and Oermann, Kardong-Edgren, and Odom-Maryon (2011) all used convenience samples in their research. Some of those samples were quite large—11,000+ in Study 4 in Eskreis-Winkler et al. (2014)—but a large convenience sample is still a convenience sample.

Although dated, one of the best examples of the problems encountered when attempting to generalize from a convenience sample is the embarrassment of the editors of *The Literary Digest* ("Landon, 1,293,669: Roosevelt, 972,897," 1936) when they used a convenience sample to predict the outcome of the 1936 U.S. presidential election. Their problem was, simply, that their prediction was incredibly wrong. They initially sent out 10 million ballots and obtained a sample of 2 million returns. Those returns indicated a 57% to 43% margin in favor of Alf Landon over Franklin Delano Roosevelt. Instead, Roosevelt obtained about 63% of the actual popular vote.

With such a large sample, even a convenience sample, someone unfamiliar with sampling theory might expect the sampling error to be very small. But that's exactly the point underlying our knowledge about sampling theory: No matter how large the sample, there is no way to estimate sampling error without a random sampling procedure. Unfortunately, the editors of *The Literary Digest* had used telephone books and automobile registration records in their sampling frame. In the mid-1930s, telephone and automobile owners tended to be among the wealthier members of the population, and wealthier voters, then as now, tended to vote Republican.

The editors' sample was composed primarily of Republicans, which explains why they predicted that the Republican candidate, Landon, would be the winner. The standard error of their sample would have been extremely small, but *only* if the editors had wanted to predict the voting patterns of Republicans. Of course, Republicans were not the only voters to vote in the 1936 election, and the editors ended up looking rather silly.

Purposive Sampling

For some research projects, particularly exploratory or pilot projects, researchers may want to obtain a sample of specific individuals. **Purposive sampling** refers to *procedures* *directed toward obtaining a certain type of element.* If one were developing a questionnaire designed to measure prejudice, for example, one might want to include in the sample both members of a known bigoted group, such as the Ku Klux Klan, and members of, say, the National Association for the Advancement of Colored People. If the questionnaire was valid, the former group ought to score considerably higher than the latter. Although the two samples would enable the researcher to assess validity, the researcher would still have no logical basis for attempting to generalize the results to any particular population.

Quota Sampling

One of the many ways in which those interested in such things attempt to predict the outcomes of elections is **quota sampling**—*selecting sampling elements on the basis of categories that are assumed to exist within the population.* At first glance, quota sampling appears to be the same as stratified random sampling, but there is an important difference. In stratified random sampling, elements are randomly selected within the stratified groups.

For those interested in predicting the outcomes of elections, quota sampling usually involves selecting voters from what are called *key precincts*, those that exhibit a good track record of outcomes similar to the overall election results. There may be a historical reason to believe that the precinct results will match the overall results, but the continuation of that match cannot be guaranteed. If there has been a shift in the population in the precinct or a shift in the thoughts or activities of the voters in the precinct, then the precinct results will no longer match the overall election results. Indeed, political scientists use changes in the predictive ability of key precincts as a measure of political shifts.

Although quota sampling may produce a sample that appears to be a miniature version of the population, the appearance is more illusory than real. It is possible to obtain certain percentages of males and females, Blacks and Whites, wealthy and poor, and so on, but failure to select randomly within those categories makes it impossible to determine the amount of sampling error. Despite its apparent attractions, research based on quota sampling should not be generalized without considerable thought given to the possibility of changes in the population.

Quota sampling led to the famous 1948 photograph of President-elect Harry Truman holding a newspaper with the headline "DEWEY DEFEATS TRUMAN." Based on the 1940 census, the correct percentages of various types of voters had been included in a quota sample, but the percentages had changed since the census. In the intervening eight years, the need to increase production to support U.S. efforts during World War II had led to a major shift in the population from rural to urban areas. The 1940 census figures did not reflect that shift, and the quota sample used by the newspaper had underestimated urban voters (who tended to vote Democrat). The early election returns from key precincts chosen on the basis of the outdated census information, coupled with the desire to be the first on the street with the election results, produced the incorrect headline.

Snowball Sampling

As initially described (Goodman, 1961), **snowball sampling**, also known as **key-informant sampling**, is *a form of random sampling in which researchers obtain suggestions for other participants from those they have already observed*. However, in more recent usage, it is most likely used as a nonprobability procedure because researchers who use the technique rarely begin with a random sample (Browne, 2005), which is why it is described here instead of among other probability sampling procedures. The procedure is quite simple: Each person who is selected to be in a study is asked to recommend someone else who can be invited to participate. The process continues until the researcher has enough participants.

Snowball sampling is a particularly effective way of reaching out to what are called *hidden populations* (Voicu & Babonea, 2011), people who generally do not want to participate in research or who make up a very small percentage of the general population. When reading about snowball sampling, you can determine whether or not to consider the sample a random sample by looking for mention of random sampling applied to the first cohort of participants to be included.

REPRESENTATIVE SAMPLES

The primary goal of any sampling procedure is to obtain a **representative sample**—*a sample that resembles the population within an acceptable margin of error*. The phrase *within an acceptable margin of error* should immediately clue you in on the fact that probability sampling procedures are required for representative samples, simply because sampling error can be estimated only for randomly selected samples.

Of equal importance, however, is the phrase *resembles the population*. Random selection, simply because it is random, may result in a sample that does not resemble the population. The odds are against such an occurrence, but some likelihood exists. In a predominantly male college, such as the U.S. Air Force Academy, for example, a simple random sample might well not include any female students. If the population evidences distinct subgroups, some stratification will be required to obtain a representative sample.

Alternatively, some types of research projects do not require that much attention be paid to sampling procedures. We already noted that exploratory projects may not require a probability sample; a convenience or purposive sample may be all that is needed. One of the more difficult practices for many to understand is the use of volunteer participants in experimental research. Consider the research conducted by Oermann et al. (2011) concerning the effect of brief practice on maintenance of cardiopulmonary resuscitation (CPR) skills.

The purpose of their explanatory research was to demonstrate the extent to which brief practice affects skill maintenance. Some students were assigned to engage in brief practice for several months, while other students were assigned to not engage in brief practice. At this point, you should realize that the students assigned to practice do represent a population of students who receive practice, just as the students who did not practice represent a population of students without practice, but we don't know anything about those populations other than whether or not they received practice. Oermann et al. used inferential statistics to estimate whether or not those two populations were different (and they were). Although they represented some population, the students who participated in the study were a convenience sample, not a random sample of all nursing students, so we cannot estimate the accuracy of the overall sample. We know that practice makes a difference among Oermann et al.'s participants, but we cannot determine how much of a difference practice would make for other people.

SUMMARY

- A unit or element is any one thing selected for inclusion in a research project. Populations are abstract collections of elements that can be defined by a sampling frame. Samples are selected from the sampling frame—the concrete representation of the population.

- Parameters are values exhibited by a population and, like the population, are abstract. Statistics—values obtained from a sample—must be used to estimate parameters. All estimates, however, contain some amount of sampling error, which must also be estimated in order to determine the accuracy of the statistic.

- A sampling distribution is a distribution of statistics that could be obtained from repeated samples drawn from the same population. Confidence intervals can be calculated by taking advantage of the nature of sampling distributions, which is defined by the central limit theorem. The standard error of a statistic is the standard deviation of its sampling distribution, and it can be estimated if the sample was selected on the basis of some random sampling procedure.

- Simple random sampling involves identifying all elements in a sampling frame and using a procedure that provides every element an equal chance of being included in the sample. Systematic random sampling also involves a listing of the sampling frame, from which elements are selected by some systematic procedure. A stratified random sample includes dividing the sampling frame into subgroups—strata—from which random samples are separately selected.

- Cluster sampling can be used whenever a listing of the entire sampling frame does not exist. Increasingly more specific elements are randomly selected until one reaches the level at which one can randomly select the elements to be included in the research project.

- Nonprobability sampling includes any sampling procedure that does not include a random selection process. Convenience sampling involves selecting whatever elements are available, whereas purposive sampling involves selecting specific units of interest. Quota sampling involves a convenience or purposive sample selected from presumed subgroups in the population. Regardless of which nonprobability sampling procedure is used, sampling error cannot be estimated.

- A representative sample is any randomly selected sample that resembles the population. Most, but not necessarily all, random samples are also representative. Whether or not a sample represents a population of interest can also depend on the purposes of the research project.

EXERCISES

1. Using your library's databases, find an article in which the authors tried to obtain a simple random sample and any of the other types of probability samples.

2. Using your library's databases, find an article in which the authors obtained a convenience sample.

3. Using your library's databases, find an article in which the authors tested the representativeness of their sample.

5

Measurement

Measure what is measurable, and make measurable what is not so.

—(attributed to) Galileo Galilei

OVERVIEW

The purpose of this chapter is to present an overview of measurement theory. You will learn in more detail about operational definitions, reliability, validity, and techniques for determining how reliable and valid an operational definition may be. You will also learn about different levels or dimensions of measurement and the implications of these levels for statistical analyses, which will enable you to decide whether or not researchers used appropriate analyses. In addition, you will learn about the construction of measurement scales: how to evaluate the appropriate use of scale, how to evaluate the reliability and validity of scales, and information about various formats for scales. Finally, you will learn more about the relationship between variables and the concepts they are used to represent.

INTRODUCTION

Everybody thinks they know what measurement is. It is what you do, for example, when you use the bathroom scale to determine how much you weigh. You step onto the scale, read the number, and you have measured your weight—simple, straightforward, uncomplicated. But using that bathroom scale is only a small part of the overall measurement process, most of which occurs long before you step onto that scale. Somewhere along the line you learned about the relationship between those scale numbers and your weight; you may not think of *relationship* in those terms, but that, too, is part of the measurement process. Also, someone designed and built the scale; that's part of the process. Someone, perhaps the same person, tested the scale for accuracy and consistency; that's part of the process as well. You may have taken the measurement process to its completion when you used the scale, but you did the easy part. For everyday purposes, being an uncritical end user of measurement may well be enough, but when trying to understand research well enough to engage in evidence-based practice, we need to understand the measurement process well enough to make critical assessments of the research under consideration.

There are a variety of different definitions of measurement, but all of them include the notion that **measurement** is *a process through which the kind or intensity of something is determined* (Adams, 1964; Allen & Yen, 1979). What kind or what intensity doesn't much matter; the process of measurement is essentially the same whether one is measuring religious denomination (kind) or weight (intensity).

The entire measurement process is a series of procedures that moves us from a theoretical concept, such as weight, to a concrete representation of that concept, such as the numbers on a bathroom scale. We all think we know a great deal about measurement because we all do it every day. But we also make a great many errors in our everyday measurement. For example, I once owned a car with a defective speedometer; it read about 15 miles per hour faster than it should. I knew about it and compensated for it. I knew that a reading of 75 miles per hour was really only 60 miles per hour. Every once in a while, however, someone riding with me would look over at the speedometer and then would begin looking around for patrol cars or would look at me as though I was crazy for driving so fast. When I noticed this, I tried to work the speedometer's inaccuracy into the conversation. I knew what the relationship between the concept of speed and the speedometer's representation of it was, but first-time passengers did not, and it sometimes caused them problems.

Dimensionality

Measurement is used to represent theoretical concepts, and most concepts in the behavioral and social sciences have more than one dimension, more than one quality that defines them. **Dimensionality** refers to *the number of different qualities inherent in a theoretical concept*. Consider, for example, the concept of social status. Some of its dimensions include occupational prestige, ethnicity (unfortunately), popularity, educational prestige, financial resources, and so on. To attempt to represent all of these dimensions in a single measurement would be impossible. Instead, those who want to measure social status select one or a few of the dimensions.

Regardless of which dimensions are selected, however, the researcher is measuring only a part of the overall concept. For example, one researcher might consider financial resources to be inadequate as a sole measure of social status and decide to combine financial resources and educational prestige. Someone else may add popularity, and so on, but no one would be able to include everything. For this reason, as well as others, measurement is always incomplete. Whatever is measured is only part of the actual theoretical concept. Measurement represents concepts, but no measure can be considered to be the same thing as the concept itself.

MEASUREMENT LEVELS

In addition to there being any number of dimensions inherent in any theoretical concept, any dimension may be measured at one of four different levels of measurement: nominal, ordinal, interval, and ratio (Stevens, 1946). While there continues to be disagreement with respect to the hierarchical nature of the levels (Cicchetti, 2014), the first three levels involve making finer distinctions within levels of the concept being measured, and each level limits the types of statistical procedures that can be used to analyze the data. The simplest level—nominal—involves distinctions among categories, such as using the school one attended to measure educational prestige. Two of the other three levels—ordinal and interval—involve finer gradations among the levels of the concept being measured, and the fourth level—ratio—includes the notion of absolute zero.

Nominal Measurement

As you might expect from the term, **nominal measurement** involves *determining the presence or absence of a characteristic; it is naming a quality*. Because naming a quality usually involves creating categories, nominal measurement is also called **categorical measurement**. By naming or labeling things, we are able to distinguish among them, just as your name distinguishes you from other people. Good nominal measurement, however, includes mutually exclusive categories. Your name, therefore, may not be a particularly good nominal measurement because other people may have the same name. If we want to distinguish among individuals, a Social Security number (in the United States) is a good nominal measurement. Unless the Social Security Administration has made an error or someone has stolen your number, you are the only person with your number, and one could use the number to distinguish you from everyone else.

Sometimes the label used in nominal measurement is a number, as in the example of a Social Security number. It distinguishes you from other people, but the number itself has no meaning beyond its use as a label. The numbers represent only categories, not intensity. A Social Security number of 123-45-6789 is no higher or lower—no more or less intense—than 987-65-4321; they are just different numbers. For this reason, nominal or categorical measurement imposes restrictions on data analyses and interpretations.

The major restriction on data analysis involves central tendency statistics or averages. The only appropriate central tendency statistic for nominal data is the **mode**, which is *the most frequent score in a set of scores*. Neither of the other two measures of central tendency, mean and median, is appropriate for nominal measures. The **mean**, which is *the arithmetical average of a set of scores*, is calculated by adding all the scores and dividing by the number of scores. The mean of a set of Social Security numbers would be meaningless. Because the numbers assigned to the verdict preferences are only labels, computing the mean makes no sense. The same applies to the **median**, *the 50th percentile score, which separates the lower and upper halves of a distribution of scores.* The "middle" in a set of ordered Social Security numbers is not the middle of anything because the ordered numbers have no meaning.

The above limitations do not mean that researchers cannot use statistical analyses on nominal data, only that they cannot use analyses that involve adding, subtracting, multiplying, or dividing the scores. When researchers use nominal or categorical measures, you will most likely read about chi-square analyses. Essentially, **chi-square analyses** are *statistical techniques used to determine whether the frequencies of scores in the categories defined by the variable match the frequencies one would expect on the basis of chance or on the basis of predictions from a theory.*

Ordinal Measurement

There are a variety of situations in which researchers want to do more than determine the presence or absence of a characteristic. Some assessment of intensity or degree is required; perhaps some way to order responses on a continuum is desired. **Ordinal measurement** involves *a level of measurement in which scores are ranked or otherwise placed in order with respect to the intensity for a quality.* Letting people know you are in the top 10% of your class, for example, is making use of an ordinal measurement scale; you are reporting your rank within your graduating class.

Ordinal measurement identifies the relative intensity of a characteristic, but it does not reflect any level of absolute intensity. If you are in the top 10% of your class, for example, I know you are doing better than most of the students in your class (congratulations, by the way). But your class ranking doesn't enable me to determine how well you would do at, say, Harvard or at Basket-Weaving State College, unless you happen to be attending one of those institutions. I also cannot determine how much better you are than the bottom 90% of your class. Ordinal measurement is like the place finishes at a horse race: The winner might be barely a nose ahead of the second-place finisher or might have won by 10 lengths. For this reason, comparisons among ordinal values are somewhat limited but not as limited as those among nominal values.

The limitations on ordinal data result from the fact that ordinal measurement involves ranking the scores. Calculating a mean for a set of ordinal scores is about as nonsensical as it is for nominal scores. The mean for ordinal scores is the center of the ordinal scale, which doesn't change. If there are 10 scores, for example, then the mean of those ranks is always going to be 5.5; if there are 20 scores, the mean is 10.5, and so on. In this case, the mean is determined by the number of scores in the set, not the values of the scores that were ranked. When you read research involving ordinal measures, you will most likely read about statistics involving the median.

Interval Measurement

When more specificity is required, researchers attempt to attain an interval level of measurement. **Interval measurement** *involves a continuum divided into equally spaced or equally valued parts.* The Fahrenheit and centigrade temperature scales are good examples of interval measurements. A change of one degree anywhere along the continuum reflects an equal amount of change in heat; the interval *degree* is equal along the entire scale. With interval data, researchers can compare different scores more specifically than they can with either nominal or ordinal measures. Recall that with ordinal measurement, you know that a value of 5 is different from a value of 10, but you don't know how much different. With interval measurement, you know that a value of 5 is five units different from a value of 10, the same difference as that between 10 and 15.

What we do not know when we use interval measurement, however, is exactly what one interval represents in terms of the quality being measured. For example, the most well-known use of interval measurement in the behavioral sciences is the intelligence quotient (IQ), even though there is some disagreement about its status (Neubauer & Opriessnig, 2014). Although it is not possible to determine exactly how much intelligence is represented by a single IQ point, it is possible to make comparisons between scores. The difference between the scores 100 and 110, for example, reflects the same amount of intelligence (whatever that is) as does the difference between 120 and 130. How much intelligence is represented by 10 points is unknown, but 10 points is 10 points anywhere along the scale.

This limitation of interpreting interval measures—not knowing the meaning of one unit—results from the fact that interval scales involve arbitrary numbers that represent anchor points on a continuum. For the centigrade and Fahrenheit scales, the arbitrary anchors are the temperatures at which water changes states (freezes and boils): 0 and 100 degrees centigrade and 32 and 212 degrees Fahrenheit, respectively. Similarly, on the IQ scale, the arbitrary anchor point chosen was 100, a point that purportedly reflects an intellectual capacity consistent with one's physical age.

Despite the arbitrary anchor values used for interval measurements, there are few limitations on the types of analyses that can be applied to interval data, provided, of course, that the analyses are appropriate for the questions being asked. When researchers wish to determine relationships between variables, you will read about correlational analyses; when they wish to examine differences among groups, you will read about statistics comparing means, such as analysis of variance.

Although the arbitrary values for interval data do not restrict the statistics that may be used to analyze the data, the arbitrariness of the anchors does limit the ways in which we may interpret statistical results. Suppose, for example, that you have one group with an average IQ of 150 and another with an average IQ of 75. It is, of course, true that the mean IQ of one group is twice that of the other, but that does not mean you can claim that one group is twice as intelligent as the other. Because the numbers of an interval scale are arbitrary, it is never clear exactly how much intensity is reflected by any given number on the scale. Thus, the values produced from interval measurement cannot be interpreted the same as numbers used to count things. If you have 10 dollars and I have 5 dollars, then you have twice as many dollars. Counting numbers have an absolute zero, which brings us to ratio measurement.

Ratio Measurement

To interpret numbers used to measure a variable without restrictions, the researcher must have used a ratio level of measurement. **Ratio measurement** involves *a continuum that includes an absolute zero, a value of zero that represents the complete absence of a quality.* When physicists measure temperature, for example, they use the Kelvin scale, on which a value of zero represents the complete absence of heat. There are no negative values on the Kelvin scale because there cannot be less heat than no heat at all. Thus, 100 degrees on the Kelvin scale represents twice as much heat as 50 degrees. The same cannot be said for either the Fahrenheit or centigrade scales. That the latter two scales contain a zero point does not make them ratio scales because the zero points on those two scales do not represent the absence of heat.

In the behavioral and social sciences, very few measurements conform to the requirements for a ratio scale, and what few there are have been constructed for the purpose of providing examples of ratio scales. Income, for example, has a zero point that represents the absence of earnings. Therefore, someone who earns $20,000 has an income twice that of someone who earns $10,000. However, income is usually used to represent some aspect of socioeconomic status, and when it does, it no longer conforms to ratio-level requirements for measurement: Someone with zero income does not have zero socioeconomic status. If you believe you have encountered a ratio level of measurement while reviewing research, you should be very skeptical; be sure that zero means *nothing*, the complete absence of the concept being measured.

Before you read on, see Table 5.1 for a summary of our discussion of measurement levels. It is important that you understand the different types of measurement levels

TABLE 5.1   Summary of Measurement Levels

Level	What's Measured	Example	Central Tendency
Nominal	Distinctions	Guilty/not guilty	Mode
Ordinal	Relative position	Socioeconomic status	Median
Interval	Arbitrary amounts	Intelligence quotient	Mean
Ratio	Actual amounts	Age	Mean

that are used in research and the implications those levels have for interpreting research results. Most researchers get it right when they are interpreting their own results, but you are very likely to be in a position to reinterpret another researcher's results. If you do not get it right, then your review of a policy may mislead others into making a policy change that has an incorrect empirical basis.

RELIABILITY

Knowing what level of measurement was used in research is only part of understanding the measurement process. Another part involves understanding how reliable or consistent the measure is. A variety of different techniques are designed for such purposes, and all of them rely on the extent to which one version of the measure is related to another version of the measure.

The extent to which two things are related can be measured through **correlations**, *statistical procedures that estimate the extent to which changes in one variable are associated with changes in another.* A positive correlation coefficient means the two variables are directly related, a zero coefficient indicates no relationship, and a negative correlation indicates an inverse relationship. When assessing the reliability of a measure, correlations involve different versions of the measure instead of different variables. What follows is a brief description of the various ways in which such assessments are typically accomplished and reported in research articles.

Interrater Reliability

Whenever subjective judgments or ratings made by more than one person are part of the measurement process, the appropriate technique for determining reliability is interrater reliability. As implied in the name, **interrater reliability** is *the consistency with which raters or observers make judgments.* Using a very simple example, interrater reliability would involve the extent to which you and a friend agree about the temperature after reading the same thermometer. If you and your friend write down your daily temperature readings for a couple of weeks, the two sets of readings could be correlated. The higher the correlation coefficient (I'm assuming it would be positive), the greater the reliability of your measurements.

Proper use of interrater reliability techniques requires observers or raters to make independent ratings. If one rater merely copies the ratings of another, for example, all that would be tested is the other rater's ability to copy correctly; that's not reliability. Collaboration among observers or judges is not allowed. Of course, collaboration does not have to be as obvious as copying one another's ratings; even minimal discussion will destroy the independence of the ratings. Raters should make their ratings as though they were taking a final exam: No copying, no idea sharing, and no peeking. Collaborative ratings tend to appear to be more consistent, but the consistency is artificial. What you will often read in a research report, however, is that ratings were made independently and then disagreements were resolved through discussion. For example, Parish et al. (2000) tested interrater reliability for judgments about cardiac arrhythmias and then resolved the few discrepancies (the correlation was above 0.90) through discussion before including the rhythm categories in their analyses. Resolving discrepancies through discussion is perfectly acceptable, so long as interrater reliability was assessed before the discussions occurred.

Test–Retest Reliability

Test–retest reliability refers to *measurement consistency estimated by comparing two or more repeated administrations of the same measurement.* Despite its name, the test–retest technique does not require using a formal test of knowledge as a measure, but it does require that the measure can be used more than once. It is based on the same principle as that involved in interrater reliability. Instead of repeating measurements by using more than one rater, test–retest reliability involves repeating measurements made on the same participant by administering the measure a second time after a period of time. Test–retest reliability, like interrater reliability, is estimated with correlations: The correlation between the two administrations of the measure is the estimate of reliability. One assumption of test–retest reliability is that the time period is long enough so that one can rule out participants' memory as the basis for the second set of scores. For example, Brookes, Hollocks, Khan, Morris, and Markus (2015) assessed the reliability of the Brief Memory and Executive Test, a measure of cognitive impairment for individuals with strokes produced by small-vessel disease, by correlating scores obtained three months apart for a subsample of their participants. Using a sample of nurses, residents, and social workers, Jansson et al. (2015) similarly assessed the test–retest reliability of their measure of patient advocacy engagement by correlating responses obtained 41 days apart.

Another required assumption of this form of reliability assessment is that the characteristic being measured does not change appreciably over the time period between administrations. While assessing test–retest reliability in a study designed to examine a technique for improving first-graders' performance in mathematics, for example, Doabler et al. (2015) separated administrations of some of their measures by only a week; much longer than a week would violated the assumption of "no appreciable change," particularly when the purpose of the study was to change the participants' understanding of mathematics.

You will most likely read about test–retest reliability in early research reports about a new measure or a new version of a measure, such as translation of a verbal measure into a different language. A general rule of thumb is that the correlation between the two administrations should exceed 0.70 to achieve sufficient reliability (see, e.g., Frost, Reeve, Liepa, Stauffer, & Hays, 2007).

Alternate-Forms Reliability

Alternate-forms reliability involves *comparing two different but equivalent versions of the same measure*. The name of this procedure is doubly descriptive, for there are two different ways to implement it. One procedure involves giving the same group of people different versions of the measure at different times; this is analogous to the test–retest procedure. The other procedure involves giving the same measure to different groups of people, which is analogous to the interrater procedure.

When it is possible to use different forms of a measure for the same group of people, scores from one version of the measure are correlated with scores from the other. The procedure is exactly the same as that for test–retest reliability, except that different versions of the measure are repeated. The required assumption is that the two different forms are, in fact, different but also equivalent insofar as they both measure the same concept. Different-but-equivalent forms might involve merely changing the order of items in a multiple-item measure, or it may involve constructing entirely different items. Different addition items on a math test, for example, would be equivalent, but addition problems on one version and division problems on the other would not be equivalent. Similarly, differently phrased questions about attitudes toward a single topic would be equivalent, but questions about two different topics, such as sex education on one form and math education on the other, would not. Bell, McCallum, Ziegler, Davis, and Coleman (2013), for example, demonstrated sufficiently reliability of two different forms of their measure of adult educators' knowledge of reading instruction.

Sometimes, it is not possible to measure the same group of people more than once. In such situations, dividing a single group into two distinct subgroups may serve the same purpose. If, for example, a researcher gave the same test to everyone in the group and then randomly divided the group into two subgroups, he or she could compare scores between the groups to estimate reliability. In addition to correlational results, however, you might read about comparisons of means, standard deviations, or some other distributional descriptors in the research report. Jones et al. (2014), for example, used three different groups in their assessment of alternate-forms reliability of a new measure of pharyngeal high-resolution manometry, which is used to study quality of swallowing.

Split-Half Reliability

When the measurement used by researchers contains more than one item, such as some sort of questionnaire, then the split-half technique can be used to assess reliability. **Split-half reliability** involves *creating two scores for each participant by dividing the measure into equivalent halves and correlating the halves*. Each half of the measure is then treated as though it were a complete version of the measure. Essentially, the split-half technique involves creating equivalent forms by dividing the measure, rather than the group of participants, in half. The scores on the two halves are then correlated, just as with the alternate forms procedure. Again, the stronger the correlation is, the greater the reliability. Hatsumi, Nozomu, Hidemitsu, and Kouhei (2015) used split-half reliability as one of the procedures for assessing the measurement properties of their measure of stigma perceived by psychiatric patients while at work.

Item-Total Reliability

When researchers use a measurement that includes more than one item, it is common to assess the reliability of the entire measure by measuring the internal consistency of all of the items included in the measure (see Table 5.2 for a summary of reliability procedures). **Item-total reliability** is *an estimate of the consistency of one item with respect to other items on a measure.* Conceptually, this form of reliability assessment correlates each individual item with a total score on the measure excluding that item. Practically, there exist formulas that are applied to measures that calculate an overall value for internal consistency. When researchers use item-total reliability, you will most often read about Cronbach's alpha, represented by the Greek letter α (Cronbach, 1951), which you may interpret the same way you would any other correlation coefficient. You may also encounter reports of KR-20 (Kuder & Richardson, 1937), which you also interpret as though it is a correlation coefficient. Sometimes, however, the KR-20 results are reported in whole numbers (0–100), in which case you need to divide by 100 to obtain the equivalent of a correlation coefficient.

TABLE 5.2   A Summary of Reliability Procedures

Procedures	Conditions	Analyses
Interrater	Multiple judges	Correlation between raters
Test–retest	No practice effect	Correlation between scores
Alternate forms		
2 forms, 1 group	Equivalent forms	Correlation between scores and/or items
1 form, 2 groups	Random assignment	Correlation and/or between-group differences
Split-half	Equivalent items	Rulon's split-half
Item-total	Multiple items	Cronbach α

VALIDITY

Reliability is a necessary condition for quality measurement, but it alone is not sufficient. Reliability is the extent to which the measure is consistent. Before accepting any researcher's use of any measure, you must make sure it is valid. **Validity** refers to *the extent to which a variable measures the theoretical concept it is supposed to measure.* Sometimes, the answer to the validity question is obvious, such as whether or not a patient was discharged alive from a hospital, and sometimes some evidence is required to convince us that a particular questionnaire measures the concept it is supposed to measure. Just as there are different ways to estimate reliability, there are different techniques for estimating validity. Which of the following techniques researchers report, or do not report because it's "obvious," depends on both the specific requirements of the study and the facilities available.

Face Validity

Suppose your instructor gave you a test in your research methods class, but the test contained only differential calculus problems. You would probably complain, claiming the test was not fair, and you might even use the phrase *not valid.* You would be using face validity as the basis of your complaint. **Face validity** is *consensus that a measure represents a particular concept.* It is sometimes called **expert validity** or **validation by consensus**. When face validity involves assessing whether a measure deals with a representative sample of the various aspects of the concept, it is also called **content validity**. Whatever it is called, it is based on the notion that a good measure should look like a good measure to those who are in a position to know; those whose opinions matter should agree that a measure is measuring what it's supposed to measure.

Face validity is a rather limited test of validity. It is, after all, not much different from claiming, "My mother said so," except that *an expert* replaces *my mother* in the claim. Although appeals to personal authority are not sufficient grounds for argument in a scientific approach, an appeal to expert authority can be used as a starting point in the process of evaluating a measure's validity. Sometimes, however, face validity is the only type of validity assessed for a particular measure. Oermann, Kardong-Edgren, and Odom-Maryon (2011), for example, relied on the expertise of the manufacturer when using a high-fidelity mannequin and associated software to measure the compression and ventilation characteristics in their study of CPR skills. When we read research in which face validity it presented, then then we must determine whether or not the validity of the measure is sufficient for our purposes.

Concurrent Validity

Just as face validity relies on authoritative experts, concurrent validity relies on authoritative measurements to establish validity. **Concurrent validity** involves *comparing a new measure to an existing, valid measure.* The difference between concurrent and face validity is that one relies on an existing, valid measure instead of the consensus of experts; one relies on data instead of expertise. Concurrent validity is a specific form of **criterion validity**: *the process in which the validity of one measure is compared* *against another measure of known validity.* The comparison is usually accomplished by correlating the old and new measures in much the same way that alternate form reliability is determined, but sometimes you'll read that the researchers used regression analyses or a Bland–Altman analysis (Bland & Altman, 1986). Concurrent validity is assessed in many research projects. Among the many validation studies for grit, the measure used by Eskreis-Winkler, Shulman, Beal, and Duckworth (2014) was research (Duckworth, Peterson, Matthews, & Kelly, 2007) in which the concurrent validity of the grit scale was assessed against educational achievement.

It is not too difficult to understand the major limitation of concurrent validity: The new measure cannot be any more valid than the old measure to which it is compared. If the validity of the existing measure was established through face validity, such as considering educational attainment as a measure of perseverance and consistency of interests, then the use of concurrent validity is actually an approximation of face validity. It is always important to determine how the validity of a measure was established empirically. For those of us who consume research, this may involve tracking a particular measure through the literature to discover the original basis for its validity. It can sometimes be a tedious process, but it is worth the tedium to avoid basing practice on results obtained from a measure that does not have demonstrable validity.

Predictive Validity

Predictive validity is another specific form of criterion validity, except that **predictive validity** is *established by comparing a measure with the future occurrence of another, highly valid measure.* The most well-known example of predictive validity is college entrance examinations and their ability to predict first-year performance in terms of college grades. For predictive validity, one simply administers the new measure, waits for an opportunity to use the comparison measure, and then compares the two. The comparison measure is usually a very different form of measurement, such as grades versus a multiple-choice test, or it is an unquestionable standard to which all other similar measures are compared (such as grades for college performance), sometimes known as a *gold standard.*

The same limitations for concurrent validity apply to predictive validity procedures: How the validity of the comparison measure was established limits the validity of the new measure. Usually, however, the limitation is not as important because the new measure is being developed specifically to predict the existing measure; that is, the existing measure is considered valid by definition. With college entrance examinations, for example, grades are by definition valid measures of college success. Whether or not that should be the case is an entirely different question, one we cannot address here. If another standard is chosen, then the new measure is compared to that. All four of the studies reported in Eskreis-Winkler et al. (2014) are examples of assessing predictive validity.

Construct Validity

Construct validity involves determining *the extent to which a measure represents concepts it should represent and does not represent concepts it should not represent.* It is similar to an essay question in which you are asked to compare and contrast two different but possibly related concepts. Construct validity involves both making comparisons between a new measure and existing, valid measures of the same concept and contrasting the new measure with existing, valid measures of a different concept. It also involves testing the extent to which comparisons and contrasts are affected by the method used for the measure (Campbell & Fiske, 1959; Hamdani, Valcea, & Buckley, 2014; Johnston et al., 2014).

The first part of construct validity is called **convergent validity**—*the extent to which a measure correlates with existing measures of the same concept.* It is similar to concurrent validity but involves one important difference: Convergent validity includes comparisons with more than one existing measure. Ideally, the existing measures should involve at least two different measurement methods, one of which is the same method as the new measure. In multiple studies, Duckworth et al. (2007) compared scores on the grit scale to other measures of personality as well as educational attainment, completion of demanding physical challenges, and performance in a spelling bee.

Using different measurement methods for the existing standards enables the researcher to test the extent to which the correlations between the new and existing measures are related to the type of measurement method used. Two measures of personality, for example, could be somewhat correlated by virtue of the fact that they are both questionnaires. If the new measure correlates both with another questionnaire and with some different method, such as educational attainment, then we can be comfortable with the new measure's validity. It is the same principle behind using multiple-choice and essay questions on the same examination: Some people might do well with one or the other simply because they are familiar with that particular answer format, but a student who does well on both formats is more likely to know the subject matter.

The second part of construct validity is called **divergent validity**—*the extent to which a measure does not correlate with measures of a different concept.* Again using the grit scale as an example, testing divergent validity could involve contrasting grit scores with valid measures of verbal IQ as well as previous experience in a study of spelling bee participants (Duckworth et al., 2007). Grit should be different from intelligence. Table 5.3 contains some of the results from the sixth study reported in Duckworth et al. (2007). It is apparent that grit is related to measures to which it should be related (self-control, success) but not related to a measure to which it should not be related (intelligence), even though all of the measures are related to success (level of advancement) in a spelling bee. You may not often come across a complete analysis of construct validity (convergent and divergent comparisons) in a single research report, but you can build your own version of Table 5.3 for measures in which you are interested by combining information from different articles.

TABLE 5.3   Correlation Coefficients for High Construct Validity of Grit Scale From Duckworth et al. (2007)

	Grit Scale	Self-Control	Verbal IQ
Self-Control	.66		
Verbal IQ	.02	(not reported)	
Success	.34	0.27	0.80

EPISTEMIC CORRELATION

At the beginning of this chapter (and in Chapter 2 as well) we learned that a measured variable represents but is not the same thing as a theoretical concept. There may be several different dimensions of a concept, of which the measure taps only some. There are also many different operational definitions for any theoretical concept, and no measure can tap all of them. Therefore, any measure, no matter how valid and reliable, represents only a portion of the total theoretical concept.

Any score obtained from a measure contains two components: a true score component and an error score component. The *true* component refers to the validity of the measure; it is the part of the measure that is doing what it is supposed to do. The *error* component reflects all of the things that can go wrong in the measurement process. The fewer things that go wrong, the smaller the error component. It is an accepted axiom of measurement theory, however, that the error component is never equal to zero; there is always, without exception, some error involved in any measure.

The theoretical relationship between the true component of a measure and the concept it represents is called an **epistemic correlation**. Despite its name, an epistemic correlation cannot be calculated; it can only be logically determined. Consider, for example, annual income as a measure of social status: Even though we all know that a higher income indicates a higher social status, it includes only one dimension of the concept. Thus, within certain limitations, we know that there is a positive epistemic correlation between income and social status. We cannot calculate that coefficient, but we can be reasonably certain that it is positive.

Before we interpret results obtained in a study using income as a measure of social status, however, we also need to know what level of measurement—nominal, ordinal, interval, or ratio—annual income represents. Annual income obviously cannot represent a ratio level because zero income does not reflect zero social status. Once you have given the matter some thought, you will realize that income probably does not represent an interval level of measurement, either. To merit interval level status, an income change of, say, $10,000 would have to represent the same amount of change in social status at any amount of income; clearly, this is not so. A change from zero income to $10,000 represents a considerably larger increase in social status than does a change from $1,000,000 to $1,010,000. The best we can do with income as a measure of social status is declare it an ordinal scale.

On the other hand, the very same measure—income—could be an interval or perhaps a ratio scale if used to represent a different theoretical concept. If, for example, someone used income to represent contribution to the tax base, it may be an interval level of measurement. Although an economist might disagree about its being at the interval level of measurement, the point is that the epistemic correlation must be evaluated before we can interpret results. Even though we cannot calculate it, we must make a logical decision, based on the concept itself, about the correlation between the concept and its measure. Understanding theoretical concepts and the measures used to represent them are equally important parts of good research consumption. We now turn our attention to more complicated forms of measurement, those involving multiple items used to measure a concept collectively.

SCALING

Because no measure is perfectly reliable or perfectly valid, researchers often use some sort of triangulation process to zero in on the concept they are trying to measure. In my high school physics class, for example, we always made three measurements and used the average of those three measurements as the recorded data value. The reason for using three measures was not apparent then, but it is now: Using the same measure three times and recording the average increases the overall reliability of measurement; an average reduces random error.

Most researchers do not have the luxury of making the same measurement more than once. Putting a ball bearing on a balance three times is very different from asking a person to answer the same question three times; the latter usually involves little more than testing someone's memory of his or her first answer. Similarly, measuring the crime rate in a city three times requires the assumption that the rate does not change over time, which is not a safe assumption.

Instead of making the measurement three times, researchers measure the same concept in several different ways. One way to accomplish this is to use a **scale**—*a measurement instrument that contains a number of slightly different operational definitions of the same concept.* If you have ever completed a questionnaire that seemed to contain many similar questions, you have firsthand experience with a scale. Simply generating a number of seemingly redundant questions, however, does not a scale make.

The key to the notion of a scale is the phrase *slightly different operational definitions.* Each item on a scale is a different operational definition of the same concept, and combining the items into a scale allows the researcher to get at the concept from a variety of different directions. All of the general measurement principles outlined above apply to scales.

For example, scales can operate at any of the four different levels of measurement—nominal, ordinal, interval, or ratio—and all must be tested for reliability and validity. Scales, however, usually provide several advantages over single-item measures; one such advantage is a higher level of measurement than any of the individual items that together constitute the scale itself.

Common Aspects of Scales

Perhaps the best way to learn how to evaluate scales is to learn how they are developed. If you understand how scales are constructed, then you will find it considerably easier to decide whether or not a particular scale is relevant to your interests regarding evidence-based practice. So, we first consider some common aspects of all forms of scales.

Face Validity of Scale Items

First among the general issues surrounding scale item generation or evaluation is the face validity of items. Although face validity is not a necessary characteristic of every item on a scale, at least some of the items must demonstrate face validity. If you have access to the actual items included on a scale, examine them for face validity: Ask yourself whether or not the items made sense to you. If you cannot understand the relevance of items included in a scale, then you should have some doubts about the validity of the scale, doubts that should be overcome by the researcher's report of reliability and validity analyses. You may have to backtrack a few research articles to find the results of such analyses, but as I noted earlier, backtracking is well worth the trouble if you plan to use the results of a scale to make recommendations concerning an important policy.

Item Bias

Perhaps the most important consideration common to all scale items is **item bias**— *the extent to which the wording or placement of an item (question, rating, etc.) affects someone's response to the item.* An item may be biased for a variety of reasons; some are more subtle than others. Perhaps the best (worst?) example of a biased item comes from a survey sent to me by my former congressional representative in the days when the Strategic Defense Initiative (SDI; also known as *Star Wars technology*) was a hotly contended issue during the 1980s. The survey was devoted to defense spending, and the first item was "Do you favor increasing defense spending to prevent Communist aggression?" This item has just about everything wrong with it that could possibly be wrong.

First, the item is a **double-barreled item**, *a single item that contains two or more questions or statements.* The item raises two issues, one concerning increases in defense spending and another about Communist aggression. Some respondents would have had opposing views on the two topics and would have found it difficult to respond. They might, for example, oppose Communist aggression but not wish to increase defense spending. You might also have noticed the item was emotionally worded. Communist aggression was an emotional flag—something few American citizens would advocate, regardless of their political views or opinions about defense spending. The item is also ambiguous; there is no indication of how much of an increase the respondent is being asked to advocate or reject. Similarly, there is no indication of the type of Communist aggression to be prevented. All of these forms of bias make it extremely difficult for someone to respond to the item in any manner other than without thinking about it.

Perhaps the most important among the item's shortcomings is the fact that few, if any, respondents would have access to the kind of information required to make a rational decision. For example, not many people had an idea about how much money was currently being expended for defense, let alone that amount of defense spending set aside specifically for preventing Communist aggression. Nor did many people have any idea how much more money might be needed to prevent Communist aggression.

Finally, the placement of the item as the first in a series about defense spending introduced bias throughout the series. The implicit link between increases in defense spending and Communist aggression made it difficult for respondents to say no to other items about increasing defense spending. Once someone has agreed with the notion that increasing defense spending is a good idea for preventing Communist aggression, for example, that person will find it difficult to disagree with other items about increasing defense spending. I was not at all surprised when the representative voted in favor of all increases in defense spending (including SDI), claiming he was simply doing what his constituents had requested. Heavily biased scale items may be politically useful, but they have no place in good research.

Formats for Scale Items

Just as there are a number of different types of item bias, there are a number of different formats through which to present an item. Because there typically is not room in a publication to include the entire scale, we often find out about the item format from a brief mention in the method section. That means we need to be familiar with the vocabulary used to describe scale items.

Perhaps the simplest format is the **forced-choice format**—*a response format in which the respondents must choose between discrete and mutually exclusive options.* The following item is an example:

	Yes	No
Should defense spending be increased?		

The respondent is forced to choose between increasing spending or not, hence the name *forced choice*. The forced-choice format is most appropriate when responses can be easily categorized.

More often than not, however, responses are not so easily categorized. One's response to changing defense spending, for example, may be more a matter of how much to change rather than simply to change or not to change. In such cases, the graphic format is the most widely used response format. The **graphic format** involves *an item on which responses are presented along a graded continuum and the respondent chooses one of the options*. Illustrated below are a number of different ways to use a graphic format:

What is your opinion on changing the level of defense spending?

1	2	3	4	5
It should definitely be decreased.		It should remain the same.		It should definitely be increased.

The respondent is still required to make a choice, but the choices reflect positions on a continuum. It is even possible for someone to choose a position between 3 and 4, and in such cases, a graphic format can include markers between the points, as shown here:

What is your opinion on changing the level of defense spending?

1————————2————————3————————4————————5				
It should definitely be decreased.		It should remain the same.		It should definitely be increased.

The above example is also referred to as a **visual analog scale**, *a type of response item with a continuous graphic display*, which is often scored by measuring the distance between one endpoint and where the respondent marked the scale. Items on the Visual Analog Mood Scales (see, for example, Kontou, Thomas, & Lincoln, 2012), usually employed in clinical settings, involve emoticons instead of words as endpoints but still include the continuous response scale.

Other versions of the graphic format include presenting only the labels for the endpoints of the continuum, presenting additional labels along the continuum, including more numbers along the continuum, and so forth. The graphic response format is often labeled a *Likert-type* item and sometimes simply a *Likert* item, after the type of item Rensis Likert (Likert, 1932) used in his explanation of scale preparation, about which you will read more later in this chapter. Regardless of the variations in its appearance, the graphic format reflects a continuum of responses. The respondent is presented with a graded choice rather than a forced choice. Whatever version of the graphic format researchers may use, however, you should be sure that the endpoints reflect legitimate responses. The extreme endpoints should not be so extreme that no one would consider them to be potential responses. Researchers will typically report the endpoint labels for items in their research reports.

Providing response alternatives in a graphic format is not the only way to present a continuum of responses. The itemized format can be used to accomplish the same purpose. Instead of presenting a continuum of responses, the **itemized format** involves *presenting a continuum of statements representing various choice options*. Each statement is a response, and together, the statements reflect a continuum of potential responses. The graphic item illustrated above could be presented through the itemized format as follows:

- ☐ Decreasing the level of defense spending is absolutely essential to the well-being of our country.

- ☐ Keeping defense spending at its current level is the best thing to do right now.

- ☐ Increasing the level of defense spending is absolutely essential to the well-being of our country.

Note that the first item represents one extreme, the second item represents a neutral point, and the third item represents an extreme that is the opposite of the first. Of course, more than three items would normally be included in an itemized format, but three are enough for illustration purposes. Instructions for the illustrated items would include asking respondents to place a mark in the box corresponding to the item that best represents their opinions. The essence of a graphic format—a continuum of responses—is presented with a series of statements. Respondents must choose one of the statements (they cannot choose between two represented positions), so the items must be very carefully chosen to represent an adequate gradation of responses.

Sometimes it makes sense to ask respondents to weigh the relative importance of specific issues. With the **comparative format**, *direct comparisons among various positions are provided to respondents*. One example of the comparative format, again using defense spending, appears here:

Which of the following ways to increase the defense budget is most preferable?

a. Increase the size of the national debt.

b. Increase income taxes.

c. Increase other types of taxes.

d. Decrease money spent on social welfare programs.

e. I prefer not to increase the defense budget.

In another version of this format, respondents could be asked to rank the presented alternatives from most to least preferable. Regardless of which version is used, however, the comparisons should be distinct and legitimate.

We've only briefly touched on a few of the many different types of item formats used in research. The formats about which you read will depend on many different aspects of the researchers' measurement decisions.

Types of Scales

Just as items should be examined critically when interpreting research, the manner in which researchers combine those items should match their research purposes and your interpretation of their research results. For this reason, some of the major types of scales currently used are presented below.

Thurstone Scales

One of the levels of measurement described previously—interval measurement—is extremely difficult to attain with a single item; equal spacing of alternatives in a graphic format is not the same as equal intervals. Interval measurement, however, can be approximated with a scale constructed using the Thurstone technique. Invented by Thurstone and his colleagues (1929, 1931; Thurstone & Chave, 1929), the formal name for the **Thurstone scale** is the **equal-appearing interval technique**; it *produces a series of items, each of which represents a particular point value on the continuum being measured.* It is an itemized format scale designed so that the items reflect specific points on the response continuum.

In the construction of a Thurstone scale, many items are generated such that each item represents a particular point of view about the concept to be measured. Items in this initial pool are rated by judges on an 11-point scale representing the full range of positions concerning the concept. After all of the items have been generated and judged, the scale values assigned by the judges for each item are tabulated and the median value used as the actual scale value of the item. The selection criteria for the final list of items are those with scale values closest to whole numbers with the smallest semi-interquartile ranges. The **semi-interquartile range** is *a measure of variability or degree of dispersion calculated by halving difference between values representing the 75th and 25th percentiles in a distribution of scores.*

The respondent is asked to check any of the items that reflect his or her opinion. Ideally, respondents should check only one item, partly because using the equal-appearing interval scale involves assuming that respondents' opinions are sufficiently defined to make it difficult for them to agree with more than one item. A respondent's score is the scale value of the item selected. Sometimes, however, respondents will choose more than one item, in which case, the respondent's score is the median of the scale values for all items selected. Arons, Krabbe, Schölzel-Dorenbos, van der Wilt, and Olde Rikkert (2012) used a Thurstone scale to measure perceptual differences regarding quality of life between patients with dementia and those who were caring for them.

Likert Scales

One alternative to the time- and labor-intensive effort required to construct a Thurstone scale is the technique developed by Likert (1932). Known as a *Likert scale*, this technique also begins with generating a pool of initial items. The **Likert scale** is *a unidimensional measure containing items reflecting extreme positions on a continuum, items with which people are likely either to agree or disagree.* The items are typically presented in a graphic format that includes endpoints labeled with some version of *agree* and *disagree*. After a pool of face-valid items has been generated, the entire pool of items is administered and an item analysis is completed, usually employing the item-total correlation. Items with the most extreme (positive and negative) item-total correlations are selected for the final version of the scale, which produces a unidimensional, interval-level measure of the concept about which the items were written. Participants are asked to respond to all of the items on the scale, and a score for the scale is calculated simply by adding the values of the responses, which is why the Likert scale is also called a **summative scale**, a label applied to *any measurement scale for which scores are calculated by summing responses to individual items.* The Grit scale (Duckworth et al., 2007; Duckworth & Quinn, 2009) is an example of a Likert scale.

Guttman Scales

The Thurstone and Likert techniques were designed to use more than one item to measure the same concept. Guttman (1944), however, criticized both techniques, claiming that neither resulted in a truly unidimensional scale.

The problem, according to Guttman, is that one respondent could obtain the same score as another respondent, even though the two respondents had agreed with or checked completely different items. To Guttman, this prevented the Thurstone and the Likert scale from being truly unidimensional. On a **Guttman scale**, *it is possible to order both the items and the respondents on a single, identifiable continuum of measurement.* The Guttman scale is also called either a **scalogram scale** or a **cumulative scale**.

Like the Thurstone method, the Guttman method begins with items written to represent a particular position on a continuum. With Guttman's technique, however, "good" items remain on the scale to the extent that respondents endorse that item and all of the items representing that end of the continuum to that point. The item analyses are complicated and include a **scalogram analysis,** which *a determination of the extent to which the pattern of actual responses fits the ideal pattern of a Guttman scale.*

The response pattern of an ideal or perfect Guttman scale, presented in Table 5.4, illustrates the concept. If the items are ordered on a continuum from easiest to most

TABLE 5.4   Proportion of Respondents Agreeing With Each Item on a Perfect Guttman Scale

Scale	Item Number									
Score	1	2	3	4	5	6	7	8	9	10
0	0	0	0	0	0	0	0	0	0	0
1	1	0	0	0	0	0	0	0	0	0
2	1	1	0	0	0	0	0	0	0	0
3	1	1	1	0	0	0	0	0	0	0
4	1	1	1	1	0	0	0	0	0	0
5	1	1	1	1	1	0	0	0	0	0
6	1	1	1	1	1	1	0	0	0	0
7	1	1	1	1	1	1	1	0	0	0
8	1	1	1	1	1	1	1	1	0	0
9	1	1	1	1	1	1	1	1	1	0
10	1	1	1	1	1	1	1	1	1	1

difficult to endorse, the pattern of responses forms two triangles. The upper right triangle consists only of zeroes, whereas the lower left consists of ones. From this pattern, it is possible to deduce exactly which items were chosen by any respondent simply by knowing the respondent's score.

Everyone who agreed with Item 10, for example, also agreed with Items 1 through 9. If a Guttman scale is perfect, only those who agreed with Items 1 through 9 would also agree with Item 10, only those who agreed with Item 1 would also agree with Item 2, and so on. Interestingly, Gnoth and Zins (2013) used the Guttman technique to create a scale of interest in learning about other cultures, and Veer et al. (2013) used the technique to develop a measure of xenophobia.

Semantic Differential Scales

The Thurstone, Likert, and Guttman scaling techniques have three things in common: They involve the preparation of a pool of items that exhibit face validity, they require some sort of analysis in order to select a final set of items, and they are designed specifically to measure unidimensional concepts or a single dimension of multidimensional concepts. In this section, we turn to a rather different measurement scale, one that does not share any of the above commonalities. The **semantic differential scale** is *designed* *to measure the psychological meaning of concepts along three different dimensions: evaluation, potency, and activity.*

Developed by Osgood, Suci, and Tannenbaum (1957), the semantic differential scale is not used to measure how much of a particular quality (such as grit) someone has or how much someone believes in a particular concept (such as xenophobia) but rather what someone understands a particular concept to be—that is, the subjective meaning of a concept. Instead of measuring respondents' attitudes toward research methods, for example, one might use a semantic differential scale to measure what people think research methods are. The meaning of the concept being measured is defined by the general dimensions of evaluation, potency, and activity.

Evaluation refers to *the overall positive or negative meaning attached to the concept in a semantic differential scale.* Such labels as *good, bad, attractive,* and *dirty* may be part of the evaluation dimension. **Potency** refers to *the overall strength or importance of the concept in a semantic differential scale.* Potency includes such labels as *strong, weak, superior,* and *useful.* **Activity** refers to *the extent to which the concept is associated with action or motion in a semantic differential scale.* Such labels as *fast, slow, active, passive,* and *deliberate* qualify for the activity dimension. Thus, an individual's subjective perception of research methods might be good (evaluation), important (potency), and exciting (activity). One of the main advantages of the semantic differential scale is that the same list of adjective pairs can be used to measure the meaning of a variety of different concepts: research methods, education, social welfare, prisons, and many other concepts. Corrigan, Bink, Fokuo, and Schmidt (2015) used semantic differential scales to measure stereotypes and stigma regarding individuals with mental illness.

Q-Sort Scales

Just as the semantic differential scale is typically used to measure the meaning of concepts, a **Q-sort** is a *scale used to measure an individual's relative positioning or ranking on a variety of different concepts.* The Q-sort technique was adapted by Stephenson (1953) and has remained popular among researchers interested in measuring characteristics of individuals. One way to further describe the Q-sort technique is to consider it to be a combination of Thurstone and semantic differential scaling, for aspects of both techniques are involved. Various items representing different concepts are generated. The respondent then sorts these items into ranked positions on the dimensions of the concepts.

Administration of a Q-sort is almost identical to the item analysis phase of Thurstone scaling, with one very important difference: With the Q-sort technique, it is the sorters who are being measured, not the items. Sorters (participants) are asked to categorize the items on the basis of some dimensional criterion. Unlike the Thurstone procedure, however, the sorter is also asked to make the number of items in the categories conform to a normal distribution. For example, if 100 items were to be sorted into 11 categories, the sorter would be instructed to distribute the items such that the number of items in each category would approximate the distribution below:

Number of items:	3	4	7	11	15	20	15	11	7	4	3
Category number:	1	2	3	4	5	6	7	8	9	10	11

Of course, the number of items to be placed in each category will depend both on the number of items in the initial pool and the number of categories. The category number assigned to each item is used to calculate correlations between the various individuals who did the sorting. That is, sorters become the variables in the calculation of correlation coefficients, and the category numbers assigned to the different concepts become the scores for the variable. The results of these analyses are usually displayed in a matrix labeled by the sorter's name or other identification along the top and side and containing correlation coefficients as matrix entries. Oliveira, Motta, Guerra, and Mucha (2015) used the Q-sort technique in their study of differences among types of members of the dentistry profession and lay people regarding smile and dental attractiveness.

Sociometric Scales

The Q-sort technique is most useful for measuring various aspects of an individual or a few individuals. The scaling technique we next consider is most prevalently used for descriptive research among groups. A **sociometric scale** is *a scale designed specifically for measuring relationships among individuals within a group* (Proctor & Loomis, 1951). Sociometric scales—sometimes called *sociometry*—have also been used to measure social choice (Kerlinger, 1973). Very simply, the technique involves asking members of a group to make choices among other members of the group.

Consider, by way of example, the other members of your research methods class. Which three people do you most like? Which three do you like the least? Such questions are the basis of a sociometric scale. If every person in your class answered these two questions, there would be enough information to be able to construct a profile of your classmates—a "who's who" in terms of popularity. Of course, the questions might just as easily be worded in terms of working with, eating with, or doing anything else with others in your class. Similarly, one could inquire about the people with the most and least financial status, intelligence, or any other concept of interest; the questions depend entirely on the researcher's purposes. The question(s) may be asked by way of a questionnaire, an interview, or observations of behavior. For example, without asking anyone anything, a researcher could observe the pattern of conversation within a group. Scores could be assigned on the basis of how many times each person talks to every other person, thereby measuring popularity, perceived expertise, friendliness, or any of the myriad of reasons why people talk to each other. If written or verbal questions are posed, the response format could be forced-choice, graphic, or any other suitable format.

Reliability and validity of the items used on a sociometric scale depend, primarily, on simplicity and face validity; that is, the simpler and more specific the question(s) used, the more reliable the measure. Similarly, the more directly the questions pertain to the theoretical concept under consideration, the more valid the measure. Stone and LaGreca (1991) used sociometric scales in their investigation of the relative popularity of students with and without learning disabilities.

SUMMARY

- Measurement is the process through which we translate the kind or intensity of a theoretical concept into a concrete variable. Most concepts include more than one dimension, not all of which can be easily included in a single variable.

- There are four different levels of measurement, all but one of which involve limitations on data analyses, interpretations, or both.

- The nominal level of measurement is the simplest and involves categorical distinctions of kind. Statistical analyses involving frequencies or the mode as the central tendency are the only appropriate analyses.

- The ordinal level of measurement involves degrees of intensity and reflects only relative amounts. Frequency analyses may be appropriate, but central tendency analyses based on the median are more likely to be the best analyses for such measures.

- The interval level of measurement represents intensity on an equal-interval continuum. The continuum, however, is composed of arbitrarily assigned values and does not contain an anchor for the absence of the quality being measured. Although there are no limitations on appropriate analyses, interpretations should not include multiplicative comparisons such as *twice as much*.

- Ratio levels of measurement are extremely rare, perhaps nonexistent, in behavioral and social sciences mainly because the zero point of the measure must represent the complete absence of the quality being measured. If achieved, however, there are no restrictions on analyses or interpretations.

- Reliability involves the extent to which a measure is consistent, and it can be estimated through a variety of different techniques. All of these techniques, however, generally involve comparisons between different versions of the measure.

- Interrater reliability can be assessed when there is more than one person making ratings or judgments. It is accomplished by correlating one rater's scores with another rater's scores.

- Test–retest reliability involves presenting the same measure to the same people at two different times and then correlating the scores. Alternate-forms reliability involves presenting the same people with two different versions of the same test and again correlating the scores. Alternatively, the same test can be given to two randomly divided subgroups and then compared with appropriate central tendency analyses.

- Split-half reliability involves comparing random halves of a multiple-item measure using a formula invented by Rulon. An alternative for multiple-item measures is item-total reliability, which involves comparing each item score with the total score using Cronbach's alpha.

- Validity refers to the extent to which a measure is related to its theoretical concept. Face validity refers to consensus about the relationship, whereas concurrent validity refers to the correlation between a new measure and one that has otherwise been demonstrated to be valid. Concurrent validity is one form of criterion validity. Another form of criterion validity, predictive validity, refers to the correlation between a new measure and a standard that is, by definition, valid.

- Construct validity refers to multiple comparisons with existing, valid measures of the same concept and multiple contrasts with valid measures of a different concept. The new measure should correlate highly with the former measure and not at all with the latter measure.

- An epistemic correlation is the derived relationship between a measure and its theoretical concept. It cannot be calculated but must be used to determine the level of the new measure.

- Measurement scales are used whenever one item is not sufficient to represent the complexity of a concept or when it is not feasible to repeatedly use the same operational definition.

- Every item on a scale has the potential to produce a biased response. Thus, every item should be examined for bias. The format for presenting a scale should be chosen to maximize respondents' understanding of the scale.

- The Thurstone scale represents the full range of positions toward the concept being measured. It, like the Likert scale, approximates an interval level of measurement. The Likert scale involves creating a series of extreme position statements to which respondents are asked to react through a graphic format. The Guttman scale ensures a true interval level of measurement.

- The semantic differential scale is used to measure the psychological meaning of a concept; it consists of a series of adjective pairs that can be categorized in terms of evaluation, potency, and activity. Unless a set of adjective pairs has already been demonstrated to be reliable and valid, factor analysis is required to demonstrate these qualities.

- The Q-sort scale is typically used to assess the reactions of a small group of respondents. The emphasis of measurement is on the relative meaning of items included on the scale.

- The sociometric scales are most often used to assess relationships within a defined group, including a general measure of cohesiveness. Although essentially a technique that measures choices among the group members, the wording of the criteria for the choices can include nearly any concept in the behavioral sciences.

EXERCISES

1. Using any of the articles you have found so far, or after finding a new article, identify the types of measurement levels reflected by the variables included in the article.

2. Find an article in which the authors report on the reliability and/or validity of at least one of the measures used in the research. Determine the type of reliability and/or validity assessment employed by the researchers.

3. Find an example of each of the different types of measurement scales.

6

Experimental Research

> *That [continuity and progress] have been tied to careful experimental*
> *and theoretical work indicates that there is validity in a method*
> *which at times feels unproductive or disorganized.*
>
> —Aronson (1980, p. 21)

OVERVIEW

The purpose of this chapter is to provide you with the information you need to evaluate experimental research, specifically, research designed to test cause–effect hypotheses. You will learn about a variety of issues that must be considered when consuming the results of an experiment. For each of the major designs discussed, appropriate questions are suggested so that you can critically evaluate them. General considerations about reading reports are addressed.

INTRODUCTION

To some people, experimental research is the highest peak of scientific research. To others, it is the valley of darkness through which promising scientists must walk before they can do meaningful research. To most researchers, **experimental research** is *the general label applied to methods developed for the specific purpose of testing causal relationships.* Other labels include **randomized controlled trial**, *randomized clinical trial, controlled study,* and similar phrases that include the words *random* or *control* or both. Like Aronson, I sometimes feel that experimental research can be unproductive and disorganized and, at other times, I feel that experimental research includes the best possible designs for almost anything; experiments, for example, are often called the *gold standard* in research (Versi, 1992). I never feel as though it is the valley of darkness, but whatever negative feelings I may sometimes have are more than offset by the thrill of finding out why something occurs the way it does. Experimental research may involve the most complicated research designs—that is, until one becomes accustomed to reading it—but it is the only way to obtain a definite answer to the question of *why* something happens. That is because experimental research is the only way to test causal hypotheses directly. Even though the word *experiment* is used in a variety of ways in everyday language—it is often used to refer to any kind of research or test—an experiment has some very specific characteristics and the word has a much narrower meaning when used by researchers. The specific meaning when used in the context of research has to do with a process called *causal analysis*.

CAUSAL ANALYSIS IN EXPERIMENTAL RESEARCH

Causal analysis—*the logical process through which we attempt to explain why an event occurs*—should not be new to you. It is, for example, the basis for explanatory research (see Chapter 1). Within the framework of experimental research, causal analysis includes a combination of three elements—temporal priority, control over variables, and random assignment—the presence of which enables researchers to test cause–effect hypotheses and interpret the results in terms of why something has occurred.

Temporal Priority

One of the requirements of causal analysis is knowledge that the suspected cause precedes the effect. Even though the simplicity of this requirement is readily apparent—something that will happen tomorrow cannot cause something that happens today—the concept can sometimes get a little confusing. For example, the unemployment figures that will be released tomorrow cannot affect today's decision to invest in the stock market; on the other hand, *speculation* about what tomorrow's unemployment figures might be *can* affect that decision. It is not tomorrow's event that affects today's behavior but today's speculation about tomorrow that affects today's behavior. **Temporal priority**, *the requirement that causes precede their effects*, is a stringent requirement, and we must be careful to understand exactly what is being considered a cause. Figure 6.1 illustrates temporal priority.

Because the requirement of temporal priority is obvious, it is often assumed that temporal priority exists when, in fact, it may not. Consider, for example, the temporal priority involved in Jacobs's (1967) research on suicide notes discussed in Chapter 1. Jacobs's content analysis of suicide notes led him to conclude that people committed suicide because they believed the uncertainty of what might happen after death was preferable to the perception of certain, continued depression in their lives. One question Jacobs was not able

FIGURE 6.1   Sensible and Nonsensible Temporal Priority

Sense			Nonsense		
Before	→	After	Before	←	After
Cause	→	Effect	Cause	←	Effect

to address directly was, "Which came first?" Did people decide to commit suicide because they preferred the uncertainty of death, or did they decide to commit suicide and then justify that decision by writing notes about the uncertainty of death? There is, of course, no way to answer this question using Jacobs's data; there may be no ethical way to answer this question with any data. Thus, as you read through reports of experiments, look for explicit justification of temporal priority. Merely assuming temporal priority does not count as critical evaluation of experimental research.

Control Over Variables

Because temporal priority is often difficult to establish through logic alone, experimental research invariably involves exerting some control over the research environment. Some of that control involves keeping certain things constant, such as the form used to collect the data or the setting (whether inside or outside of a laboratory). Some things cannot be held constant, and they are called, sensibly, *variables*. One way to establish temporal priority is to manipulate the **independent variable**—*the suspected cause under consideration in a research project*. In order to test Jacobs's hypothesis experimentally, then, we would have to be able to depress a group of people to the point at which they were suicidal and then compare them to a group of people who were not depressed. Obviously, such research would violate just about every known principle of ethics. Let's continue this discussion with a more feasible experiment.

Oermann, Kardong-Edgren, and Odom-Maryon (2011) exerted control over the amount of practice in their study of cardiopulmonary resuscitation (CPR) skills by assigning some nursing students to a practice condition and other students to a no-practice condition. They ensured that the students in the practice condition received practice by having them go to a skills laboratory each month and engage in six minutes of practice on a mannequin that provided automated advice about the quality of the practice. Students in the no-practice condition were not given opportunities to practice on the voice-advisor mannequin. Thus, their independent variable had two levels: (1) practice and (2) no practice.

The **dependent variables**, *the effects under investigation in the experiment*, in Oermann et al. (2011) were measured during a three-minute performance of CPR on a mannequin that could record depth of compression, ventilation volume, and other variables of interest. Because Oermann et al. (2011) had control over the timing of the independent and dependent variables—they scheduled the testing session several months after the practice session began—they were able to both establish temporal priority and demonstrate control over the variables. If you read Oermann et al. (2011), however, you will not find the phrase *We established temporal priority by . . .* ; critical reading requires that we take in the information that is presented and use it to establish temporal priority and control. We do read, for example, that "site coordinators ensured that the study protocol was followed" (Oermann et al., 2011, p. 2), which is how they indicated that they exerted control over the variables, how they made sure that the practice group received practice and the no-practice group did not receive practice. The research hypothesis is illustrated in Figure 6.2.

FIGURE 6.2   An Example of an Experimental Research Hypothesis in Oermann et al. (2011)

Practice (Yes or No)	→	Depth of Compression
Independent Variable	→	Dependent Variable
Suspected Cause	→	Effect Under Investigation

Random Assignment

Despite the use of monitors to control the practice sessions by Oermann et al. (2011), there remain other, plausible explanations for the different CPR skills exhibited by students who received practice and those who did not. It is possible, for example, that students who received practice already had better CPR skills or, perhaps, had even completed a previous CPR course. To attempt to control all of these other possible causes by manipulating them and including them as additional independent variables would soon require more groups of people than would be possible. Instead of attempting to control all other possible explanations through manipulation, investigators rely on **random assignment**, which includes *any procedure that provides all participants an equal opportunity to experience any given level of the independent variable*. In Oermann et al. (2011, p. 2), for example, we read that students were "randomly assigned" to receive either practice or no practice in CPR skills.

Random assignment is a critical part of experimental design because it ensures that participant differences that are not otherwise controlled are equalized across the levels of the independent variable. If there happened to have been some nursing students who already knew how to do CPR, for example, then they would be just as likely to be assigned to the practice group as to the no-practice group. Thus, any differences in the mean skill performance exhibited by the two groups would not be attributable to students who already knew how to do CPR. Similarly, differences between the two groups could not be attributed to differences in age, proportion of men and women, motivation, intelligence, health, nutrition, strength, or any of the hundreds of other possible reasons why someone might perform CPR better than someone else. Because of random assignment, the only thing that systematically differed among the groups was the amount of practice they received.

DEMONSTRATION VERSUS DEMOGRAPHY

The combination of temporal priority, control of variables through manipulation, and random assignment is what makes a research study an experiment, what makes it possible to test cause–effect hypotheses. That same combination, however, tends to produce a somewhat artificial environment. If other institutions chose to use brief practice sessions to maintain CPR skills, for example, there probably would not be monitors in the practice rooms at all times to make sure that the people practicing were really practicing. Other practice rooms might not contain exactly the same make and model of practice mannequins as those used by Oermann et al. (2011). Would those differences necessarily mean that brief practice would not be effective in a different environment? The answer is a resounding *no*.

Experimental research is not supposed to produce an exact replica of natural phenomena. That's not heresy but rather a recognition that experimental research has a very specific purpose—to test cause–effect hypotheses—and conclusions drawn from experimental research are drawn about the cause–effect relationship. In Oermann et al. (2011, p. 6), for example, among the conclusions was the line "the findings of this not study only confirmed the importance of practicing CPR psychomotor skills to retain them but also revealed that short monthly practices could improve skills over baseline." Note the use of "could" in the second half of the sentence. They are not promising that brief practice will improve skills—there is no guarantee. Instead, they are reporting that brief practice has been shown to improve skills.

The issue here is the difference between *demonstration* and *demography*. In their experiment, Oermann et al. (2011) *demonstrated* brief practice improved CPR skills among their participants under the described experimental conditions. *Demography*, on the other hand, involves the question of how often we can expect those same differences to occur with different participants and under different conditions. *Demonstration* relies on the extent to which the independent variable is the only systematic difference among the groups. If the mean skills levels are different and the brief practice is the only variable that could have caused those differences, then they have demonstrated a cause–effect relationship between brief practice and skill improvement.

Demography, on the other hand, relies on **mundane realism**, which refers to *the extent to which the experience of research participants is similar to the experiences of everyday life*. If others are highly similar to the students who participated in the research and experienced the same type and amount of practice, then we would expect those individuals also to exhibit improved CPR skills (but there is still no guarantee that doing the same thing would produce exactly the same results). Different people, difference types and amounts of practice, different practice conditions, and other differences might produce different amounts of skill improvement. How much the skill improvement might change would depend upon those other differences and additional research would probably tell us more about that, but for now, we know that brief practice *can* produce skill improvement. We cannot, however, claim that brief practice *will always* produce skill improvement. Of course, replicating the experiment—for example, with a different amount of practice or with different students—and obtaining the same set of results would add to the generalizability of the cause–effect relationship demonstrated in the first experiment. Enough replications would eventually enable us to develop some idea as to just how much brief practice is enough or just what types of mannequins are effective or how long the brief practice needs to be continued. The results of the additional studies would help us understand the demography of brief practice.

ALTERNATIVE EXPLANATIONS FOR RESEARCH RESULTS

When the purpose of research is explanation—testing cause–effect hypotheses—every effort must be made to ensure that the independent variable is the only systematic influence on the dependent variable. The results of experimental research typically involve detecting differences among groups as measured by the dependent variable. Therefore, we need to be sure that the independent variable is the only preexisting difference among those groups. Temporal priority, manipulation of variables, and random assignment are the general requirements of an experimental design, but sometimes those requirements are missing from a study that we want to use to draw conclusions about cause–effect. In those cases, we need to consider alternative explanations. An **alternative explanation**, simply, is *any number of defined reason why an independent variable is not the only suspected cause of changes in a dependent variable*. As a critical consumer of research, you need to understand alternative explanations before you can determine whether or not a causal conclusion expressed in a research report is warranted.

For the following discussion, let us pretend that Oermann et al. (2011) did not conduct an experiment. Instead, let is imagine they conducted a simple demonstration study in which they asked a single group of nursing students to engage in brief practice of CPR skills and measured their skills before and after practice. For reference purposes, let's call this the Fake Practice Study. Let's also assume that the results of the Fake Practice Study were such that CPR skills were better after brief practice than they were before the brief practice. Finally, I should also note that Campbell and Stanley (1963) literally wrote the book on alternative explanations, and much of the following discussion relies heavily on their classic volume.

History Effects

A **history effect** is *a potential alternative explanation to the results of the experiment, produced whenever some uncontrolled event alters participants' responses.* Usually the event occurs between the time the researcher manipulates the independent variable and the time the researcher measures the dependent variable. Sometimes a history effect is caused by a truly historical event, but more often than not, it is produced by more commonplace events.

Suppose, for example, that the American Heart Association issued new guidelines about CPR during the Fake Practice Study. Those new guidelines might have motivated the participants to work on their CPR skills, and it might be that work, rather than the brief practice, that caused the improvement in the students' CPR skills. Of course, a history effect is not always caused by an historical event. The participants in the Fake Practice Study could just as easily have been motivated by one of their instructors saying, "You know, CPR skills are an important part of nursing," which is not a particularly historic event. The key aspect of a history effect is that something other than the independent variable happened and that "something" caused the observed effect in the dependent variable.

Generally, random assignment and a control condition enable researchers to eliminate the influence of a history effect. Oermann et al. (2011) had two groups of students, those who did and those who did not receive brief practice, and randomly assigned students to those groups. If there were something that happened—a historical event, an instructor's comment, or anything else—then it would be equally likely to affect both groups of students. If both groups of students were equally affected, then there would be no group differences in the dependent variable. Thus, random assignment and a control condition don't eliminate a history effect (that would be impossible), but they do ensure that whatever history effect might have occurred is not the reason for group differences in an experiment.

Maturation Effects

In some sense, maturation is a catchall alternative explanation. **Maturation** refers to *any process that involves systematic change over time, regardless of specific events.* From a causal point of view, the passage of time is not the cause of maturation but is merely the most convenient indicator of whatever process may be affecting participants. Most experiments do not last long enough for maturation to occur in the everyday sense of the word—people growing older—but maturation also includes such things as fatigue, boredom, thirst, hunger, and frustration as well as positive outcomes such as greater knowledge, wisdom, enhanced decision skills, and so on. If, for example, in the Fake Practice Study, the yearlong duration of the study convinced the students that CPR skills were very important, then they might start practicing CPR more diligently. Or, if the students became stronger as a result of practice, then they could achieve greater compression depth when tested. Either realization of CPR importance or greater strength would be a maturation effect in the Fake Practice Study and could account for better CPR skills instead of the brief-practice sessions.

Any design involving random assignment to different conditions provides some protection against maturation effects because all groups should experience about the same amount of maturation, but random assignment alone is usually not sufficient protection. Maturation effects could remain an alternative explanation of results if Oermann et al. (2011) did not ensure that both groups were otherwise treated equally during the experiment, such as testing CPR skills the same number of times in the practice and the no-practice groups.

At this point, you should realize that control over much more than the independent variable is necessary for good experimental research. Not only did Oermann et al. (2011) need to control the independent variable (amount of brief practice), they needed to control the number of testing sessions, ensure that the students' classes were continued as usual, and make sure that the same mannequins were used. The need for even more control will become apparent as we continue to consider additional alternative explanations of research results.

Testing Effects

You may recall from Chapter 2 that measurement always involves some sort of error; measurement is never perfect. How one phrases questions, for example, can affect the responses one receives. Simply asking a question, the measurement itself, can affect more than the response to the question. In experimental research, **testing effects** are *changes in responses caused by measuring the dependent variable.* Testing effects can occur in a variety of ways. One might, for example, measure the dependent variable more than once, thereby creating the possibility that responses on the second measurement reflect memory of the first responses. In the Fake Practice Study, for example, knowing that they are being tested may cause some students to perform CPR better than they would perform if no one was watching. Similarly, testing effects can occur when there is more than one dependent variable: One cannot measure all of the dependent variables simultaneously—one of them has to be measured first—and participants' responses to the first dependent variable might alter their responses to measures of other variables.

The most obvious means for eliminating testing effects are to measure dependent variables only once and to measure the primary dependent variable before any other measures. Oermann et al. (2011) used mannequins that automatically measured compression depth and rate as well as ventilation volume and rate at the same time. From the participant's viewpoint, the dependent variable was simply "performing CPR." Oermann et al. (2011) did measure the dependent variable more than once, but they used different, randomly selected subgroups of students to measure CPR skills at 3, 6, 9, and 12 months into the experiment. Thus, no students received extra practice at CPR from being measured. When reading research in which the dependent variable was measured more than one time, read carefully to find out how the investigators dealt with the possibility of testing effects.

Instrumentation Effects

Beginning researchers, and even some experienced ones, can become confused about the difference between testing effects and instrumentation effects. Such confusion likely occurs because the two terms seem to refer to the same problem. They are not the same, however, and should be considered separately. **Instrumentation effects** are *changes in the manner in which the dependent variable is measured*; they are problems caused by inconsistent operationalization of the dependent variable or by inconsistently measuring participants' responses. Testing effects, on the other hand, are produced by the act of measuring something, even if the measurement itself is consistent.

In the context of the current example, instrumentation effects would be a viable alternative explanation if Oermann et al. (2011) had used different types of mannequins to measure CPR skills. (They did not; they used the same exact make and model mannequin for all measurements.) Different types of mannequins might be more or less accurate, or more or less reliable, and therefore could bias the results. In other experiments, instrumentation effects might be cause by changing the questions on a questionnaire, having different groups use different questionnaires, or not calibrating equipment before each use.

To avoid instrumentation effects, control over operationalization of the dependent variable is critical. The logic of experiments may fall apart completely if those who experience different levels of the independent variable also experience different dependent variables. It may seem obviously foolish to use different versions of the dependent variable for different groups, but there are circumstances that might make such foolishness relatively easy to overlook. Even something as apparently innocuous as differences in the quality of copies of the form used to record the dependent variable can cause instrumentation problems. If one group has copies that are more difficult to read than the other group's copies, that discrepancy violates the logic involved in having the independent variable as the only systematic difference between the groups. Of course, as a consumer of research, you probably are not going to have access to the kind of detailed information that enables you to determine whether or not instrumentation effects have occurred in any particular study. Nevertheless, you should be attuned to potential clues of instrumentation effects when reading the method section of an article. If researchers use alternative versions of the same scale, perhaps one version before the manipulation and a different version after, then you should make sure the article contains information about the equivalence of reliability and validity of the different versions.

More often than not, instrumentation effects become a problem when the operational definition of the dependent variable depends on someone's judgment. Subjective measures, such as someone's rating of the quality of an essay, are subject to various problems. For example, the person making the judgments may grow tired, bored, or careless, and such changes are, in fact, changes in the dependent measure. In this case, because the instrument is the person making the rating, changes in the rater become instrumentation effects.

Not allowing raters, judges, or others in a study to be aware of the level of the independent variable experienced by the participant reduces the likelihood of instrumentation effects. **A blind rater** is *someone who is unaware of either the research hypothesis or the experimental group from which the responses came.* When you read research reports containing such phrases as *the observers were blind to conditions* or *blind raters were used*, it doesn't mean the observers had a vision deficit. Rather, it means the observers or raters did not know to which experimental group those being observed belonged. In Oermann et al. (2011), the raters were blind because the "raters" were mannequins, so they lacked awareness.

Statistical Regression Effects

In the context of alternative explanations of research results, *statistical regression effect* does not refer to a particular type of data analysis. Originally described by Galton (1886), **statistical regression effect** is *an artifact of measurement that occurs when extreme scores are obtained and the participant is tested again at a later time.* Someone who scores extremely high or extremely low on a measure, if tested again, is likely to obtain a second score that is closer to the average than was the first score. The person's score is said to regress toward the mean because the score moves back to the average score, either from an extreme high or an extreme low. A less-extreme second score doesn't always happen; it depends on the amount of measurement error.

Most continuous variables, such as a rating from 1 to 10, an intelligence quotient (IQ) score, and crime rates, include the assumption that the overall distribution of responses should conform to the normal distribution, the bell-shaped curve. Most scores bunch together near the mean of the distribution, and the frequency of scores decreases as the scores become more distant from the mean. Therefore, the probability of obtaining extreme scores is lower than the probability of obtaining scores closer to the mean. Think of the distribution of grade point averages (GPAs) of undergraduates at your school. Most undergraduate students have a GPA somewhere between a 2.5 and a 3.5; the number of students with a 4.0 or a 0.5 is relatively low. Thus, the probability of your running into someone with a 4.0 GPA is considerably lower than the probability of your encountering someone with a 2.5 GPA. If you know someone who earned a 3.9 GPA last semester, statistical regression means that he or she would be less likely to earn a 3.9 or higher this semester, too.

Statistical regression effects, like testing effects, are a problem only when the dependent variable is measured more than once. Only random assignment can be used to avoid them. However, statistical regression effects can become a problem even when an implicit measure of the dependent variable is used. For example, a teacher might select students he or she believes to be the brightest students and give them special assignments designed to further improve their abilities. If, subsequently, the students exhibit no change in their abilities, perhaps as measured by an alternate-form examination, then the lack of difference could be due either to the fact that the assignments were ineffective or due to statistical regression. That is, some of the brightest, as measured by the teacher's perceptions, may not be as bright as the teacher perceived them to be (there is measurement error in the teacher's perception). Subsequent measurement would produce a score closer to average. But if the special assignments are actually making the students brighter, then the combination of independent variable plus regression might produce a net result of no change. Statistical regression brought the scores down, and the assignments brought them back up again, leaving the scores right where they started. Of course, the students did receive some benefit—improved abilities—from the assignments, but statistical regression prevented that benefit from being reflected in their scores. Note that such an experiment would also be subject to instrumentation effects; a teacher's perception and a written examination are not the same operational definition of the dependent variable.

In general, we should be suspicious about any results in which very high scores became lower, or very low scores became higher, unless the researchers provide information that enables us to rule out regression toward the mean as an alternative explanation. As noted earlier, Oermann et al. (2011) avoided statistical regression effects by selecting different groups of students to receive the repeated measures in their study and by repeating the measurements more than once. Over time, the students in the brief-practice condition improved, and their scores showed continual improvement instead of a one-time change.

Selection Effects

The brightest-student example in the preceding section also involves a specific example of alternative explanations known as *selection effects*. A **selection effect** is *produced by the manner in which the participants were recruited or recruited themselves.* That is, selection effects occur because some characteristic of the participants differs systematically across the groups. In the Fake Practice Study, students who volunteer to participate in the study may also be the kind of students most interested in improving their CPR skills. Once again, random assignment to conditions eliminates selection effects because the selection characteristic, whatever it is, should be equally distributed across the randomly assigned groups. Oermann et al. (2011) included students of different ages and genders, but those differences were overcome by random assignment to conditions. By now, you should be getting the idea that random assignment to conditions is an integral part of any experiment.

Sometimes, however, random assignment is practically or ethically impossible. In such cases, you may read about a technique called matching, which is a second-best alternative. **Matching** is *an attempt to equalize scores across groups on any relevant variable.* Suppose, for example, Oermann et al. (2011) were not able to assign students randomly to the practice and no-practice conditions in their study, perhaps because students were free to choose whether or not they wanted to practice CPR skills. Under such conditions, the researchers would probably make sure that they included about the same proportion of men and women in each condition, the same range of ages in each condition, the same distribution of experience in school in each condition, and so on. When there are many different variables on which to match participants, you may read about the use of propensity scores (see, for example, Rubin, 2001), which involves statistical matching. **Propensity scoring** involves *statistically matching participants on a variety of variables or measures to rule out those variables as alternative explanations*. Although more complicated than simple matching technique, propensity scoring is still a form of matching.

The issue with using matching to overcome selection effects is, very simply, that we can never be sure that the researchers have included all of the relevant variables in the matching process. If someone were to replicate Oermann et al. (2011) without random assignment, they would have to match the students in terms of gender, age, amount of previous education, amount of experience with CPR, arm strength, general physical condition, and so on. There may be no limit to the number of different things that might affect CPR skills, so there may be no limit to the number of different variables on which the participants would have to be matched. Even though matching does provide an alternative when random assignment is not possible, it is not as effective as random assignment. Thus, we should be much more critical, and skeptical, about tests of cause–effect explanations that include matching instead of random assignment. Sometimes matching is the only available technique to a researcher, but that doesn't mean that it is as good as random assignment in controlling selection (or other) effects.

Attrition Effects

Attrition effects are *changes in the dependent variable caused by the loss of participants during a research project*. (Sometimes the loss is *caused by the death of participants during the project*, in which case the term **mortality effects** is used.) Attrition is a specific type of selection effect, one due to participants' leaving, rather than joining, the research project. Oermann et al. (2011) did have attrition in their study; some students quit participating over the 12-month course of the experiment. That attrition occurs in a study, however, does not mean that attrition effects have occurred. That is, just because some participants left the study doesn't mean that the study is ruined, but it does mean that we should read critically to find out what the researchers did to rule out attrition effects.

Random assignment is considered a safeguard against attrition effects because the number of participants likely to drop out of a study should be roughly equal across groups, as was the case in Oermann et al. (2011). Random assignment, however, cannot be considered a *cure* for attrition effects, for one experimental group could in fact contain a disproportionate number of dropouts. When you read a study with disproportionate attrition among conditions, then you should add the phrase *for those who remained in the study* to any interpretation of the results. As consumers, we cannot know the reasons for the disproportionate attrition, but we can wonder about attrition effects as an alternative explanation.

When you read a study in which attrition effects are likely to be of concern, either because the procedure was long or there are multiple sessions, read carefully to find mention of comparing the dropouts across conditions or comparing the dropouts to the remaining participants. Look for results in which the researchers compared proportions of genders, ages, or other variables. Look for wording such as *the average age of the attrition group was the same as the average in the continuing group* or *those who withdrew consent in the experimental group were slightly older than those in the control group*. Such comparisons will enable you to decide whether or not attrition effects are a reasonable alternative explanation for the results.

Participant Bias

We have already noted that research participants can be affected by **self-presentation**, the *concern for the impression one makes upon others*. This is one example of **participant bias**—*any intentional effort on the part of participants to alter their responses for the purpose of self-presentation*. Another example may involve participants' concerns about revealing sensitive information simply because they believe it is none of the researcher's business what they think. Generally, any **evaluation apprehension**—*concern about being observed*—can produce participant bias. In the Fake Practice Study, participants might be concerned that poor CPR performance could affect their grades in their courses and be more motivated to perform well. Thus, the results would be due to participant bias instead of brief practice.

Random assignment to conditions helps to reduce participant bias because, as usual, random assignment equalizes the distribution of apprehensive participants across experimental groups. The only way to avoid participant bias completely is to prevent the participants from being aware that they are being observed, but this invokes the ethical issue of disregarding informed consent. Participants sometimes are unaware that they are in a research project, but this occurs very infrequently.

In addition to evaluation apprehension and related forms of participant bias, participants may intentionally attempt to help or hinder the research efforts. The **beneficent subject effect** *occurs when participants are aware of the research hypothesis and attempt to respond so as to support it*. Suppose, for example, that students in the Fake Practice Study wanted to perform CPR well because the researcher was one of their favorite faculty members. In this case, the results would be caused by participant bias instead of brief practice. The opposite effect, known as the **maleficent subject effect**, *occurs when participants are aware of the research hypothesis and attempt to respond so as to undermine it*.

The only way to prevent either effect is to prevent participants from becoming aware of the research hypothesis. This is known as keeping the participants "blind" and is analogous to keeping raters of subjective dependent measures in the dark about the hypothesis. In some projects, a **double-blind procedure** is used; *the raters (or investigators) and participants are unaware of the research hypothesis or of group memberships related to that hypothesis*. Blind and double-blind studies may involve concealment of the research hypothesis by preventing awareness of participation itself or they may involve some sort of **deception** (*providing false information about the research project*). It is common to keep participants and raters unaware of the specific hypotheses in research, but deception poses ethical problems and is considered only after it has been determined that simply withholding information about the specific research hypothesis will not prevent participant bias.

Experimenter Bias

Participants are not the only people who may alter their behavior during an experiment. **Experimenter bias** refers to *the researcher's differential treatment of experimental groups*. There was, for example, considerable potential for experimenter bias in Oermann et al. (2011). The researchers and site coordinators could have especially encouraged students in the brief practice groups to improve their CPR skills. Oermann et al. (2011) conducted their study across ten different schools, however, and the chances that such a breach of research protocol happened at all ten schools are extremely low.

The logic of the experiment requires researchers to treat all groups exactly the same; the only systematic difference between the groups should be the manipulated independent variable. As you read, therefore, pay particular attention to efforts to avoid experimenter bias and all of the previously discussed alternative explanations. Just because researchers are not blind to conditions, for example, does not mean that there was experimenter bias exerting effects upon the results. Experimenters who are not blind, participants who are not randomly assigned, or any of the other aspects of the research that might alert you to potential alternative explanations, however, should be considered very carefully so that you, as the consumer of the research, can decide whether or not any of these alternative explanations pose a problem for interpreting the results. You should not assume there is experimenter bias simply because the results section did not contain the phrase *the experimenter was blind to conditions*, but you also should not assume that there are no alternative explanations just because the study was published.

EXPERIMENTAL DESIGN

Fortunately, not every experiment is subject to every alternative explanation described above. On the other hand, every alternative explanation must be considered a potential problem until logic, control, or experimental design enables you to rule it out.

In this section, we'll consider the various experimental designs that can be used to rule out alternative explanations. **Design** refers to *the number and arrangement of independent variable levels in a research project*. Although all experimental designs involve manipulated independent variables and random assignment, different designs are more or less efficient for dealing with specific alternative explanations.

The design a researcher uses depends upon the research hypothesis the researcher has tried to test. Therefore, being familiar with a variety of different designs enables you to critically consume a variety of research projects as you attempt to inform your practice empirically. The major factor in examining a design critically is not its complexity but the extent to which it provides internal validity. **Internal validity** refers to *the extent to which the independent variable is the only systematic difference among experimental groups* (Munn, Lockwood, & Moola, 2015; Shadish, Cook, & Campbell, 2002). That is, the internal validity of an experiment allows you, as the research consumer, to conclude that the independent variable produced the effects measured with the dependent variable. Just as every poker hand either wins or loses the pot, every design is either a winner or loser at internal validity, depending on the specific research hypothesis being tested

The Basic Design

The basic design is the simplest design that still qualifies as a true experimental design. Campbell and Stanley (1963) refer to it as the *posttest-only control group design*, while others call it a *randomized trial* or a *randomized comparative trial*. If we were to add a no-practice group to the Fake Practice Study and randomly assign volunteers to receive either practice or no practice, then we would have an experiment with the basic design, as illustrated in Figure 6.3. When one of the levels of the independent variable is a **control condition**—*the absence of the manipulation*—then the design is sometimes called a *randomized control trial*. Sometimes researchers will use a **placebo**, *a treatment that appears to be real but is not effective*, instead of a control group, and the design may be called a *randomized placebo trial*. For example, instead of "Do Not Engage in Brief Practice" in Figure 6.3, researchers might have participants engage in a brief practice of inserting an IV or some other activity that is not related to CPR. That way, both groups engage in about the same amount of activity, but only one group practices CPR skills.

The basic design is not necessarily limited to two groups. Researchers could include brief practice of CPR, brief practice of IV insertion, and no practice at all in a single study. The key aspects of the basic design are that participants are (1) first randomly assigned to two or more groups and (2) measured on the same dependent variable.

The basic design is most efficient for research in which the pre-manipulation state of participants—what they are like before they experience a single independent variable—is either not of interest or can be assumed to be unrelated to the independent variable. Neither change over time nor differential reactions to the independent variable as a

FIGURE 6.3 The Basic Design for an Experiment

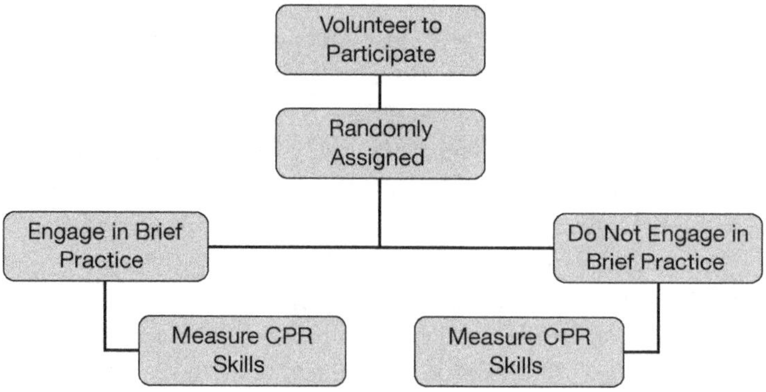

function of some preexisting characteristic can be studied with the basic design because there is no way to know anything about the participants before they experience the independent variable.

The Basic Pretest Design

The basic pretest design, as the name implies, involves adding a pretest measure to the basic design. A **pretest** is *a measure of the dependent variable that is administered before intervention or treatment so that change can be determined.* The obvious reason for using a pretest measure is to examine how much the independent variable causes participants to change. The basic pretest design, illustrated in Figure 6.4, is the design Campbell and Stanley (1963) call the pretest–posttest control group design. In Figure 6.4, our fictitious researchers would measure everyone's CPR skills, the randomly assign the participants to engage or not engage in brief practice, and then measure the same CPR skills again. Change would be measured by comparing skills displayed after the intervention to the skills displayed during the pretest. Although not depicted in the figure, the basic pretest design can include more than two levels of the same independent variable.

The obvious advantage of the basic pretest design over the basic design is the ability to obtain information about the pre-manipulation state of the participants, to examine the change in scores. The disadvantage is that the pretest measure may affect participants' reactions to the independent variable—that is, asking participants first to display their CPR skills could sensitize them to take greater advantage of the practice opportunities later in the experiment, which could produce a type of testing effect.

Random assignment enables us to overcome the possibility of general testing effects, but the combination of pretest measures and manipulation of the independent variable may create another alternative explanation for the results. Campbell and Stanley (1963) call this alternative explanation a **testing–treatment interaction**, in which

FIGURE 6.4   The Basic Pretest Design, in Which the Dependent Variable Is Measured Both Before and After Manipulation of the Independent Variable

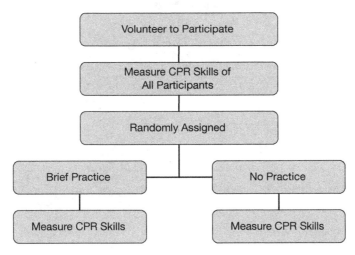

participants experiencing one level of the independent variable may be more sensitive to testing effects than participants experiencing a different level of the independent variable. Essentially, the pretest measure may make one of the levels of the independent variable, such as the brief practice, more forceful than it would have been without the pretest. This increased forcefulness of that particular level of the independent variable, then, is an artifact rather than a valid test of the variable's impact. The dependent variable in such cases measures both the effect of the independent variable and its combination with the pretest instead of measuring the effect of the independent variable only. It is also possible that the pretest measure may make participants wonder about the purpose of the study and increase participant bias.

The Solomon Four-Group Design

The most effective design for dealing with the problem of testing–treatment interaction is the Solomon (1949) four-group design, illustrated in Figure 6.5. Although there are only two levels of the independent variable, four groups are required to assess the extent to which testing effects have occurred. It is important to realize, however, that this design does not eliminate the testing–treatment interaction but rather enables the researcher to determine whether or not it has occurred and, if it has, assess its impact. This design also enables one to determine whether or not overall testing effects have occurred; it enables the researcher to assess the effectiveness of the random assignment procedure.

When there are control conditions, then comparing the control with pretest (Group 2) to the control without pretest (Group 4) provides a test of the overall testing effect.

FIGURE 6.5   The Solomon Four-Group Design

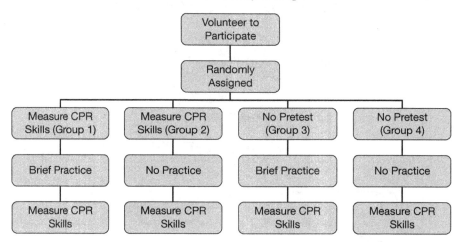

The only difference between these two groups is the existence of a pretest measure, and any difference between these two groups would be due to the pretest. Comparing the difference between change in Group 1 and change in Group 3 provides an estimate of the testing–treatment interaction effect. If there is no interaction between testing and treatment, then the effect of the treatment should be the same with and without a pretest. If, however, there is a testing–treatment interaction, then you will probably read about statistical analyses used to adjust for the interaction. Critical reading, however, will also involve being able to notice when a four-group design should have been used but was not used.

Unfortunately, the Solomon four-group design is not, in general, a very efficient design. It requires twice as many groups as the basic pretest design to examine essentially the same cause–effect hypothesis. The four groups depicted in Figure 6.5, for example, include only two levels of a single independent variable. The loss of efficiency is related to the need to test for the testing–treatment interaction. In general, the more the researcher needs to know, the more groups or participants will be required. Oermann et al. (2011), for example, used a version of the Solomon four-group design by randomly selecting some participants to be measured at various times throughout their yearlong study. Because they had many participants, they were able to check for a testing–treatment interaction effect even though they did not actually include a pretest in their study.

Factorial Design

Many research questions require inclusion of more than one independent variable in the design. Hagger, Wong, and Davey (2015), for example, manipulated both mental simulation (or visualization) and self-control building in their study of mechanisms for reducing binge drinking among college students. Their design allows participants

FIGURE 6.6 A Factorial Design Based on Hagger et al. (2015)

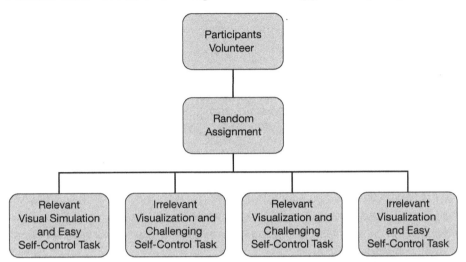

to experience mental simulation alone, self-control building alone, both together, or neither mechanism.

Designs that include more than one independent variable are called **factorial designs**. In terms of our diagram scheme, a simple factorial design is illustrated in Figure 6.6. Hagger et al. (2015) manipulated mental simulation by having participants either (a) visualize behavior related to reducing alcohol consumption or (b) visualizing behavior related to going to the movies or going shopping. They manipulated self-control building by having participants regularly engage in (a) tasks that involve challenging exercises in self-control or (b) tasks that involve very easy exercises in self-control. Within the design, participants collectively experience all possible combinations of the two independent variables, but each participant experiences only one of these combinations. As with other designs, each of the independent variables can have two or more levels.

Often, the notation used in Figure 6.6 is not applied to factorial designs. As you probably discovered while attempting to decipher Figure 6.6, the notation is a little cumbersome. Instead, the notation used in Figure 6.7 is adopted for factorial designs in which the combination of independent variables forms a kind of matrix. I have added identification numbers to the groups, called *cells* in the design, to make it easier to refer to them in further discussion, but you will usually see means, standard deviations, or some other summary statistics when reading research articles.

In Cell #1, participants will receive irrelevant mental simulation instructions and will be presented with easy self-control tasks, which serves as the control condition. In Cell #2, the mental simulation is irrelevant but the self-control task is challenging; this cell, together with Cell #1, is comparable to a basic design for self-control building alone. In Cell #3, participants engage in relevant visualization and are presented with easy

Figure 6.7 The Factorial Design of Hagger et al. (2015) in Matrix Notation

		Type of Self-Control Task	
		Easy	Challenging
Type of Visualization	Movies or Shopping	1	2
	Reducing Drinking	3	4

self-control tasks; this condition, together with Cell #1, is comparable to a basic design for mental simulation alone. Finally, participants in Cell #4 engage in relevant visualization and presented with challenging self-control tasks. Cell #4 enables the researchers to assess the combination of both independent variables. The design depicted in Figure 6.7 is called a *2 × 2 factorial design*—two levels of one independent variable combined with two levels of another independent variable.

The advantage of a factorial design is that interactions between independent variables can be tested. An **interaction** is *a result that occurs when the effect of one variable depends upon which level of another variable is present*. Interactions are sometimes called **moderator effects** (Baron & Kenny, 1986). Hagger et al. (2015) noted that a number of researchers have demonstrated the utility of mental simulation on reduction of unwanted behavior, including binge drinking, and a number of other researchers have demonstrated the utility of self-control building on improving healthy behavior, but they reported that no studies have examined the combination of both strategies. That is, they expect that the effect of mental simulation will be even greater when paired with self-control building. It is equally reasonable to write that they expect the effect of self-control building to be even greater when paired with relevant mental simulation.

Figure 6.8 contains four different fictitious results from Hagger et al. (2015). In Panel A, neither type of visualization nor type of self-control task has much of an effect upon the number of binge-drinking episodes per month. In Panel B, it is clear that mental simulation about reducing drinking does reduce the number of binge episodes compared to visualization about shopping. This is known as a *main effect* for the type of visualization. Generally, a **main effect** *occurs when different levels of one independent variable evidence different results in the dependent variable*. Panel C contains fictitious results for a main effect for type of self-control task. Panel D in Figure 6.8 illustrates an interaction effect. There appears to be a main effect for type of visualization and for type of self-control task, but notice that visualizing drinking less combined with a challenging self-control task reduces the number of binge episodes more than one would expect from the mere combination of both main effects. That is, mental simulation and self-control training together produce an extra strong effect, a greater effect than either variable could produce on its own. The nonparallel lines in Panel D are another indicator of an interaction effect.

FIGURE 6.8   Fictitious Results From Hagger et al. (2015) Illustrating Effects on Binge Drinking

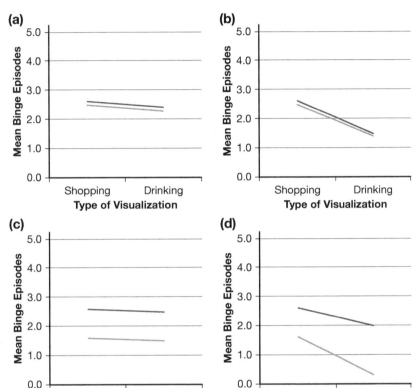

The ability to detect and interpret interactions is the primary advantage of factorial designs. As you read articles, keep in mind that no matter how complicated a design may appear to be, factorial designs include only two types of effects, main effects and interaction effects. Don't allow yourself to be overly confused when trying to understand complicated factorial designs; interpret the results one main effect at a time and one interaction at a time.

Within Subjects Design

A **within subjects design** is *a design in which the same participants are exposed to more than one level of an independent variable.* This is often done so that each participant (sometimes called *subject*) serves as his or her own control; that is, the independent variable is manipulated within, rather than between, the participants. A within subjects design also involves **repeated measures design**, in which *the dependent variable is measured more than once for each participant.* The basic pretest design, for example, is the simplest form of repeated measurement design, but that design does not involve exposing any participant to more than one level of an independent variable.

Kim, Gordon, Ferruzzi, and Campbell (2015), for example, were interested in testing whether or not the lipid content of eggs would enhance absorption of carotenoids contained in vegetables. Their participants consumed a salad to which zero, one and a half, or three scrambled eggs were added and provided hourly blood samples for 10 hours after consumption. The participants consumed each type of salad on different days, thus being presented with all three levels of the independent variable. Kim et al. (2015) also employed repeated measures of their dependent variables by drawing blood from the participants over a ten-hour period. Figure 6.9 contains an illustration of the major parts of the design, which included random assignment to the different orders in which the participants consumed the salads.

As is evident from Figure 6.9, each participant consumed all three types of salads, but the salads were consumed in different orders so that Kim et al. (2015) could assess whether or not the order of consumption made a difference. This is known as **counterbalancing**, *a methodological tactic in which all orders of levels of an independent variable are employed in a within-subjects design to assess the impact that order may have on the dependent variable.* When reading studies in which within subjects designs are used, always look for an indication that counterbalancing was used; without it, there is always the possibility that the order of the levels of the independent variable had an impact on the dependent variable.

For some variables, repeated measures designs are simply not possible. Some independent variable effects may last so long that they interfere with later, different levels of the same variable. Kim et al. (2015), for example, waited 14 days between consumption of the different salads to ensure that lipid intake from a preceding salad did not affect the absorption of carotenoids. Critical reading of within subjects designs also includes consideration of the amount of elapsed time between different levels of the independent variable.

Participant Characteristics

Before we leave design, let's consider the use of participant characteristics as independent variables. **Participant characteristics**, sometimes called **subject variables**, *are variables that differentiate participants but cannot be manipulated and are not subject to random assignment.* Participant characteristics include such variables as gender, age, ethnicity, amount of formal education, height, and so forth. They can be included in an experimental design, but because they are not subject to manipulation or random assignment, they cannot be considered true independent variables in an experimental design.

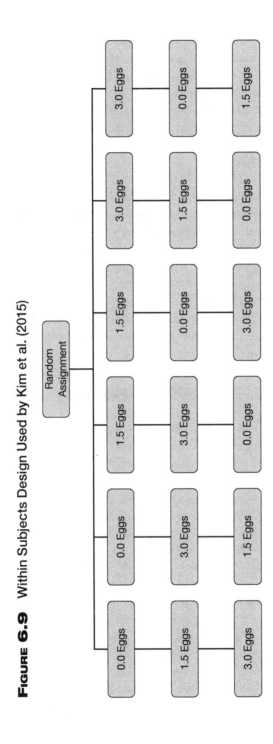

FIGURE 6.9 Within Subjects Design Used by Kim et al. (2015)

When reading research reports, however, you will often find that they are described as *independent variables* or sometimes called *subject variables*.

Oermann et al. (2011), for example, included gender and degree type (diploma, associate, baccalaureate) as participant characteristics in their study of brief practice for resuscitation skills among nursing students. They obviously could neither manipulate nor randomly assign students to gender or degree groups, but they did include both variables in their initial analyses to assess the extent to which men and women and different degree aspirations might be related to performance of resuscitation skills (neither variable evidenced a relationship with performance).

When participant characteristics are included in an experimental design, conclusions about cause–effect relationships cannot be drawn from any effects associated with such variables. Despite this restriction, you would not have to look very long before finding a research article in which the author(s) did exactly that. Drawing cause–effect conclusions about participant characteristics seems to be an almost irresistible temptation to many researchers. When this happens, it usually results from a very logical consideration of the effect and the researcher's knowledge about related research. Suggesting potential explanations for a gender effect, for example, is certainly within the realm of scientific research. On the other hand, concluding that a gender effect results from, say, differential attitudes when attitudes have not been manipulated in the design falls well outside the logic of experimental research.

DEMONSTRATION VERSUS DEMOGRAPHY AGAIN

Earlier in the chapter, the primary purpose of experimental research was described as testing whether or not a cause–effect relationship can be demonstrated. This purpose does not automatically rule out generalizing the results of the experiment, but generalization (demography) is secondary to testing the relationship (demonstration). If generalizing well beyond the experimental environment is an important part of your intentions as a consumer, you need to ensure that your efforts in that direction are not affected by the internal validity of the experimental design. If random assignment is not consistent with generalization, for example, then you should not generalize as though random assignment didn't occur.

Overgeneralization is also something to avoid. Although overgeneralization is a potential problem in any research method, experimental research seems particularly prone to the phrase *research has proved*. Random assignment is critical to experimental research, but experimental research is a process that also depends on replication for its effectiveness. Like any procedure based on probability theory, random assignment works in the long run but may not be effective on a one-time-only basis. Any research requires replication before we can rely heavily on the results.

You should realize that a single experiment does not *prove* that a cause–effect relationship exists; rather, it *demonstrates* the existence of the relationship under the conditions created by the experimental procedures. Those conditions include the specific experimenter, participants, operational definitions, and a host of other potential factors that differ from one experiment to another. A demonstration that something *can* happen does not mean it always *will* happen. Consuming a valid experiment requires paying attention to all aspects of experimental research, and that includes looking for additional studies in which the cause–effect relationship has been demonstrated under a variety of different circumstances.

SUMMARY

- Experimental research methods are the only methods designed specifically to test cause–effect hypotheses. Experiments are accomplished by manipulating the independent variable, randomly assigning participants to the various levels of the independent variable, controlling or eliminating alternative explanations, and measuring responses via the dependent variable. The independent variable is the suspected cause; the dependent variable is the effect of interest.

- Generalizing the results of an experiment well beyond the experimental situation is logically impossible, for the major purpose of most experiments is to demonstrate that the cause–effect relationship *can* occur, not that it always occurs.

- The logic of experimental research is that any difference between groups of participants as measured by the dependent variable is caused by their different experiences with the independent variable. Therefore, an experimenter must maintain internal validity—he or she must rule out alternative explanations of any obtained differences.

- Alternative explanations are generally ruled out through the use of random assignment to conditions created by manipulating the independent variable. These alternative explanations include history effects, maturation effects, testing effects, instrumentation effects, statistical regression effects, selection effects, attrition effects, participant bias, and experimenter bias.

- Control over the experimental situation can be used to rule out instrumentation effects, participant bias, and experimenter bias.

- The basic design of an experiment includes different groups representing different levels of a manipulated independent variable to which participants are randomly assigned. Adding a pretest to this design enables us to measure change as a function of the independent variable. Care must be taken, however, to avoid an interaction between treatment and testing.

- The Solomon four-group design can be used to measure testing effects, including a testing–treatment interaction. This added ability to test effects decreases the efficiency of the design with respect to testing the research hypothesis.

- When more than one independent variable is of interest, factorial designs are used to assess both main effects and interaction (moderator) effects. Main effects are simple effects due to one variable, whereas interaction effects are those caused by a combination of two or more independent variables.

- Within subjects design measures may be used with any experimental design, but only if the effects of an independent variable are not so long lasting as to interfere with subsequent levels of the same or another independent variable. Within subjects designs, which almost always include repeated measures of the dependent variable, should also take into account the possibility of order effects.

- Although often used in experimental research, participant characteristics cannot be considered valid independent variables. Also called *subject variables*, they may indicate the presence of a systematic difference, but they are not themselves considered to be causal agents.

EXERCISES

1. Find a research article in which the authors identify the research as an experiment. Determine whether the investigators established temporal priority and used random assignment.

2. Using the same or a different article, identify the design used in the research.

3. Using the same or a different article, examine the design and procedure carefully for each of the alternative explanations described in the chapter.

4. Find an article in which the authors describe an interaction (moderator) effect. Identify the variables involved in the interaction and try to explain the interaction to someone who has not read the article.

7

Quasi-Experimental Research

Participants were randomly assigned to the high and low IQ groups.

—Confused student's paper

OVERVIEW

Quasi-experimental research, as the name implies, includes research designs that approximate but are not truly experimental designs. In this chapter, you will learn about the major types of quasi-experimental designs as well as correlational research in general. You will also learn about designs that involve only a single participant.

INTRODUCTION

For a variety of different reasons, some of which were not understood by the student quoted at the beginning of this chapter, it is simply not possible to assign participants randomly to the different levels of many independent variables. It is also not possible to manipulate many independent variables. Researchers cannot, for example, manipulate participants' levels of intelligence; even if someone found a way to make such a manipulation, doing so would be well beyond the boundaries of ethical research. On the other hand, researchers can manipulate participants' knowledge about specific topics—which is what the confused student did—but that's not the same as manipulating levels of intelligence. Similarly, a researcher cannot assign participants to different gender categories. For these and other variables that cannot be controlled, true experimental research is not possible. It is possible, however, to test research hypotheses with approximations of experimental research. But don't let such labels as *quasi* and *approximations* lead you to think that quasi-experimental designs are somehow not quite as good as "real" experiments for adding to our knowledge. Like all research designs, quasi-experiments are excellent for some, but not all, research questions. Understanding such designs, including their limitations, will enable you to expand greatly the amount and types of research you can add to the information that guides your evidence-based practice.

In this chapter, we will concern ourselves with **quasi-experimental designs**— *research designs that approximate experimental designs but do not include random assignment to conditions* (Shadish, Cook, & Campbell, 2002). Although quasi-experimental designs do not involve as rigorous a test of cause–effect hypotheses as do experimental designs, they do provide worthy alternatives when experiments are impossible, impractical, or unethical. Many of the designs discussed below are used to avoid a number of alternative explanations fully described in Chapter 6. Quasi-experimental designs cannot, per se, avoid all of the alternative explanations that threaten internal validity; instead, logical analysis replaces random assignment.

As alternatives to experimental designs, quasi-experimental designs can be used to ask nearly the same questions as those asked through true experimental designs. Indeed, you may find that a quasi-experiment is sometimes called a **found experiment** or a **natural experiment**. Testing cause–effect questions is also the main purpose of quasi-experimentation. Although the questions are pretty much the same, the specificity of the questions differs greatly. Recall from Chapter 6 that experimental research involves asking whether the independent variable can be demonstrated to cause the dependent variable—whether, for example, brief practice can improve cardiopulmonary resuscitation (CPR) skills (Oermann, Kardong-Edgren, & Odom-Maryon, 2011). In quasi-experimental research, the cause–effect aspect of the question remains, but its emphasis changes. Instead of finding out whether the independent variable *causes* the dependent variable, consumers of research find out whether an independent variable *is an indicator* of whatever the real cause may be. You cannot sensibly ask, for example, whether gender causes performance differences; gender per se is not a legitimate cause. Instead, when we read quasi-experimental research, we find out whether performance differs as a function of gender, whether gender is an indicator of some unknown cause (whatever that cause may be). Gender does not cause the difference, even though that might be the way we talk about it in everyday conversation. Instead, we learn from research that men and women differ in terms of the cause of performance as well as performance itself; gender is an indicator of both the cause and the effect.

A more realistic example of quasi-experimental research is research conducted by Dane, Russell-Lindgren, Parish, Durham, and Brown (2000) to assess the extent to which nurses' being trained in advanced cardiac life support (ACLS) made a difference in patient survival of in-hospital resuscitations. In that study, we identified all in-hospital codes that were called by a nurse and determined through hospital employment records whether or not the nurse who called the code was certified in ACLS. We also found out, again from hospital records, whether or not the patient was discharged alive from the hospital. There were other aspects to the study, but the primary purpose of the study was met by using the quasi-experimental equivalent of the basic design described in Chapter 6 and depicted in Figure 7.1

FIGURE 7.1 Design of Dane et al. (2000)

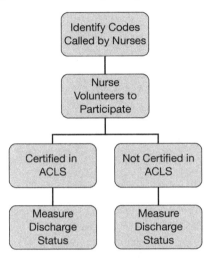

The primary difference between Figure 6.3 and Figure 7.1 is that the quasi-experiment does not include random assignment as part of the method. In the hospital in which Dane et al. (2000) did the research, about 75% of the nurses were already certified in ACLS before the study began, so it would have been difficult and time consuming to assign some nurses randomly to undergo certification and then wait for a patient to need resuscitation, and then wait one of the nurses in the study to be the person to discover the patient in need. More importantly, because ACLS certification for nurses was a best practice in some areas of the hospital, it would have been unethical to assign some nurses not to be certified.

Because Dane et al. (2000) did not randomly assign nurses to be ACLS certified, that variable is only an indicator of group difference and cannot be concluded to be the cause of the results, which were that patients discovered by an ACLS-certified nurse were four times more likely to be discharged alive than patients whose code was called by non-ACLS-certified nurses. As tempting as it might be to think, "Of course it was the certification," there could be many other differences between the two groups of nurses. ACLS-certified nurses could be more experienced, for example, or more confident or better at basic CPR. Critically engaging in evidence-based practice means that we have to withhold conclusions until the research has been done, and in the case of conclusions about causality, quasi-experimental research is not sufficient, no matter how logical or desirable the causal conclusion might be. Nevertheless, quasi-experimental research helps us to begin to narrow down possible causes, so it is worthwhile to consider other types of quasi-experimental designs.

TIME-SERIES DESIGNS

Time-series designs are *a type of extended repeated measures design in which the dependent variable is measured several times before and after the introduction of the independent variable*; that is, a series of measures is taken over a period of time. There are two types of time-series designs: interrupted time-series and multiple time-series.

Interrupted Time-Series Design

Interrupted time-series designs take their name from the notion that *the implementation of the independent variable is experienced as a change in the normal stream of events in participants' lives*. For example, Jewkes et al. (2014) used an interrupted time-series design to examine the effectiveness of a program intended to improve economic conditions, reduce intimate partner violence (IPV), and otherwise improve the lives of residents living in informal urban settlements in Durban, South Africa. (According to Sheuya [2010], informal settlements are unplanned communities generally characterized by inadequate sanitation, overcrowding, lack of property ownership, poor structural quality, and diverse populations.) The intervention used by Jewkes et al. (2014) involved a combination of programs that took about 12 weeks to deliver. They collected data 2 weeks before the intervention as well as immediately before implementation of the intervention, and then again at 28 weeks and 58 weeks after the first data collection (24 and 54 weeks after the intervention was completed). Jewkes et al. (2014) referred to their design as a "shortened" interrupted time-series because most time-series studies involve more than two data-collection points on either side of the intervention.

As is evident from Figure 7.2, the percentage of women in the sample who reported IPV decreased over the course of the study. From a design perspective, however, we see that data were collected repeatedly before the intervention, which occurred during Weeks 2 through 14 as well as repeatedly after the intervention. It is also apparent that it took

FIGURE 7.2   Interrupted Time-Series Results From Jewkes et al. (2014)

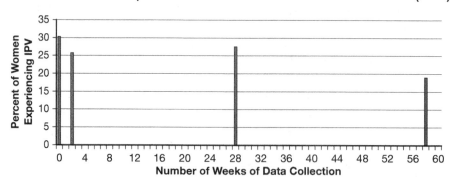

a while for a change in the IPV rate to occur. To find out if the change in IPV rate was permanent, Jewkes et al. would have had to continue data collection beyond 58 weeks. As noted earlier, however, the fact that the residents were not randomly assigned to the intervention and the absence of a control group who did not receive the intervention means that we cannot assign causality to the intervention. It is obvious from Figure 7.2 that something affected IPV rates and that the effect was contemporary with the intervention, but a contemporaneous effect does not mean that the intervention was the specific cause of the reduction in IPV rate. The possibility of a history effect is clear.

Multiple Time-Series Design

One variation of the interrupted time-series design is the multiple time-series design. In this design, two sets of observations are compared. Feigl, Salomon, Danaei, Ding, and Calvo (2015), for example, compared smoking rates among high school students with those of slightly older individuals to examine the potential impact of a law in Chile making it illegal to smoke or to sell cigarettes within 300 meters of a high school. The adults serve as a quasi-experimental control group for the intended target of the ban, the high school students. The existence of the control group provides information about a history effect, but without random assignment, other alternative explanations described in Chapter 6 may come into play. The data were obtained from separate biennial surveys.

As is evident Figure 7.3, Feigl et al. (2015) obtained data for several years before the smoking ban went into effect on January 1, 2006, and again for several years after the ban. The trend lines indicate that smoking rates decreased immediately after the ban to a greater extent among high school students (~5%) than among older adults (~2.5%). Both groups continued to reduce smoking after the immediate reduction, perhaps because of the ban or perhaps because of other effects to reduce smoking. The *perhaps* in the previous sentence is a reminder that quasi-experimental designs do not enable clear conclusions about causality.

FIGURE 7.3 Multiple Time-Series Results From Feigl et al. (2015)

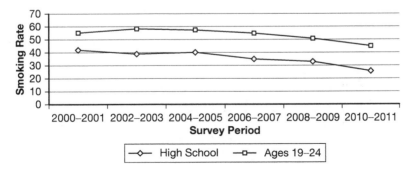

REGRESSION–DISCONTINUITY DESIGNS

Time-series designs are **longitudinal designs**—*designs in which the same partici-pants are repeatedly measured over time*. For some research projects, however, it is too expensive or otherwise undesirable to make repeated measurements. In such instances, cross-sectional designs are more appropriate. A **cross-sectional design** involves *one measurement of different groups that represent different time periods*. It might involve, for example, grouping participants according to the number of years they have lived in the community where the research is occurring. Such a design, called a *regression–discontinuity design* (Thistlethwaite & Campbell, 1960), is illustrated in Figure 7.4, which contains a very simplified version of results obtained from a recent study of the rela-tionship between number of additional school counselors and rate of four-year-college admission for high school students (Hurwitz & Howell, 2014).

The underlying logic of the regression–discontinuity design is the same as that for the multiple time-series design. Instead of repeatedly measuring variables in the same sample, however, regression–discontinuity designs involve different samples repre-senting different levels of the variable. In Figure 7.4, the number of full-time teach-ers indicated on the **abscissa** (*the horizontal axis of the graph*) does not represent an increase in teachers from the same schools but instead represents different schools with different numbers of teachers. Some school have more teachers than others, and Hurwitz and Howell (2014) found that schools with more full-time teachers tend to send more students to four-year colleges. When an additional school counselor was added, however, the rate of four-year-college acceptance increased by about 10%. From Figure 7.4, we are able to conclude that the impact of adding a counselor is independent of the size of the school and the number of full-time teachers in the school. That is,

Figure 7.4 A Regression–Discontinuity Design Illustrated With Results Adapted From Hurwitz and Howell (2014)

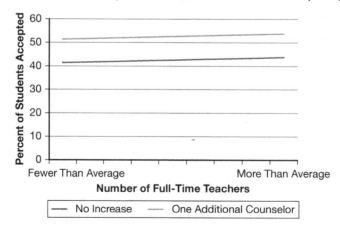

the apparent effect of an additional counselor is not simply due to the fact that larger schools tend to have more counselors.

Although the regression–discontinuity design may seem to be more efficient than the time-series design, the relative efficiency of being able to obtain all measures at the same time is offset by the requirement of additional assumptions about the participants. Experience with the independent variable may be determined equivalently under both designs, but the regression–discontinuity design requires one to assume that the different samples did not change during the time period of interest. Hurwitz and Howell (2014), for example, also measured and corrected for changes in the gender ratio in the schools, the number of students receiving free lunches, the proportion of underrepresented minority members, and the overall size of the schools, all of which are known to be related to the proportion of students attending college. Thus, they were able to ensure that the schools with an added counselor, for example, did not also have a higher ratio of women.

NONEQUIVALENT GROUPS BASIC PRETEST DESIGNS

When it is not possible to make multiple measurements over time, to measure a relatively large number of different groups of participants, or to assign participants randomly to different levels of an independent variable, then an abbreviated combination of time-series and regression–discontinuity designs may be used. The design in Figure 7.5 should remind

FIGURE 7.5   The Nonequivalent Groups Basic Pretest Design Based on Cerdá et al. (2012)

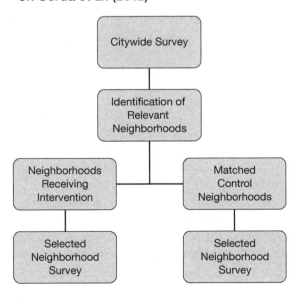

you of the basic pretest design described in Chapter 6. Except for the fact that participants are not randomly assigned to different conditions (a very important exception), the non-equivalent groups basic pretest design is identical to the basic pretest design. Cerdá et al. (2012), upon whose research the figure is based, took advantage of an urban transportation development project. They were fortunate that a citywide survey of residents' perceptions of crime was accomplished before the development project was completed. Cerdá et al. repeated the survey in their selected neighborhoods after completion of the project, which enabled them to compare survey responses before and after the intervention. The use of pretesting enabled them to determine whether any change exhibited by those experiencing the intervention also would have occurred in its absence.

Of course, the nonequivalent groups basic pretest design, similar to the time-series and regression–discontinuity designs, is subject to selection effects because it lacks random assignment to conditions. When researchers use this design, critical readers must look for information in the report about how the researchers ruled out alternative explanations through logical analysis rather than through random assignment and control over variables.

Matching, also discussed in Chapter 6, provides an alternative to random assignment but is not as effective as random assignment for dealing with selection effects. Matching, you should recall, involves an attempt to equalize scores on variables of interest among groups. There is no end, however, to the number of potential variables that may require matching, and therefore, one can never be sure one has matched participants on all relevant characteristics. Cerdá et al. had the added advantage of having all of the pretest results available while they chose the control neighborhoods and so were able to use propensity scores, also discussed in Chapter 6, to match the intervention and control neighborhoods statistically on all of the variables of interest. On those posttest measures on which there were differences (including homicide rates), one would need to construct an alternative explanation based on a variable that was not measured in the study to discount the results.

SELF-SELECTION

Although it may seem that random assignment is always preferable to quasi-experimental designs, such is not the case. There are a number of situations in which self-selection is the primary interest rather than an alternative explanation to be avoided. **Self-selection** refers to *any circumstances in which the participants are already at different levels of an independent variable*, usually because they have some desire to be at that level. Your own experience with class scheduling is an example. Unless you are very different from most students, you would rather be in a position to choose your courses than to have them randomly assigned to you by the registrar's office. When a research hypothesis involves a similar self-selection component, then a quasi-experimental design provides greater **external validity**—*the relationship between the research experience and every-day experience; the similarity between the physical and social aspects of the research environment and the target environment; the extent to which the data may be generalized beyond the research project*—than does an experimental design. Self-selection is not always an alternative explanation; it may sometimes be the independent variable.

The key distinction between experimental and quasi-experimental research is the manner in which the participants experience the independent variable. Experimental participants are randomly assigned to conditions, whereas quasi-experimental research involves capitalizing on preexisting differences among participants. Whenever such preexisting differences are the focus of research, quasi-experimental designs may be more appropriate than their experimental counterparts.

CORRELATIONAL RESEARCH

In some ways, any research in which relationships between two variables are explored can be considered correlational research. That includes experiments and quasi-experiments in which the relationship between independent and dependent variables is investigated. However, **correlational research** is a label generally reserved for *empirical studies in which the relationship between two (or more) quantitative variables is examined*. It is important not to confuse the design with the statistic; correlational research does not have to include reports of correlation results nor does reporting of correlation results necessarily mean that the design was correlational research. Generally, correlational research does involve comparing two or more measures obtained from the same participants.

Hudgins (2015), for example, used a correlational design to assess the relationship between resilience and intention to remain with the same employer using measures of resilience, job satisfaction, and anticipated turnover. Similar to most other correlational research, the concepts of interest to Hudgins could not be manipulated. It would be unethical to manipulate an employee's resilience or job satisfaction or intentions to remain in the same job. The only way to investigate those concepts, then, is to measure them as the already exist among available individuals. Similarly, it would be unethical to manipulate how much teasing children received for their body mass index (BMI) or their levels of self-esteem, so Bang et al. (2012) measured those concepts to investigate the extent to which parental teasing was related to the connection between BMI and depression.

Bang et al. (2012) used a technique called **mediation analysis**, in which *the importance of a given variable is examined as part of a suspected chain of variables in an existing relationship*. The link between BMI and self-esteem, particularly in terms of physical appearance, was well documented before they initiated their study; children with higher BMI tend to exhibit lower self-esteem. Bang et al. (2012) did find that parental teasing is a part of suspected chain—higher BMI → more parental teasing → lower self-esteem—from which we may critically infer that parental (and presumably other) types of teasing should be considered whenever we attempt to affect the link between BMI and self-esteem. That is, we have a better understanding of a suspected causal chain, but we still do not have a demonstration of the causal chain because the children were not randomly assigned to manipulated levels of the suspected causal variables.

Another technique used to further clarify but not demonstrate suspected causal relationships involves controlling for or statistically eliminating the influence of variables that might alter a relationship. Essentially, controlling for an additional variable is the opposite of mediation analysis; instead of putting variables into a suspected relationship (mediation), variables are taken out of a complicated relationship to target a simpler relationship. For example, Cox and Roche (2015) knew of research linking the use of vasopressors, a class of drugs that raise blood pressure by contracting muscles surrounding arteries and capillaries, with susceptibility to pressure ulcers (bed sores) among patients in critical care hospital units and were interested in testing which of five different vasopressors might exhibit the effect. There are, however, a number of conditions related to pressure ulcers for which vasopressors might also be prescribed, so a simple link between a particular vasopressor and pressure ulcers would not be a sufficient test of the relationship. To clarify the relationship, Cox and Roche used statistical techniques to control for variables such as cardiac arrest, length of time on a ventilator, cardiac disease, and shock; that use of one vasopressor was still related to development of pressure ulcers when the other variables were statistically controlled provides stronger evidence for, but not demonstration of, a causal link.

META-ANALYSIS

Meta-analysis is *the collective name for the various quantitative techniques used to combine the results of empirical studies; integrating research findings by statistically analyzing the results from individual studies.* The term was coined by Glass (1976) and, since its initial development, has come to be used for a variety of different purposes. What all of these purposes have in common, however, is that researchers use the results of others' (and perhaps their own) research instead of collecting new data (Wachter & Straf, 1990). Because meta-analysis can be used to describe quantitatively the current state of research on a given topic, it has become quite popular. A recent search for the key word meta-analysis on EBSCOhost.com produced more than 100,000 entries, and the topics are seemingly endless: suicidal thoughts (Calati, Laglaoui Bakhiyi, Artero, Ilgen, & Courtet, 2015), anti-platelet therapy (Costa et al., 2015), prostate cancer risk (Fan, Zhou, Gong, & Zou, 2015), computerized cognitive training (Motter et al., 2016), specific medications (Savarese, De Ferrari, Rosano, & Perrone-Filardi, 2015), advertising repetition (Schmidt & Eisend, 2015), lifestyle change (Taylor et al., 2015), and food safety programs in developing countries (Young et al., 2015). For research consumers, understanding a recent meta-analysis is a very effective way of delving into the state of empirical literature on a given topic.

Meta-analysis researchers use **effect size**, which is *a statistical term for the estimate of the magnitude of the difference between groups or the relationship between variables.* The effect size from each study is combined with effect sizes from all of the other studies on the same phenomenon in order to determine, among other things, the average effect observed in the reviewed literature. In meta-analysis reports, you will read about an evaluation of the methodological rigor of the included studies; results from more rigorous studies are often given greater weight in the results. You will also read about estimating **publication bias**, which is *an estimate of the influence produced by the tendency of journal editors to be more likely to publish manuscripts in which statistically significant effects are included.* Publication bias is assessed by describing the distribution of the effect sizes obtained from the literature; the distribution should be consistent, without major gaps in the continuum from smallest to largest effect sizes. Critical reading of reports of meta-analyses also includes an assessment of the key words and electronic sources used in the search process. You should assess the extent to which the search included all of the literature relevant to your interest; you may have to read more than one meta-analysis to cover the breadth of your interests.

SINGLE-PARTICIPANT DESIGNS

Known also as single-subject design, case study, or a single-case experimental design, a **single-participant design** is *a design specifically tailored to include only one participant in the study.* Whenever research interests center on a single person—perhaps a client experiencing therapy—single-participant designs are appropriate. They are also appropriate when the population of interest is so highly homogeneous that studying more than one member of the population is redundant. Learning studies involving experimental animals, for example, generally involve the assumption that one animal's reaction to the independent variable will be the same as any other animal's reaction. There are three types of single-participant designs: case study, baseline, and withdrawal.

Case Study Design

As the name implies, a **case study** involves *intensive study of a single participant over an extended period of time.* The most common example of such design involves a provider monitoring a client's or patient's responses to treatment (e.g., Iqbal, Younis, & Saeed, 2015), but case studies can be about students (e.g., Smith, 2016), a forest (e.g., Joshi, Tripathi, Jinnah, Bisht, & Upreti, 2016), or anything else of interest to a researcher. By definition, treatment begins as soon as the provider and participant meet, so there is usually no opportunity to make direct observations before the independent variable—treatment—is experienced. Of course, self-reports from the participant provide some information about pretreatment experiences, but that is not the same as directly measuring the dependent variable prior to the initiation of treatment.

By now, you should realize there are a host of alternative explanations to this design, which is essentially the basic design without random assignment. However, a series of logical assumptions may enable a researcher to rule out most of the alternative explanations (Dermer & Hoch, 1999). For example, in a treatment situation, it is reasonable to assume that a problem existed before the treatment began or the participant would not have sought treatment. Thus, a measure of the dependent variable before initiation of the independent variable is not always necessary, although it can be used when appropriate and possible. More importantly, a case study involves a series of intensive in-depth observations, and many of those observations may provide information that can be used to rule out additional alternative explanations.

For the most part, case study designs are utilized when the researcher is interested in what happens at the level of a specific individual, the specific conditions experienced by the participant. Similarly, as in all research, conclusions drawn from a case study should be limited to similar situations or participants. Although it is certainly possible to generalize from a case study, generalization comes from **replication**, *any repetition of a study—* in this case, with a different participant. The major assumption underlying generalization is that the research participants represent the individuals to whom the generalization is applied, and a single research study rarely represents any larger group of people. Animals bred for research may be sufficiently homogeneous to allow generalizations, but people are rarely that homogeneous.

A case study can certainly be used to develop research hypotheses to be examined in later studies. Indeed, hypothesis generation is probably the most common purpose of case studies. Piaget's (1984) famous theory of child development, for example, came about through his case studies of individual children. Since he first began proposing hypotheses generated from case studies, many of his theoretical formulations have been supported empirically through a variety of different methods. The key to critical consumption of a case study is careful examination of all of the information presented to understand the limits of internal as well as external validity of the study.

Baseline Design

The baseline design is, to some extent, an elaboration of the case study. In a **baseline design**, *pre-independent variable measures are compared with post-independent measures for a single participant.* Except that only one participant is included in the study, the baseline design is very similar to a time-series design. Multiple baseline measures may be taken, and one can use repeated measurements after a change in the independent variable regardless of whether or not the independent variable is manipulated. Indeed, the use of multiple measures as a baseline design is one of the ways in which researchers obtain sufficient data to rule out alternative explanations (Dermer & Hoch, 1999).

Farmer, Allsopp, and Ferron (2015), for example, used dozens of pretreatment baseline measures in their study of the relationship between The Personal Strengths Program and self-determination among college student with learning disabilities and attention deficit hyperactivity disorder. In contrast, Rahn et al. (2015) used a single baseline measurement and multiple intra- and postintervention measures of letter-sound fluency in their study of two English-learning children. The number of measurements during a study may differ considerably, but the hallmark of the baseline design is that at least one preintervention measure and at least one postintervention measure are included.

The strength of the baseline study is that the measure of the dependent variable before the change in the independent variable enables one to assess its effects. With the case study, for example, one can only guess about the preexisting state of the individual participant, even if that guess is based on self-reports from the participant. The baseline design allows one to measure preintervention levels directly. Despite this strength, critical consumption of baseline studies necessitates looking for replications to assess generalizability of the results. Remember that if the researcher is interested only in that one specific participant, there is no need for the researcher to generalize the results, but you need to generalize results in order to use them to engage in evidence-based practice, unless your practice happens also to be limited to those same participants.

Withdrawal Design

Despite the strength of the baseline design, it is not the most powerful among the single-participant designs. That distinction belongs to the **withdrawal design**, in which *the treatment (independent variable) is presented and removed several times for a single participant*. Known also as an *A–B–A–B design*, the withdrawal design involves measuring the dependent variable before the independent variable is manipulated, after it has been manipulated, again after the manipulation has been removed, and so on for as many repetitions as seems appropriate. Mitchell et al. (2015), for example, used a withdrawal design to measure the impact of the Good Behavior Game, typically used with children in special education classes, on disruptive classroom behaviors among general education students in high school.

Usually, the *A* condition refers to the baseline state of the participant, the state without the treatment or manipulation; Mitchell et al. measured the number of disruptive behaviors in the classroom before the Good Behavior Game was introduced. The *B* condition refers to the state of the participant while experiencing the treatment; Mitchell et al. measured the number of disruptive behaviors while the game was played. At some point, the treatment is withdrawn and the participant returns to baseline, after which the independent variable is manipulated again. Of course, this design may be used only if the independent variable can be manipulated. Even if the independent variable creates a permanent change in the participant, the withdrawal design enables one to measure its permanence, and additional measures can be used to assess how comprehensive the permanent effect may be.

The withdrawal design also can be used to assess the impact of combining different manipulations. Axelrod, Tornehl, and Fontanini-Axelrod (2014), for example, used the withdrawal design to examine the combination of a urine alarm and simple reinforcement on nocturnal enuresis (bed wetting). They measured a baseline, then measured while using a urine alarm, then measured again without the urine alarm, then measured again using both alarm and reinforcement, and finally measured again without either treatment. As with other single-participant designs, the withdrawal design can be used to rule out a number of alternative explanations but cannot be used to assess the strength of the effect across a variety of participants except through replication.

SUMMARY

- Although experimental designs provide the best way to test cause–effect relationships, there are times when experiments are not possible. At such times, quasi-experimental designs are preferred. Quasi-experimental designs lack random assignment.

- Time-series designs are longitudinal designs involving repeated measures of the dependent variable before and after implementation of the independent variable. The repeated measures can be used to assess maturation and testing effects.

- History effects can be assessed through multiple time-series designs, which involve simultaneously measuring more than one group of participants.

- Regression–discontinuity designs involve a single measure of the dependent variable across groups that differ along a dimension defined by the independent variable. They are cross-sectional designs that can be used when longitudinal designs are not feasible.

- When repeated measures or a large number of groups cannot be included in a research project, the nonequivalent groups basic design may be used to approximate an experimental design. In this design, two or more groups that have not been randomly assigned to conditions are measured before and after implementation of the independent variable.

- Correlational designs are quasi-experimental designs in which the relationships between continuous variables are examined.

- Single-participant designs are generally used to test hypotheses about a specific participant or involve the assumption that the participant represents a homogeneous group of others.

- In a case study, the participant is observed after the independent variable is introduced. A baseline design involves measuring the dependent variable before and after the independent variable is manipulated. In a withdrawal design, measures are taken sequentially with successive presentation and removal of the manipulation.

- If the independent variable can be manipulated and the research environment controlled, single-participant designs may be used to test cause–effect hypotheses but may lack the generality of more traditional experimental designs.

- All quasi-experimental designs are subject to selection effects as an alternative explanation. Selection may, however, be considered a function of the independent variable if self-selection is part of the phenomenon being studied.

EXERCISES

1. Find an article in which the authors report on research based on a quasi-experimental design. Identify the variables that could not be manipulated.

2. Find an article in which the authors report on a study involving a time-series design. Determine which type of time-series design was used and identify the length of time the participants were observed.

3. Find an article in which the authors report on research involving a single-participant design. Consider each alternative explanation and decide whether any of them could have an effect on the conclusions drawn by the authors.

8

Qualitative Research

To define "science" only in terms of measurement, experimentation,
and prediction would be narrow indeed.

—Gergen, Josselson, and Freeman (2015, p. 7)

OVERVIEW

In this chapter, you will learn about methods that researchers use to conduct qualitative research, which include a wide range of methods that focus on the subjective nature of human experience. You will learn about underlying philosophies of qualitative research as well as specific methods involving phenomenology, ethnography, grounded theory, history, and case study. You will also learn more about critical evaluation of qualitative research, including application to evidence-based practice, as well as concepts and processes related to field research in general.

INTRODUCTION

One of the continuing themes of this text is that every one of us conducts research every day but that scientific research is more systematic than the informal research that merely satisfies our curiosity. In this chapter, you will learn about research methods that may, at first glance, seem more similar to those of informal research than any other method. One of my goals in this chapter is to enable you to appreciate the systematic foundations of qualitative research. Understanding the principles and practices of qualitative research provides you with the skills necessary to move beyond the notion of passive reception of everyday experience. However, don't let the label *qualitative research* lead you to believe that the methods described in this chapter can be used only outside the laboratory or that research conducted outside the laboratory can be accomplished only through these methods. The label refers to a preference for words over numbers, but qualitative research is much more than simply research without numbers. As a consumer of research, understanding the methodology underlying qualitative research enables you to include qualitative results in your evidence-based practice.

Qualitative research is *the general label applied to a collection of methods used to obtain information about lived experience. Lived experience* refers to trying to understand events from the viewpoint of people who were part of the events, to understand their experience instead of imposing another person's viewpoint. The events, however, need not necessarily be live events; part of our discussion will include various methods for accessing historical or remembered events. Still, whether reported live or remembered, the emphasis is on observing events as they unfold.

One characteristic of lived experience as viewed within qualitative research is the continuum of naturalness. Within the context of research, a **natural event** is *an event that is not created, sustained, or discontinued solely for research purposes* (Tunnell, 1977). The viewpoint used to assess naturalness is that of the research participant, which is why naturalness needs to be conceptualized as a continuum: The more the participant perceives the event to be part of the normal stream of experiences, the more natural the event is. The emphasis on natural events in qualitative research is why the methods are sometimes called *naturalistic methods.* Qualitative researchers exert considerable effort to get to know their participants so that the interviews that make up the most common means of data collection are as natural as possible; they are experienced more as conversations than as formal interviews. Hampshire, Iqbal, Blell, and Simpson (2014) provide a particularly good description of the process of developing rapport with informants such that conversations move from the artificiality of, say, a job interview to the naturalness of a conversation with an acquaintance. Their description of moving beyond rapport to what they described as "reverse interviewing" (Hampshire et al., 2014, p. 221) enables considerable insight into the effort researchers put forth to develop the desired level of naturalness. When reading qualitative research articles, look for a description of how the researcher(s) developed rapport with the participants.

In addition to providing context and more detailed description, what Clifford Geertz (1973) called *thick description,* one of the purposes of qualitative research is **social action**, *research conducted to solve a social problem* (Betancourt, Frounfelker, Mishra, Hussein, & Falzarano, 2015; Lewin, 1946; Sallee & Flood, 2012; White, 2004). Of course, a single research study is not likely to solve a social problem. Just as with theory development, however, each research study adds to the existing collection of results, the accumulation of which may be applied to solve the problem. The depth of information and context obtained from qualitative research makes it much easier to understand a problem as well as reactions to attempted solutions.

Philosophically, modern qualitative research grew out of the rejection of a now-outdated philosophy of science called **logical positivism**, which *asserted that theories could be demonstrated to be correct, or at least confirmed, through sufficient collection of* *quantifiable data* (Gergen et al., 2015; Mesel, 2013). Qualitative research is entirely consistent with nonjustificationism (Weimer, 1979) as presented in Chapter 2: All research is based on observations that are interpreted by researchers and related to concepts, some of which are included in theories. Qualitative research, therefore, is not designed or intended to prove a particular theory or viewpoint. Rather, qualitative research describes the world, either contemporaneously or historically, and those descriptions sometimes give rise to consideration of the future.

Another key to the critical use of qualitative research is understanding the **social constructionist** viewpoint, which *holds that all knowledge is changing and must be situated within a particular community* (Gergen et al., 2015). That is, the assumptions and beliefs, as well as the history of groups of individuals, affect what those individuals understand knowledge to be. The notion that facts change, even scientific facts, is not new (Fleck, 1979); it has long been recognized that changes in knowledge are more of a topic for research than they are the results of research designed to find the "real" or "true" facts (Kuhn, 1962). Thus, as a community changes, so changes the knowledge of that community; equally, different communities have different knowledge. The constructionist viewpoint is that there is no single, correct description of knowledge. Therefore, qualitative research, as does all research, expands our knowledge about our own as well as others' communities.

Robinson-Wood et al. (2015), for example, applied a social constructionist viewpoint to the data they collected from highly educated Black women regarding their experience of **microaggressions**, which *are insults and other types of denigration directed toward individuals or groups*. Robinson-Wood et al. used thematic analysis, a form of content analysis, to identify commonalities within the information provided by the participants. In their words, "We wove an analysis of narratives with data extracts while contextualizing our work within the existing research literature" (Robinson-Wood et al., 2015, p. 229). That is, the researchers relied on their own community for knowledge with which to interpret the information provided by the research participants. Critical reading of social constructionist research includes gleaning from the article the communities with which the researchers are associated, which requires a careful reading of the introduction of the article.

Qualitative research generally involves a rich verbal description and analysis of individuals' contextualized understanding of their environment. It is usually conducted in natural settings and is not designed to prove or confirm a particular theory. There are many different methods used to conduct qualitative research: phenomenological, ethnographic, grounded theory, historical, and case studies.

PHENOMENOLOGICAL METHOD

The essence of **phenomenology** can be defined as *the philosophical position that there are individual differences with respect to the experience of reality* (Hansen, Holstein, & Hansen, 2009). It includes the notion that the subjective experience of the individual may be just as, and sometimes more, important as the objective experience registered via physical measurement. Equally important is the notion that different people experience the world differently and that those differences do not necessarily result from errors. Our different life experiences mean that we interpret the same phenomenon differently. Different philosophical positions within phenomenology vary about the relative importance of the objective and the subjective as well as differ about the extent to which the subjective can be separated from the objective, but one of the philosophical keys to evaluating qualitative research is the recognition that accessing an individual's interpretation of an event is an important part of understanding both the event and the person (Gergen et al., 2015).

As you might expect, phenomenological research involves **recording** (*making a permanent copy of the observation, usually in field research but relevant to all research*) and analyzing people's stories; their beliefs, perceptions, and memories; and their lived experience. Phenomenological research is, of course, done for a purpose and is always associated with a particular experience or state of being. The questions are generally of the form "What is it like to be you?" but are more specific to the research purpose. Indeed, the questions are generally not as important as the participants' responses to the situation. You will more likely read that participants *were interviewed* than you are to read a list of specific questions presented to the participants.

Because phenomenological researchers understand that one's own past affects one's experience of the present, they take great lengths to avoid introducing their own experience into their participants' experiences. This is accomplished through processes generally called **bracketing**, *whereby the researcher identifies his or her own experiences, assumptions, and other beliefs relevant to the participant's and sets them aside temporarily during the research.* Basically, the researcher puts brackets around and shelves his or her lived experience while dealing with the lived experience of others. Phenomenological researchers present a discussion of their bracketing so that readers can understand the researcher's involvement in the research process (Fischer, 2009). As you might expect, bracketing is an involved process. Fischer (2009) provides several examples, and Snelgrove (2014) provides a detailed description of continued attempts at bracketing during a phenomenological longitudinal study of individuals experiencing chronic pain. When reading phenomenological research, look for descriptions of the researcher's attempts to understand how the researcher's experiences may have imposed meaning on the information obtained from the research participants. It is not possible for an individual to be free of biases—that would mean the individual has no knowledge at all—so critical consumption of qualitative research includes consideration of the extent to which the researcher's knowledge contributed to the understanding and presentation of the information provided by the participants. Equally important, it helps to think about our own experiences, assumptions, and beliefs as we read about research. As consumers, we are as likely to impose meaning as anyone else, and critical reading of research includes being mindful of the possibility that we are interpreting research through our own experiential filters.

ETHNOGRAPHY

Related to both phenomenology and the social constructionist viewpoint is **ethnography**, *a research method involving lengthy observation of and interaction with members of a group to understand their culture* (Adams, Carryer, & Wilkinson, 2015; Dalsgaard & Morten, 2013; Mead, 1969). Ethnography is, essentially, based on the notion that watching people is not sufficient for understanding them. One must also talk to them, find out what they have to say, look for patterns in what is said, and otherwise draw meaning from what they say and do. It is also based on the notion that similarities among people both result from and make up culture. Generally, "experience from the standpoint of people in [one] locality is used to provide clues and information about how people's lives are coordinated and organized within society" (Adams et al., 2015, p. 22). As Hampshire et al. (2014) report, ethnography also involves developing deep relationships with the individuals participating in the study, the **informants** (*usually in field research, anyone who is knowledgeable about the participants to be observed*). In their study, the informants included 108 Pakistani men and women in Northeast England who were interviewed to understand better the experience of infertility within a cultural context. As with phenomenological research, critical reading of ethnographic studies includes understanding the relatedness of the researcher(s) and the informant(s). For Hampshire et al., for example, whether or not the researchers had children resulted in different interactions with the informants, which they discuss in considerable detail in their article.

Thompson, Cupples, Sibbett, Skan, and Bradley (2001), for example, conducted interviews with physicians in Northern Ireland to understand the known phenomenon of physicians' reluctance to seek treatment for their own health issues. Through extensive interviews with 27 physicians, they were able to better describe the physician culture with respect to (a) a perceived need to appear healthy for patients, (b) the influence of medical knowledge in dealing with symptoms, and (c) a work culture that made it difficult to take time away from the practice. Years later, Wallace and Lemaire (2009), through interviews with physicians in Western Canada, observed the same cultural themes related to physicians' beliefs that the state of their own health is not related to the care they provide their patients. One physician, for example, remarked "Well I think we're all aware of it on one level, but I mean, I don't think any of us, or I don't think very many of us, are aware that it can actually affect us" (p. 548).

As we do with phenomenological research, critical consumers of ethnographic research pay attention to the researchers' assumptions and their own while reading. None of us are culture free, so we need to be aware of the influence of our own culture when reading about other cultures. This can be particularly difficult when we read about our own culture, but efforts to set aside preconceptions when we read ethnographic research enable us to more critically consume that research.

GROUNDED THEORY

Developed by Glaser and Strauss (1967), **grounded theory** generally *involves an inductive process of developing explanations from data.* That is, instead of deciding which data to collect based on a hypothesis derived from a developed theory, researchers using grounded theory prefer to collect the data, using as few assumptions as possible, and then develop theory from the observations and information provided by the research participants. As might be expected, there has been, and probably will continue to be, considerable development in grounded theory philosophy as well as methodology since the 1960s, but the key component of grounded theory research remains: Theory is not tested; instead, theory is developed from comparison of observations to theoretical concepts as the latter are coded through analysis of the information provided by participants (Higginbottom & Lauridsen, 2014; Rudnick, 2014). The philosophical positions that researchers bring to grounded theory research also involve some different methods and language (Ralph, Birks, & Chapman, 2015), which is all the more reason why grounded theory research articles should be read carefully and critically.

Spoorenberg et al. (2015), for example, in their study of the experiences of older adults as they participated in one particular implementation of the World Health Organization's Chronic Care Model, comprehensively described their participants, the interview process, the coding process, and even the bases for selecting illustrative quotations. The extensive quotes from the informants enable the reader to understand more fully the themes identified through the grounded theory method. When evaluating grounded theory research, you may find it useful to employ the checklist provided by Tong, Sainsbury, and Craig (2007). The checklist does not tell you which aspects of the research are good or bad—only you can decide that. Instead, it contains an outline of aspects of grounded theory research that should be carefully considered by those consuming the research.

Hakel (2015) provides a comprehensive description of both the process and results of grounded theory research regarding students' study habits. The article includes the researcher's background regarding research as well as the particular theoretical approach adopted for grounded theory research. Quotations are used effectively to illustrate the theoretical concepts developed from interviews and the theory itself is described in sufficient detail to be available to most readers. The article also contains a comprehensive discussion of the limitations of the research as well as multiple suggestions for future research. The latter are useful for consumers in that they help us to recognize what we don't yet know about the research area.

Similarly, Milsom and Coughlin (2015) provided information about their backgrounds so that readers could better understand the bracketing in which they engaged in their study of students' satisfaction and dissatisfaction of their college majors. The model that was built from the grounded theory analysis of interviews included continual reflection upon one's major as students increased experience with and learned more about their chosen majors. Neither satisfaction nor dissatisfaction turned out to be a linear process in the resulting model. Milsom and Coughlin also provided many quotes, both short and long, through which they illustrate concepts within their model, which you should now recognize as a hallmark of grounded theory research.

As with all research, critical evaluation of grounded theory research involves careful reading of the entire manuscript. Look for a description of the research process itself, including a discussion of how the authors coded the information using inductive methods. Cooney (2011) reminds us of the three major criteria by which we can evaluate grounded theory research: credibility, auditability, and transferability. The use of quotes brings **credibility**, *the extent to which the research enables the consumer to understand (and perhaps visualize) the research participants*, to the manuscript, as does an indication that the researchers returned to the participants to authenticate that **coding** (*attaching some sort of meaning to the observation*) reflects the original material. Similarly, **auditability** *refers to the use of memos to maintain an audit trail of the research process* and should be mentioned in the article, as should presentation of the researchers' assumptions and bracketing. Finally, **transferability**, sometimes called *fittingness*, *refers to the extent to which the research is relevant to the consumers' interests*. As we have noted before, it is not the similarity of research participants or the research setting that establishes transferability; it is the relationship between the theory and your practice needs. Research has *fit* when the theory developed from the primary source materials is relevant to your practice and interests and enables you to understand your interests better.

HISTORICAL RESEARCH

As the name connotes, **historical research** is *the investigation of the past based on primary or secondary sources for the purpose of enhancing current knowledge*. Historical research can involve interaction with documents or people, and it always includes analysis or synthesis relevant to the present, which is how history becomes relevant to current practice (Chase, 2011). Thus, the goal is not only to describe some aspect of the past but to use the past to promote change to the present. Nortje and Hoffmann (2015), for example, not only wrote about ethical violations among South African psychologists during a 7-year period (2007–2013), they also provided information that practicing psychologists can use today to avoid ethical misconduct. They also noted that the number of violations was quite small (5–9 per year) relative to the number of South African psychologists (6,391–7,352 per year), a finding that is consistent with research in other countries. Note also that *history* doesn't necessarily mean *long ago*.

When reading historical research, it is important to note whether the researchers accessed primary or secondary sources. **Primary sources** are *period artifacts that may include an original, direct account created at the time being considered*. For example, Nortje and Hoffmann (2015) used the documents published by the Health Professions Council of South Africa as their sources. Similarly, the diary of an eyewitness to an event would be considered primary source material. The key aspect of a primary source is that any analysis or interpretation contained in the source material is contemporary with whatever has been interpreted. That does not, of course, mean that the source material is more accurate or otherwise a better source than other material; accuracy is an entirely different issue. In contrast, a **secondary source** is *any material that is not contemporary with the time in question and not produced by those who were present*. The descriptions in this chapter about the research conducted by Nortje and Hoffmann (2015), for example, are secondary source material (their published article is the primary source). Similarly, a diary entry or an interview produced years after an event can be considered secondary source material. Even though the individual may have been an eyewitness or may have been present at the event, the production of the diary or interview years later means that interpretations based on subsequent experience may have been imposed on the event description. Again, the key issue is not whether a primary or secondary account is more accurate but rather that the primary account is contemporary with the events being described.

Harris, Bennett, and Ross (2014) used a mixture of contemporary and reminiscent interviews in their study of the impact of Dame Muriel Powell, a nurse matron at St. George's Hospital in London from 1947 to 1969. Using some of Powell's writing as well as recorded interviews from an oral history project (Carol, 2010), Harris et al. were able to describe a number of leadership themes that current nurses could use. Historical research relies on accounts of what happened, but one should always keep in mind that all accounts involve some form of memory, all accounts are subjective, and all accounts represent the narrator's understanding at the time the account was recorded (Shopes, 2011). Similarly, Talbot and McMillin (2014) used a mixture of primary and secondary sources in their study of how the University of South Dakota came to offer the first masters in social work (MSW) in that state. They had access to archives of original minutes from meetings, correspondence, newspaper accounts, and audio recordings of legislative hearings. They also interviewed a number of people who were involved in various aspects of the four-year development process that began in 2006, and both Talbot and McMillin were able to use their own recollections because they were participants in and witnesses to the development of the MSW program.

I earlier noted that the labels *primary* and *secondary* as applied to sources are not necessarily indicative of accuracy; that is, a primary source is not considered a priori to be more or less accurate than a secondary source. The main reason is that the phenomenological approach of qualitative research includes the realization that any individual's account represents that individual's understanding of the event. That is, we are interested in the individual's understanding, regardless of whether that understanding was articulated at the time of the event or years later. Much like grounded theory, our critical analysis of historical research involves consideration of transferability rather than accuracy. As consumers of historical research, we must decide upon the extent to which the research is relevant to our interests and how well the research fits our efforts to engage in evidence-based practice. Allow me to use an extreme example to illustrate further: Suppose we read a reminiscent article about an event in which the author explicitly states in the method section that source material consisted almost entirely of interviews with people who were not at the event, who were not even alive at the time of the event. Even under such extreme circumstances, the information provided by those interviewed does represent their understanding of the event. We are not philosophically in a position to disagree with that understanding. We are, however, philosophically in a position to decide whether or not descriptions obtained and conclusions derived from people who were not present are relevant to our practice and can be transferred to our interests. That is, we might not consider the research relevant to our purposes, but it is not philosophically consistent to reject the research as inaccurate. Someone who is interested in the development of fiction (for example, of self-representation) might find the research highly relevant and transferable. Another reason why it is difficult to talk or write about accuracy of qualitative historical research is that there are very many different ways to analyze oral and written material (Peräkylä & Ruusuvuori, 2011). As with other research, it is important to read the method section carefully and critically as you decide on the relevance and transferability of a particular historical research project.

CASE STUDY

In Chapter 7, **case study** was defined as *intensive study of a single participant over an extended period of time*, a definition that fits the use of the phrase in qualitative research so long as we keep in mind that *participant* does not have to be a person. Case studies also include organizations and institutions as the subject of the investigation, but in keeping with the philosophy of qualitative research, the emphasis is on the understood meaning of the participant. As indicated in the definition, however, the key components of a case study are in-depth investigation and extended time period—a multicamera video instead of a single-camera photograph. Case study methodology is employed in just about every discipline, and many disciplines—administration, business, education, engineering, medicine, and psychology, to name a few—include entire journals devoted to publishing case studies.

Reading a case study critically involves understanding all of the information presented in the study and relating that information to your interests; the entire case should be considered evidence with which to inform your practice. Bain, James, and Harrison (2015), for example, completed a case study of an early-years (preschool) teacher in a rural school in the United Kingdom. Their introduction includes a great deal of background regarding the importance of promoting communication during the early years, including oral communication, which sets the stage for the study focus on a teacher's communication with parents about the importance of communication for their children. That is, the authors quite clearly explain why the study was done and how it relates to existing literature and policy. The method section contains relevant detail about the teacher, which is also identified as one of the study authors; those details enable you, as the consumer, to begin to determine the extent to which the results of this study are relevant to your practice. You do not, for example, have to be a teacher for this study to be relevant; communicating with parents of young children as part of your role may be sufficient to realize transferability. The results contain detailed information about how the teacher chose to communicate with parents, including information about what messages she communicated. Also included in the results are details about what the teacher does in her classroom to enhance the children's communication skills. The discussion section includes placing the results in context within the literature, which further enables the reader to learn about additional research that may be relevant to one's practice. The authors include the standard caution that the results may be representative only of the particular research setting, but that is where critical consumption of the details contained in the article comes into play. Only the reader can decide the extent to which the information in the article is relevant to his or her interests and can be used to inform his or her practice. Also of interest in this particular case study is commentary provided by the teacher about her involvement in the study and what she learned from her participation in the study. Her reflection provides some useful tips about how anyone might benefit from reading her case study.

Instead of a single individual, Mazurenko, Zemke, Lefforge, Shoemaker, and Menachemi (2015) used an entire hospital as their case in a study of satisfaction among postoperative patients and staff. In an effort to better understand patient satisfaction, Mazurenko et al. (2015) conducted focus groups with patients simultaneously with focus groups that included providers, staff, and administrators in the same hospital. To maintain confidentiality, the researchers did not identify the hospital nor did they provide demographic information about those who participated in the focus groups, but they provided considerable information about the professions and roles of the participants. The method section contains a great deal of information about how the researchers analyzed the content of the interviews, and the results include some quotes from the interviews as well as a detailed presentation of the themes that emerged from the focus groups. Interestingly, the primary themes—staff relationships, technology, and staffing—produced similar reactions among the different participants; staff relationships were perceived quite positively, while technology and staffing were not perceived positively. The authors were also able to identify themes of interest to patients and staff that are not included in the U.S. government's Hospital Consumer Assessment of Healthcare Providers and Systems (HCAPS). Careful reading of the limitations described in the discussion section also provides critical consumers with information relevant to determinations of transferability.

Although originally developed to investigate only a single participant, case study methodology has been applied to small groups of participants, which then involves the use of the phrase *case series* (Abu-Zidan, Abbas, & Hefny, 2012). A **case series** is *a study of several (usually similar) participants*. Like case studies, the study period for a case series may be lengthy. Abu-Zidan et al. (2012) report that the number of participants included in a case series is highly variable, ranging from one (which is not exactly a series) to 6,432, with a median value of seven. Regardless of the number of participants, the focus of a case series remains the commonalities among the participants.

MIXED METHOD RESEARCH

A **mixed method study** is *one in which both quantitative and qualitative research is included in a single project.* Mixed method research has been controversial, primarily because there are some who believe that the philosophical basis for quantitative research is incompatible with the philosophical basis for qualitative research; to these, mixing philosophically incompatible methods makes no sense (see, for example, Howe, 1988). As we have already noted, however, both quantitative and qualitative methods are consistent with nonjustificationism (Weimer, 1979). Johnson and Onwuegbuzie (2004) and Feilzer (2010), among many others, supported mixed method research using the philosophy of pragmatism as developed by Charles Peirce (1905), William James (1907), and John Dewey (1929). In contrast, Mertens (2010) provided philosophical justification for mixed method research through the transformative paradigm, the major tenet of which is that research should be done to promote social justice. Christ (2013) also provides a combination of justifications for mixed method research. Thus, there are multiple philosophical justifications for mixed method research. There is, of course, also the more practical justification for learning about it—people are doing it (Archibald, Radil, Xiaozhou, & Hanson, 2015) and it is therefore important to know how to evaluate it.

Mixed method research can be done either sequentially or concurrently. Sequential mixed method research occurs when either a qualitative or a qualitative method is employed first and the results of that first implementation are used to inform the next phase of the research, which may be in the same study or in a subsequent study. Sometimes the two phases are published in a single article, and sometimes the phases are published in separate articles. When done concurrently (sometimes called *parallel implementation*), both qualitative and quantitative methods are implemented at the same time and the results are integrated in the final discussion section of the article. Concurrent mixed method research, however, may sometimes appear to be sequential (one or the other phase of the study must be presented first), so careful reading of the method section is required to determine whether a mixed method study is sequential or concurrent.

Collins (2012), for example, completed a concurrent (sometimes called *parallel*) mixed method study on the purposes of mixed method research and presented it at an annual meeting of the American Educational Research Association (AERA). The quantitative aspect of the research dealt with frequencies of sponsoring divisions and special interest groups within AERA as well as frequencies of the conceptual components of the presentations. The qualitative aspects of the research dealt with developing a map of the ways in which mixed method research contributes to scientific knowledge. Collins described the sampling process by which she selected presentations for inclusion in the study as well as a comprehensive description of the mapping process she employed in the qualitative phase of the study. Feilzer (2007, 2010) used a sequential mixed method to complete a study on the impact upon public perception of crime from a weekly crime column in a local newspaper. The goal of the project was to assess the impact of factual information from a criminologist. A public opinion survey was used to gather quantitative data about the impact of the weekly column using a Solomon four-group design (see Chapter 6). When participants began writing comments on the returned survey, Feilzer decided to content analyze the comments as well as implement an in-depth interview to learn more about the survey responses. The in-depth interviews also provided information about participants' experiences completing a lengthy, public-opinion survey. In contrast, Khoiriyah, Roberts, Jorm, and Van der Vleuten (2015) used qualitative methods first in their sequential study to develop a quantitative self-assessment scale of active learning and critical thinking for use in problem-based learning curricula. In their project, in-depth interviews were conducted with medical students and tutors, followed by a thematic analysis that produced themes regarding self-assessment of experiences in a program using problem-based learning. The authors used those themes to direct their writing of quantitative scale items, which in turn were subjected to content validation by a panel of experts and then administration to 270 students for eventual factor analysis of the responses. The results of the factor analysis were compared to the results of the thematic analysis to develop a better understanding of the experience of problem-based learning than could have been obtained from either method used alone.

SUMMARY

- Qualitative research is research in which understanding of experience, rather than quantity, is the primary purpose. It can include any research purpose but often is focused on greater description or social action.

- The social constructionist viewpoint holds that knowledge changes and is best understood in the context of a particular community.

- Phenomenology refers to the philosophical position that someone's subjective experience of an event is of more interest than the physical reality of the event.

- Ethnography is a research method used to understand a particular culture or the cultural context of a person's or group's experience.

- Grounded theory refers to the methodology of interpreting or coding information or data obtained through qualitative research. It involves a process of dynamically interpreting and reinterpreting themes based on analysis of the verbatim text of interviews.

- Historical research involves enhancing understanding of the present through examination of the past and can include both primary and secondary sources of information concerning the past.

- Case studies involve intensive examination of a single participant, which can include examination of a person, an organization, or an institution. The methodology can be extended to include study of several participants.

- Mixed method research involves including both qualitative and quantitative methods in a single project. There can be philosophical challenges in such combinations, but these are generally resolved through an appeal to pragmatism.

EXERCISES

1. Find an article in which the authors report on qualitative research and determine the primary method used in the research.

2. Using the same or a different article, determine the purpose(s) of the research and decide whether or not the method and procedure were sufficient to the purpose(s).

3. Find an article that seems relevant to your interests or practice and figure out how applicable the results are.

9

Conceptual Overview
of Statistical Analyses

Aristotle could have avoided the mistake of thinking that women
have fewer teeth than men by the simple device of
asking Mrs. Aristotle to open her mouth.

—Bertrand Russell (Peter, 1980, p. 457)

OVERVIEW

Research consumers need to understand the statistics used by the researchers whose work they are consuming. Fortunately, at least for those who shy away from statistics and other mathematical topics, research consumers don't need to know how to *calculate* statistics. Instead, you only need to know enough about statistics to decide whether or not the researchers chose their statistics correctly and to critically assess the researchers' interpretations of their results. Thus, this chapter deals with what I refer to as *conceptual statistics*, which includes basic theory and principles; no calculations or formulas are included. For those of you who have yet to complete a course in statistics, the material will serve as an introduction to the concepts of statistical results, enabling you to understand statistical results presented in the research reports you read. The discussion is organized around the major types of data analyses: single sample, relational, and group differences.

INTRODUCTION

Research design and data analyses are interdependent; one makes little sense without the other. As a consumer of research, you need to know enough about statistics to determine that a researcher did not choose just any old analyses. As well, you need to know enough about statistics to interpret the results presented in empirical articles, even those written by researchers who knew exactly how to analyze their data. Thus, even though you don't have to worry about analyzing data, you do need to be able to figure out whether a researcher analyzed the data properly and how the results of those analyses can be used to inform the practice you are addressing. The purpose of this chapter is to help you deal with others' analyses and results by providing an overview of current research strategies and the analyses most appropriate to them. The chapter is organized around the major types of data—categorical and continuous—within the general purposes to which statistics are applied: descriptive, relational, and intergroup comparisons.

Types of Data

Categorical data are *values presenting discreet qualities that cannot be meaningfully subdivided, typically measured as counts of things.* Even when categorical data are represented numerically, it makes no sense to think of in-between values. Identification numbers are one example: If you are identified as #1 and I am labeled #2, then it makes no sense to think about the value 1.5; there is no person who is halfway between the two of us. Affiliations of various sorts are also likely to be categorical. Academically, I am affiliated with Jefferson College of Health Sciences and one of my friends is affiliated with Mercer University. It makes no sense to think about some mythical institution that is somewhere between the two institutions. They are two different institutions; there is no value (name) that could represent some combination of the two. We could assign the data value of 1 to Jefferson and 2 to Mercer, but the in-between value of 1.5 or 1.3 would not make any sense.

Continuous data, on the other hand, are *values representing placement along an ordered range; values representing positions on some interval.* With continuous data, in-between values do make sense logically, even if in-between values are not physically possible. While Jefferson College and Mercer University are differing institutions, the size of each can be represented by enrollment. As of this writing, Jefferson enrolls about 1,100 students; Mercer enrolls about 8,500. It is easy enough to imagine an academic institution enrolling 3,000 students or 5,200 students and so on. Age is another measure that can be represented by continuous data. We usually think of age in terms of whole numbers of years (such as 12, 57, or 99), but it makes sense in some contexts to refer to someone's age as 12.5 years or 57.33 years or 99.997260273972603 years (the day before one's 100th birthday).

TYPES OF STATISTICS

Statistics are generally classified as descriptive or inferential, which refer to the purposes to which the statistics are put. As the label implies, **descriptive statistics** are *used to summarize or represent some aggregate value from a set of data and are not used* *to make inferences about a larger data set or population.* When I write that Jefferson College has about 1,100 enrolled students, that statistic refers to a quality of Jefferson College and has no implications for any other academic institution. In contrast, **inferential statistics** are *values calculated from a sample and used to estimate the same value for a population.* As you learned in Chapter 4, random samples are used to represent the greater population from which they were selected, and inferential statistics are used to represent the population numerically. For example, if the average grade point average (GPA) of a random sample of University X students is 2.9, then I can use inferential statistics to estimate, within a margin of error, the average GPA for all University X students.

Inferential statistics are used for two major purposes, estimating a confidence interval and statistical decisions, both of which are based on probabilities. A **confidence interval** is *the inclusive, probabilistic range of values around any calculated statistic* and is associated with a specific probability that the population value is within that range. When you hear or read political polling results indicating that Candidate X has 55% of the vote with a 3-point margin of error, for example, the *margin of error* refers to the confidence interval. Guerra, Stringhini, Vollenweider, Waeber, and Marques-Vidal (2015), for example, studied thousands of Swiss participants over a period of five years and reported that after controlling for age and gender, individuals classified as obese (based on body mass index or BMI) were 1.95 times more likely than healthy-BMI participants to gain at least 10 pounds over the study period. The number 1.95 is quite specific; Guerra et al. (2015) also reported that the 95% confidence interval for that value was 1.57–2.43, which means that there is a 0.95 probability that the population value is somewhere between 1.57 and 2.43. Thus, in generalizing from their results, we can be 95% confident that residents of Switzerland with an obese BMI are more likely to gain weight than residents with a healthy BMI.

When inferential statistics are used for statistical decisions, the decision is generally about a specific hypothesis know as a *null hypothesis.* Often represented by the symbol H_o, the **null hypothesis** is *a proposed result indicating that there is no difference between groups or no relationship between variables.* Generally, H_o represents the position that nothing is happening in the data. Guerra et al. (2015), for example, were testing the null hypothesis that there was no difference in weight gain between healthy-BMI and obese-BMI individuals. Inferential statistics are used to test the probability that the null hypothesis is a reasonable conclusion based on the obtained data. Table 9.1 represents the outcomes that can occur with statistical decision making.

As is evident from Table 9.1, there are four possible outcomes from the statistical decision process, two of which are wrong. Type I error, the probability of which is represented by the lower-case Greek letter alpha (α), is the error researchers make when we reject the null hypothesis when it really is true, when there really is nothing going on in the data. Type II error, the probability of which is represented by the lowercase Greek letter beta (β), is the error researchers make when we accept the null hypothesis when it is false, where there really is something going on in the data. The catch is that we never really know the

TABLE 9.1 Statistical Decision Making Based on the Null Hypothesis, H_0

		Statistical Decision	
		Accept H_0	**Reject H_0**
True (Unknown) State of H_0	H_0 is True	Correct Decision $(1 - \alpha)$	Type I Error (α)
	H_0 is False	Type II Error (β)	Correct Decision $(1 - \beta)$

true state of the null hypothesis; all that researchers are able to do is decide that the probability of an error is so low that they are willing to risk making the wrong decision. As a critical consumer of research, you also need to be willing to accept the risk of making the wrong decision when you incorporate research results into your evidence-based practice.

When *p values* are reported in research reports, such as $p < .05$ or $p < .001$, you are reading the probability of making a Type I error when rejecting the null hypothesis. The phase *statistically significant*, in turn, generally means that the probability of a Type I error is so small that we are willing to risk being wrong about rejecting the null hypothesis. When a researcher reports that the mean for women is significantly ($p < .01$) higher than the mean for men, for example, that language means that there is a less-than-one-percent chance that it is wrong to reject the null hypothesis; that there is a .01 probability of being wrong when rejecting the notion that there is no difference between men and women.

As you look again at Table 9.1, notice that $1 - \alpha$, or one minus the *p*-value, is not the probability of correctly rejecting the null hypothesis. That is, based on the fictitious results in the preceding paragraph, it is *not* correct to say that there is a 99% chance that women scored higher than men. The probability of correctly rejecting the null hypothesis is $1 - \beta$, which is also called *statistical power*, is sometimes described as the probability of finding an effect that really is in the data. In research reports, **power** (*the probability of correctly rejecting the null hypothesis or the probability of finding an effect that really is there*) is generally not reported unless the researcher has not rejected the null hypothesis or has decided that there are no differences or that there is no relationship. Power is much more likely to be used by the researcher to decide how large a sample to obtain to make sure that there are enough observations to detect an effect of a certain size, and those decisions are not usually reported in the manuscript.

SINGLE-SAMPLE STATISTICS

As we move to our discussion of single-sample statistics, keep in mind that they might be either descriptive or inferential, depending upon whether or not the researchers want to generalize to the population. Single-sample statistics are generally about central tendencies, also known as *averages*, and measures of variability.

Central Tendency

There actually are three kinds of statistical averages: mean, median, and mode. The **mean** is *the arithmetical average of a set of scores* and is the statistic to which we refer when we use the word *average* in everyday language. It is calculated by adding up all of the values in a set of scores and then dividing that sum by the number of values. Thus, your GPA is calculated by adding all of the grade points you earned and dividing by the number of credits that you attempted. The mean age of a group of people is calculated by adding all of the ages and dividing by the number of ages that were added. The **median** *is the 50th percentile score, which separates the lower and upper halves of a distribution of scores*. If we have only three people in a sample of ages 20, 25, and 27, then the median age is 25, the middle score. If, instead, the ages are 20, 25, and 80, then the median age is still 25, because 25 is still the middle of the ages in the sample. The median is usually reported when there are extreme scores and when the distribution of scores is not normally distributed. The **mode** refers to *the most frequent score in a set of scores* and is the simplest of the averages. Staying with a sample of ages, 20, 20, and 25 would yield a mode of 20; that's the most frequently observed age. As you might guess, mode is not reported very often in the literature.

Variability

Variability refers to how spread out or dispersed scores are in a data set, and each measure of central tendency has an associated measure of variability. The variability statistic for the mode is the **range**, *which is the mathematical difference between the highest and lowest score in a set of scores*. Using 20, 20, and 25 as our age data again, the range is 5 (25 − 20). For the median, the measure of variability is known as the **interquartile range**, which is *a measure of variability or degree of dispersion calculated by the difference between the values representing the 75th and 25th percentiles in a distribution of scores*. One fourth of ordered scores in a data set are higher than the 75th percentile, and one fourth of the ordered scores are lower than the 25th percentile: For the scores 21, 22, 23, and 24, for example, the 25th percentile is 21.5 and the 75th percentile is 23.5, so the interquartile range is 2. Sometimes, researchers report the **semi-interquartile range**, which is *a measure of variability or degree of dispersion calculated by halving the difference between the values representing the 75th and 25th percentiles in a distribution of scores*. The variability statistic for the mean is the **standard deviation**, which is *the square root of the value produced by dividing the sum of squared deviation from the mean by one less than the sample size*. If the preceding sentence aroused a little math anxiety, then try to relax; this is conceptual statistics, so no calculations are required. It is important to understand that larger values for any of the variability statistics mean that the scores are more spread out and exhibit more dispersion. Greater variability, in turn, means that the people or things that were measured are less alike.

Graphic Presentations

Other useful descriptive analyses include stem-and-leaf displays, histograms, and frequency polygons. All of these are ways of presenting a sample graphically. Stem-and-leaf displays (Tukey, 1977) are a little less common, so we will discuss them in greater detail. A **stem-and-leaf display** *allows a view of the entire data set as a distribution of scores without having to lose information about what the specific scores are; it also enables informal examination of differences among groups.* Figure 9.1 contains a stem-and-leaf display for the publication dates of the references cited in a brief social psychology textbook (Dane, 1988b). The stem—the left side of the display—contains the root of the date, such as 187 for the 1870s or 196 for the 1960s. The leaf, the right side of the display, contains the remainder of the number, such as 1 in 1871. By examining the stem and the leaf, one can reconstruct the original score: 187 on the stem together with 1 in the leaf indicates the year 1871.

Traditionally, the digits in the leaf are ordered, increasing from left to right, as in the figure. Although not shown in this figure, one may use the same stem more than once if that makes the display easier to read. However, when doing so, researchers will usually use every stem the same number of times. Longer leaves indicate more data points, so researchers use the same spacing for all of the leaves. That way, the leaves represent the distribution of scores much as a histogram does but without masking the actual numeric values of the data.

As you can easily see from Figure 9.1, the majority of references in the book were published within a few years of the publication date. One can count exactly how many references were published in a specific year—2 in 1980 for example—and it is easy to see that the author only included one citation before the 1930s. The same data presented in

FIGURE 9.1 A Stem-and-Leaf Display of the Publication Years for the Citations Included in Dane (1988b)

187	1
188	
189	
190	
191	
192	
193	57
194	6
195	89
196	11112788
197	122334444556667777889999
198	001111111222333444455555555555555555556666666666666666667

FIGURE 9.2   A Histogram of the Publication Years for the Citations
Included in Dane (1988b)

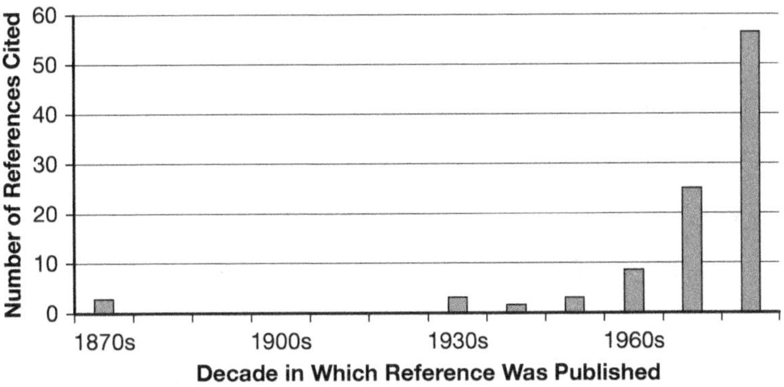

Decade in Which Reference Was Published

a histogram can be seen in Figure 9.2, in which it is obvious that some detail is lost when compared to the stem-and-leaf display. You can still see that most of the references were contemporary with the publication year, but it is no longer possible to know the exact year within each of the depicted decades.

Chi-Square Test of Fit

Chi-square analyses are *statistical techniques used to determine whether the frequencies of scores in the categories defined by the variable match the frequencies one would expect on the basis of chance or on the basis of predictions from a theory.* Chi-square analyses are used to make inferences when the data are categorical or nominal—when they involve measuring participants in terms of categories such as male–female, voter–nonvoter, and so forth. Chi-square procedures can be used to determine whether the size of categories obtained from one sample are similar to theoretical or hypothesized sizes. Stager, Freeman, and Brauna (2015), for example, reported chi-square results in their study of the consistency of different types of identification for stuttering: self-identification (asking someone whether or not he or she stutters), family identification (asking relatives whether or not someone stutters), and expert identification (classification by a qualified professional). Using expert identification as the comparison, they found that neither self- nor family-identification were particularly reliable.

RELATIONAL STATISTICS

Relational statistics generally involve testing the null hypothesis that two variables have nothing in common. When the null hypothesis is rejected, it usually means that the two variables measure, to some extent, the same theoretical concept. In Chapter 7, for example, you read about Hudgins's (2015) research, in which she demonstrated that resilience is related to a nurse's intention to remain in the same job. The ability to overcome and recover from temporary setbacks (resilience) is part of one's ability to avoid becoming dismayed when things don't go one's way at work, which in turn means one is more likely to want to continue working at the same place. There are many different kinds of statistics that are used to study relationships among variables.

Chi-Square Test for Association

Like the test of fit, the chi-square test for association involves categorical data but compares the categories of one variable to the categories of a different variable. Parish et al. (2000), for example, reported a relationship between type of arrhythmia and survival in their examination of in-hospital resuscitations. Not surprisingly, less severe arrhythmias were more likely to be associated with a successful resuscitation attempt. When the results of chi-square analyses are reported, you are likely to see text that looks something like $X^2(2) = 5.7$, $p < .05$, where X^2 is the symbol for chi-square, the number in parentheses—in this case, 2—reflects the degrees of freedom for the analysis, and the number after the equal sign reflects the actual value for the statistic. This value is then compared against values that should be obtained if the null hypothesis is correct, and this comparison is then used to determine the probability that the data represent the null hypothesis. The p, of course, is the symbol used to indicate the probability that the obtained result is due to chance or random error, which is then followed by the value for that probability.

Correlation

When research measures involve continuous variables, such as income, GPA, age, intensity of emotion, and so on, correlational procedures are used to make inferences about relationships between variables. For example, the relationship between the size of a city and its crime rate can be described with correlational analyses. **Correlations** are *statistical procedures that estimate the extent to which the changes in one variable are associated with changes in another*. Hudgins (2015) reported the correlation between job satisfaction and resilience was 0.51 in her sample. Correlation values range from −1.00 through 0.00 to +1.00. Negative values indicate an inverse or indirect relationship; as one variable increases, the other decreases. Positive values indicate a similar or direct relationship; both variables change in the same direction, whether they increase or decrease. A correlation of zero means that the two variables are not related; they have nothing in common.

Essentially, a correlation coefficient is a number summarizing what may be observed from a **scatterplot**, *a graph in which corresponding codes from two variables are displayed on two axes*. When data analyses involve correlations, you are likely to see something like this: $r(42) = .37$, $p < .05$. The r is the symbol used for the correlation coefficient, the number in parentheses represents the degrees of freedom for the statistic—usually the number of pairs of scores minus one—and the number after the equal sign is the actual value of the correlation coefficient.

FIGURE 9.3 A Scatterplot of the Relationship Between Scores on a Measure of Cynicism in the First and Second Years of Medical School (Roche, Scheetz, Dane, Parish, & O'Shea, 2003)

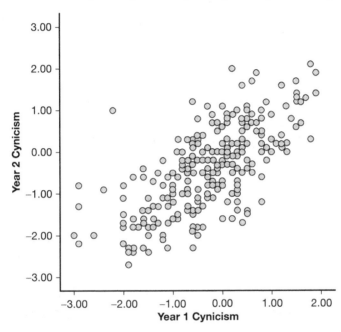

Figure 9.3 is a scatterplot representing a positive correlation using data from a study of medical students' scores on a measure of cynicism at the beginning of their first and second years of medical school (Roche, Scheetz, Dane, Parish, & O'Shea, 2003). In Figure 9.3, it is clear that students who were more cynical than their peers during their first year of medical school were also more cynical than their peers in their second year of medical school. Notice that there are more overlapping data points in the center of the graph than at the edges of the graph, which also illustrates the general tendency for most of the students to have an average score on the measure of cynicism. If I could make Figure 9.3 a three-dimensional figure, you would see the higher frequency data points appear to come out from the page toward you.

Factor Analysis

A very specialized type of correlational analysis is called **factor analysis,** *a statistical technique used to separate continuous variables into groups of variables that can* *be interpreted as single dimensions of a multidimensional concept.* Another statistical procedure, known as principle components analysis, is conceptually similar to factor analysis; the math is somewhat different (Lindeman, Merenda, & Gold, 1980), but interpretation is essentially the same for our purposes. The principle underlying factor analysis is that any given variable probably measures more than one theoretical concept and that the variance produced by employing more than one such variable can be rearranged so that all of the "pieces" of variance can be rearranged to reflect the different concepts measured by the collection of variables. Typical reports of results from factor analysis include a table in which factor loadings are used to show how strongly each variable is associated with the various dimensions (concepts) represented by the collective responses to the variables. An example of a factor analysis, including results, may help to make this descriptive procedure more understandable.

You are probably familiar with course evaluation forms, sometimes called *student opinion forms*, through which students have an opportunity to provide evaluative ratings about the course and instructor at the end of the semester. At one of my previous universities, there were 21 primary feedback items (variables) included on the form, and these items are organized into sections about (1) instructor involvement, (2) student interest, (3) student–instructor interaction, (4) course demands, and (5) course organization. One question that can be asked about student responses to these variables is whether the students in my classes consider the separate sections of the instrument to be, indeed, separate. That is, we can ask whether the five separate sections measure five different aspects of the course experience or whether there is some smaller number of dimensions that can be used to describe students' reactions to my courses. The results of the factor analysis are displayed in Table 9.2, in which the section numbers and items are listed in the left column and the rearranged pieces of the items—the factors—are displayed in the five right columns. Each of the factors represents a concept measured by the pieces of the items. The numbers in those columns—the factor loadings—represent the extent to which the item contributes to the concept measured by the factor. Loadings can range from −1.00 to +1.00; generally, a loading of .4 or higher indicates a sizable contribution to that factor.

Although the results of the factor analysis contain five different factors, the items are not grouped statistically exactly the same way they were grouped on the course evaluation form. The four instructor items (Section 1) are grouped together in Table 9.2 on Factor 1, but the "student has become more competent" item loads on the same factor. Thus, we can conclude that a student's belief in his or her increase in competence is tied to his or her reaction to the qualities of the instructor. Similarly, from the loadings on Factor 2, we can conclude that students' opinions about how intellectually challenged they felt are related to the organization of the course. Factor 3 clearly involves the difficulty of the course and is the only factor that corresponds entirely to the section on the questionnaire.

Factor 4 represents the opportunities for participation provided to the students, but interestingly, the instructor's stimulation of class discussion is not a part of this concept.

TABLE 9.2   Factor Loadings Derived From Students' Responses to a Course Evaluation Form in Which the Items Were Arranged Into Five Separate Sections

Loadings in bold type indicate a sizable contribution of the item to that factor.

Section Number. Course Evaluation Item	Factor Loadings				
1. Instructor was enthusiastic	**.874**	.194	−.128	.270	.171
1. Instructor was interested in teaching	**.831**	.317	−.097	.162	.052
1. Instructor's examples were helpful	**.887**	.196	−.114	.106	.129
1. Instructor was concerned with students' learning	**.687**	.370	−.106	.239	.096
2. Student was interested in learning	.143	.151	−.108	.133	**.889**
2. Student was attentive in class	.218	.268	−.057	.240	**.832**
2. Student felt challenged intellectually	.383	**.489**	−.129	.263	.346
2. Student has become more competent	**.421**	.298	−.143	.226	.225
3. Instructor encouraged idea expression	.287	.336	−.011	**.621**	.207
3. Instructor explained conflicting viewpoints	.176	.030	−.116	**.644**	.183
3. Student had opportunities to ask questions	.174	.191	−.004	**.963**	.075
3. Instructor stimulated class discussion	.362	.185	.034	.046	.098
4. Instructor covered too much material	−.139	−.080	**.938**	.000	−.121
4. Instructor presented material too rapidly	−.102	−.024	**.926**	−.078	−.039
4. Out-of-class assignments were too time consuming	−.053	−.029	**.971**	−.035	−.038
4. Assigned readings were too difficult	−.027	−.226	**.716**	−.064	−.021
5. Instructor covered concepts systematically	.198	**.618**	−.124	.033	.069
5. Course was well organized	.350	**.712**	−.156	.142	.164
5. Instructor's presentations were clear	.444	**.665**	−.161	.287	.198
5. Direction of course was adequately outlined	.314	**.923**	−.023	.142	.168
5. Student enjoyed going to class	.326	**.544**	−.019	.351	**.462**

Factor 5 represents the students' interest and attentiveness, which is partly related to how much the students enjoyed the course. Interestingly, the student's overall enjoyment of the course is pieced into the student's interest and the organization of the material, but this is independent of course difficulty, the instructor's enthusiasm and interest in teaching, and the opportunities for participation. We could, of course, continue discussing these results for a long time, but you should have enough knowledge about factor analysis to understand how it can be used for descriptive research purposes.

Regression

Sometimes researchers interested in relationships between or among variables are interested in predicting one of those variables from a subset of other variables. Under those circumstances, you are likely to read the results of regression analyses, which produce a regression equation. A **regression equation** is *a formula for predicting a score on the response variable from the score on the predictor variable*. In general, regression equations take the form $Y' = bX + c$, where Y' is the predicted score, b is the regression coefficient, X is the score on the **predictor variable** (*the measure one hopes will predict the response or outcome variable in predictive research*), and c is a constant (the point at which the prediction line crosses the ordinate or Y axis on a graph). One example of a regression equation with which you are probably familiar is the expression used to convert Fahrenheit temperatures into centigrade temperatures. For centigrade to Fahrenheit conversions, the equation is $F = 1.8C + 32$. Predictions from a regression equation are approximate and depend on the strength of the relationship between the two variables: The stronger the relationship—the closer the correlation coefficient is to either -1.00 or $+1.00$—the more accurate the prediction. Fahrenheit and centigrade temperatures are highly correlated simply because they are both highly valid and highly reliable measures of the same thing (heat). The amount of prediction error is very small; however, it is not zero. There is always some error in any measurement, and therefore, there is always some error in any prediction made from a measurement. Estimating the margin of error associated with predictions also falls under the category of regression analysis. Although the mathematics involved are beyond the scope of this text, almost any basic statistics text contains the information you would need.

There are times when more than one predictor variable is used in research, such as when a college admissions board uses SAT scores, high school grades, and high school ranking to predict first-year college grades. In such instances, the analysis known as **multiple regression** (*a statistical technique for estimating simultaneous correlations among any number of predictor variables and a single, continuous response variable*) is used. Although considerably more complicated in terms of mathematics, multiple regression relies on the same basic principles as correlation and simple regression. When there is more than one predictor variable, the regression equation is expanded to reflect this, and a multiple regression equation might look something like $Y' = b_1X_1 + b_2X_2 + b_3X_3 + c$, where b_1 refers to the regression coefficient for the first predictor, X_1, and so on through c, the constant.

Researchers are not likely to report the results of regression analyses in the form of an equation. The results are more likely to appear in the form of Table 9.3, which come from a study of medical students' attitudes about people in general (Roche et al., 2003). The **response variable** (*the measure one would like to predict in predictive research, the outcome variable*) in this analysis is cynicism in the first year of medical school, and the predictor variables include beliefs about people's trustworthiness, strength of will, and altruism (also measured in the first year of medical school). Notice that all three variables are significant predictors of first-year cynicism, but trustworthiness is the strongest predictor. The column labeled t reflects the fact that a type of the t test (see below) is used to determine whether or not the regression coefficient for each predictor is significantly different from zero.

TABLE 9.3   Results of a Multiple Regression Analysis in Which First-Year Cynicism Among Medical Students Is Predicted From Beliefs About (1) the Trustworthiness of People, (2) the Strength of Will Displayed by People, and (3) How Altruistic People in General Are

Variable	Coefficient	t	p
Constant	−.030	−0.646	.519
Altruism	−.346	−6.788	.001
Trustworthiness	−.680	−12.693	.001
Strength of will	−.107	−2.191	.029

Regression analyses, both simple and multiple regression, come in many different forms, but the essence of each form is that one or more predictor variables are tested for its relationship to the response variable. In logistic regression, for example, the response variable is a **nominal measurement** or **categorical measurement** (*determining the presence or absence of a characteristic; it is naming a quality*), which requires different mathematics to calculate the results but produces the same kind of results (regression coefficients). In path analysis, one or more intermediate variables are included in the model such that predictors are used to predict the intermediate variables, which in turn are used to predict other response variables. This enables researchers to understand the sequencing of the predictors; for example, high school grades predict SAT scores, and SAT scores predict first-year college grades. This sequencing enables researchers to understand the process by which one variable influences another, but the results are interpreted the same way one would interpret a simple regression result. Similarly, structural equations analysis is used to examine the predictive power of factors derived from factor analysis, but the results are interpreted much the same way one interprets multiple regression results.

GROUP DIFFERENCES

Much experimental and quasi-experimental research involves trying to determine whether two (or more) groups differ according to some quality, such as whether women or men tend to commit more crimes or whether psychology majors or chemistry majors perform better on the Graduate Record Exam. Essentially, such research involves comparing the central tendency of one group with the central tendency of another group and deciding whether the difference between the groups is large enough to reject the null hypothesis that the groups are the same.

The principle underlying group-differences tests is the assumption that both (or all) groups, whatever they may be, represent samples from the same population. Men and women, for example, represent two different samples from the same population (humans). If that assumption is correct—that is, if there are no fundamental differences between men and women; they are just humans—then the two samples should have the same central tendency, the same mean. To the extent that the two groups are different, one can conclude that the assumption about them being from the same population is wrong. Of course, that doesn't mean, in the case of men and women, that one group is not human. Instead, it means that, on whatever variable is being measured, the two groups represent very different populations of humans; they are not the same on whatever the measurement dimension may be. Group-differences statistics are also used to assess change over time, say in study that involves both a pretest and posttest, in which case, the assumption is that the participants are the same at both times. Generally, group-difference statistics involve two groups or more than two groups.

Comparison of Two Groups

The most common way to compare two groups statistically is the t test (Student [William Sealy Gossett], 1908). A *t* **test** for two groups is *a parametric statistical analysis used to determine the probability that two group means are different* and compares the difference between the two means against the overall variability of the scores. If the mean difference is larger than what would be expected on the basis of sampling error, then the null hypothesis is rejected. When researchers report the results of a t test, you will see something like this: $t(45) = 3.67, p < .05$. Of course, t is the symbol for the t test, and the number in parentheses represents the degrees of freedom for the statistic. The number after the equal sign is the calculated value of the statistic.

The t test requires that the distributions of the scores display certain characteristics, and when those requirements are not met, researchers will use and report **nonparametric**

group comparisons, which are *statistics that compare groups based on medians or other distributional characteristics than means*. When two unrelated groups are compared, the Mann–Whitney U (Mann & Whitney, 1947) is used; again, you will read whether or not the null hypothesis is rejected. When the two groups are related or the two sets of scores are repeated measures of the same group, the Wilcoxon signed rank test (Wilcoxon, 1945) is used.

Comparison of More Than Two Groups

When more than two groups are compared, **analysis of variance** (Fisher, 1921), sometimes abbreviated **ANOVA**, is used to assess the extent to which means among the groups are different. ANOVA is *a statistic in which the variance among the means is compared to the variance among the observations to determine whether or not the groups represented by the means are too different to be considered samples from the same population*. In a research article, you may see something like $F(2, 27) = 3.50$, $p < .05$. F is the symbol for ANOVA and the number after the equal sign is the actual value of the statistical test. ANOVA has two indicators for degrees of freedom within the parentheses. The first of these represents (but is not equal to) the number of groups compared, while the second indicates the degrees of freedom for the error term.

Like other mean-comparison statistics, ANOVA can be used to compare independent groups, or it can be used to analyze repeated-measures data and compare the same group over time. Patel et al. (2015), for example, used ANOVA to compare scores at various times during a year on a measure of medication adherence. They found that medication adherence rises immediately after admission for acute coronary syndrome but then levels off within a month and slowly declines over the course of the year (but remains higher than preadmission adherence).

One of the more complicated forms of ANOVA is **multivariate analysis** of variance (**MANOVA**), which is *employed whenever two or more dependent variables are analyzed simultaneously, usually because there is reason to believe that the multiple dependent variables are related in some way* (Lindeman et al., 1980). Essentially, MANOVA is analogous to employing ANOVA except that the variable analyzed is the factor, or common variance, of the several dependent variables that actually were measured. Imagine, for example, comparing the course evaluations of several members of a single department. In such a study, MANOVA would be used on each of the factors identified in Table 9.2 above.

ANOVA and MANOVA also have requirements for the distributions of scores that are analyzed, and when those requirements are not met, researchers use nonparametric analyses. For independent groups, you will read about the Kruskal–Wallis test (Kruskal & Wallis, 1952) or nonparametric analysis of variance. As with ANOVA, a rejected null hypothesis means that there are differences among the groups. When researchers are using repeated-measures data and must use a nonparametric test for analysis of variance, you will read about the Friedman test (Friedman, 1937).

SUMMARY

- Research design and analyses are interdependent. How a project is designed partly determines the statistics the researcher uses to analyze the resulting data. However, lack of familiarity with statistical procedures may limit your ability to interpret a particular set of research results.

- Designs can be categorized in terms of their purposes: exploration, description, prediction, and explanation. Different purposes involve different designs and, therefore, different statistical analyses.

- Generally, statistical analyses can be categorized as single-sample, relational, and intergroup analyses.

- Single-sample analyses tend to be simple statistics, either descriptive or inferential, that enable the researcher to summarize the data he or she has obtained, usually through measures of central tendency, as well as to estimate values for the population to which the researcher wishes to generalize.

- Relational analyses are based on the concept of correlation but can become complex mathematically. When questions about interrelatedness of variables are addressed, factor analysis may be used to describe relationships. When specific predictions are required, regression analyses can be used to construct prediction equations.

- Group-comparison analyses include t tests and various versions of analysis of variance. Generally, you will read about the extent to which some distributional characteristic, such as mean or median, exhibited differences between or among the groups.

EXERCISES

1. Using your library's databases, search for and read an article containing a stem-and-leaf display.

2. Using your library's databases, search for and read an article containing results from a multiple regression analysis.

3. Using your library's databases, search for and read an article containing results from an analysis of variance (ANOVA).

4. Go to the web site of the American Statistical Association (http://www.amstat.org), the Statistical Society of Canada (http://www.ssc.ca), or the Royal Statistical Society (http://www.rss.org.uk) and explore the site to find ways to obtain additional information or contacts when you need statistical information in the future.

10

Archival Research

[B]ut there is still no [person] who would not accept dog tracks in the mud against sworn testimony of a hundred eyewitnesses that no dog passed by.

—Prosser (1964, p. 216)

OVERVIEW

This chapter is about archival research—methods in which the sources of data are various types of documentation. You will learn about content analysis, a method for determining the meaning of recorded communication, as well as some special sampling problems relevant to content analysis. You will also be exposed to some of the techniques used to quantify information derived from content analysis. You will learn about the uses of existing data—measures that have been obtained by other researchers—as well as some ways in which such data may be used and analyzed. Finally, you will learn about meta-analysis, a method for investigating trends within a collection of related studies.

INTRODUCTION

The label *archival research* may suggest an image of an elderly scholar (with bad eyes, of course) bent over an ancient, dusty manuscript in the decrepit basement of a library. Indeed, many behavioral scientists have some disdain for archival research, the type of disdain reflected in the opening quote. One of the early reviewers of another text in which I described content analysis as a research technique (Dane, 1990), for example, commented, "I prefer to leave archival research to librarians and historians." Such images and comments notwithstanding, archival research has been firmly established as a research tradition in many different disciplines and, therefore, is a type of research that you will encounter in your efforts to engage in evidence-based practice. Archival research is an important part of qualitative research (see Chapter 8), and it is no small part of quantitative research. One reason why archival research has gained acceptance may be that there are times when a researcher cannot find any "tracks in the mud" and must rely on the testimony of others. Such testimony may be found in dusty old manuscripts, but it is also found in newspapers, songs, novels, memoirs, movies, magazines, government reports, research reports, and a variety of other sources.

Archival research, in some ways, is something every one of us does informally every day. We all read, watch, and listen. We may even be exposed to such statistical summaries as the gross national product, crime rates, or the batting averages of our favorite baseball players. Formal archival research, however, involves systematic examination of archives in order to formulate or test hypotheses and theories. For our purposes, then, **archival research** is *any research in which a public record is the unit of analysis*. What distinguishes archival research from other methods is that the researcher deals with information that was generated before the research began, and archival researchers deal with people's products rather than with the people themselves.

Archival research involves attempting to answer questions about people by investigating a portion of the seemingly infinite amount of recorded information they generate. Specific methods have been developed to allow researchers to find such records, obtain a sample of them, transform the collected information into usable data, analyze those data, and use the results to draw conclusions. Sometimes, research was not a consideration of those who originally compiled the information; in other instances, the original information was gathered through the use of some research method. Literally any record of information is fair game for archival research.

Systematic archival methods can be separated into two types: content analysis and existing data analysis. Content analysis may involve interpreting any communication medium, whether written, pictorial, oral, or audiovisual. By studying such archives, researchers test and formulate hypotheses about a variety of different phenomena, which, in turn, you can use to inform your practice. Existing data analysis generally involves using data for purposes other than those for which the data were gathered. Various archives, for example, may contain information about trends that could not have been detected when the data were first collected. Because the above descriptions are very general, more specific discussions follow.

CONTENT ANALYSIS

The amount of communication each of us experiences throughout a typical day is incredible. We converse with others; read what others have written; listen to live or taped conversations, movies, and songs; watch the actions of others on a television, computer screen, or phone; and pay attention to the various signs and signals that surround us. All of this communication has some meaning for us, and content analysis is one research method that can be used to study that meaning.

The stuff of content analysis has been described very succinctly by Lasswell, Lerner, and Pool (1952) in the question, "Who says what, to whom, how, and with what effect?" (p. 12). Holsti (1968) later added "Why?" for the sake of completeness, although discovering why a particular message was sent is not always a part of content analysis. More formally, **content analysis** is *a research method used to make objective and systematic inferences about theoretically relevant messages.* Let's examine this formal definition in order to appreciate what we can learn from reports derived from the use of content analysis as a research method.

As noted above, our world is full of messages—communication directed by someone to someone else for a specific purpose. These messages are the observations researchers investigate in content analysis. Messages contained in any medium can be analyzed, although the medium chosen for analysis depends on both theoretical and practical concerns. When content analysis is used to test research hypotheses, the content of archives serve as operational definitions of theoretical concepts. Some media are easier to analyze than others, however, and practical concerns also become part of the planning process. As consumers of research, however, those practical concerns only affect us in terms of the availability of research; we might not find specific kinds of content analysis because it was not practical for someone to do that research.

Like all research, we use the results of content analysis to make inferences about events related to theory, policy, program, and/or practice. Before we can do that, the researcher's ability to make inferences depends on the sample studied. If a researcher wanted to investigate the violent content of television programs (including streaming) during the last 10 years, for example, that researcher would have to select a sample of the programming; no one could analyze everything that was broadcast or streamed (Bureau of Labor Statistics, 2016). Like all other research, then, we should evaluate the researcher's sampling technique as part of our critical consumption of content analysis research (for more information about sampling, see Chapter 4).

In addition to being systematic, inferences must be objective; the inferences one makes about messages should be similar to the inferences someone else would make if he or she had access to the same information. Part of this objectivity is accomplished through careful construction of the operational definitions used in the research, so it is important to consider those definitions critically when reading the research. Another part of objectivity results from the consistency with which one uses the operational definitions one constructs, the reliability of measurement. Although reliability is important in any research project, the ease with which communication can be misunderstood makes reliable measurement more difficult in content analysis. Look for information in the method section about what the researchers did to ensure reliability of their operational definitions.

The range of potential topics for content analysis is considerable but finite. Just because any question of the form "Who says what to whom, how, with what effect, and why?" can be answered through content analysis does not mean that content analysis is always the most appropriate method for such questions. Specifically, content analysis is best used as a comparative technique. It cannot, for example, be used to measure how conservative a particular newspaper's editorial policy is, but it can be used to determine whether one newspaper is more conservative than another.

Who—The Source of Messages

When the research question involves the *who* part of the Lasswell et al. (1952) question, the researcher is concerned with describing the individual(s) who created the archives. The research hypothesis may concern disputed authorship or may involve making inferences about characteristics of the author(s). One example of disputed authorship was resolved by using content analysis of *The Federalist*, a series of 85 essays originally published under the *nom de plume* Publius. Alexander Hamilton, James Madison, and John Jay all wrote the essays to persuade people to throw over the Articles of Confederation in favor of the Constitution. The authorship of 12 of the essays (Essays 49–58, 62, and 63) was uncertain; either Madison or Hamilton could have written them.

Mosteller and Wallace (1964) compared the relative frequency of certain common words—*and, in, the*, and *enough*—in essays known to have been written by the two authors with the same words in the disputed essays; their results were clearly consistent with the conclusion that Madison was the author. They demonstrated that even in the least convincing paper (No. 55), the odds were 80 to 1 in favor of Madison's authorship. Subsequently, Rokeach, Homant, and Penner (1970) compared values expressed in the papers—freedom, honor, equality, and comfort—and arrived at the same conclusion concerning authorship.

More recently, Markowitz and Hancock (2014, 2016) demonstrated how writing in fraudulent empirical publications differs from writing in valid publications. When they compared a single author's fraudulent papers and his valid papers, Markowitz and Hancock (2014) observed that the author used more words related to research process and methods as well as use more expansive modifiers (e.g., *extreme, exceptional*) and fewer restricting modifiers (e.g., *somewhat, slightly*) in the fraudulent articles. The author's fraudulent papers also tended to have fewer adjectives, which is consistent with deception in general. In their follow-up study, Markowitz and Hancock (2016) compared scientific publications retracted for fraud to scientific papers in the same journal, along with some papers retracted for reasons other than fraud. In the later study, they were not able to compare specific authors' fraudulent and valid papers. They did find that greater obfuscation (more jargon, lower readability, more causal terminology, and less positive emotion) was associated with fraudulent papers, but the accuracy rate was not encouraging. When classifying fraudulent versus valid papers for a single author, the accuracy rate was about 70%, but accuracy was only about 57% for the collective-author analysis.

In the above research projects, the researchers were able to address the questions of authorship and fraud only because they had access to material known to have been written by the authors of interest; neither authorship nor fraud could have been clarified without the comparison manuscripts. Indeed, using content analysis in the absence of comparative standards can cause a number of problems. Morton (1963), for example, used seven characteristics of an author's style to analyze the Epistles of St. Paul and concluded that there were at least six different authors for the Epistles. Responding to Morton's published challenge to others to repudiate his results, Ellison (1965) used the same procedure to demonstrate that Morton's own articles exhibited multiple authorship. Morton was repudiated, rather cleverly. Attempting to determine authorship in the absence of comparative standards usually leads to more ambiguity than clarity, and you should be wary of researchers who claim to have done so.

Says What—The Content of Messages

Perhaps the most prevalent use of content analysis has been to investigate the content communicated in a message. Holsti (1968) separated this question into three distinct components: (1) changes in content over time, (2) the relationship between author characteristics and content, and (3) the extent to which content conforms to some external standard. Zimbardo and Meadow (1974) provided a simultaneously encouraging and disconcerting example of the first of these components. The starting point for their research was the phenomenon known as **nonconscious ideology**, *a prejudice that has lost its label as prejudice and has become an implicit assumption that strongly affects the roles of certain members of a society* (Bem & Bem, 1970). For example, a man would consider the expectation that his male roommate would do all the cleaning to be unfair but might be perfectly willing to expect a female roommate to do the same. That there is apparently nothing wrong with expecting a female to do all the housework is a nonconscious ideology.

Zimbardo and Meadow (1974) reasoned that humor may be the most effective medium for preserving prejudicial attitudes and, therefore, changes in the content of humor should reflect the prevalence of a specific prejudice. They focused on stereotypes about women and analyzed the content of jokes taken from the "Cartoon Quips" and "Laughter, The Best Medicine" sections of *Reader's Digest* from 1947–1948, 1957–1958, and 1967–1968. After identifying jokes with relevant bias, they discovered that the frequency of such jokes had declined over the 20-year period. Approximately 28% of the jokes were sexist in the 1940s, followed by 10% and 6%, respectively, for the 1950s and 1960s. The total number of jokes in the sections increased over the years, but the proportion and absolute number of prejudicial jokes decreased. That's the encouraging aspect of Zimbardo and Meadow's (1974) research: General sexism declined over the years.

The disconcerting aspect of their research involves the analyses of specific stereotypes represented in the sexist jokes. Zimbardo and Meadow also indicated that the sentiments expressed in the jokes remained relatively constant. The stereotypes remained current and understandable, even if they were becoming less popular among the editors of *Reader's Digest*.

More recently, Moran, Lucas, Everhart, Morgan, and Prickett (2016) sought to understand the persistence of **vaccine hesitancy**, *the parental desire to delay or refuse vaccinations for their children*, by studying the content of anti-vaccine websites. Their analysis compared the content of almost 500 anti-vaccine sites to well-researched theories of persuasion. Through reliable coding of the content of the sites, Moran et al. were able to describe several tactics used to maintain vaccine hesitancy, primarily relating anti-vaccine messages to healthy lifestyles and promoting mistrust of government and scientific sources. "By understanding how these sites go about persuading parents to resist or delay vaccinating their children, pediatricians, public health organizations, and others who communicate about vaccines can better develop effective pro-vaccination messages" (Moran et al., 2016, p. 161). That is, knowing the theory behind the messages enables one to use the very same theories to develop effective counter messages.

Using content analysis to investigate what is said can involve any one of three components outlined by Holsti (1968). Zimbardo and Meadow's (1974) study is just one example of temporal trends in content. Jacobs's (1967) content analysis of suicide notes (described in Chapter 1) is another example of archival research in which the content and author's characteristics were related. Moran et al. (2016) showed us that content is not necessarily related to effectiveness of messages; use of standard persuasive techniques can occur in many different types of messages. In the next section, the focus shifts to what we can learn from receivers of messages.

To Whom—The Audience of Messages

It is no great revelation that people communicate different messages to different audiences. We all, for example, talk about different topics with fellow students than with non-students, and we talk about different topics with friends than with strangers. One purpose of content analysis is to determine the extent to which audience-specific messages really are different.

Berkman (1963), for example, analyzed the content of advertisements in *Life* and *Ebony* magazines and found that the major difference was the presumed economic status of prospective buyers. *Life* included a greater proportion of higher-priced products in its advertising. However, within any given price range for products, the only difference in the ads in the two magazines was the race of the models: Whites for *Life* and Blacks for *Ebony*. In all other respects, the content of the advertisements was similar.

Using very different methodology, Hall et al. (2015) reviewed existing research and concluded that healthcare providers were just about as likely as the general public to exhibit negative implicit attitudes about people of color. (**Implicit attitudes** are *evaluations of specific objects that occur without the individual's general awareness of the* *existence of the evaluation.*) Providers holding implicit attitudes had different interactions with Black and Hispanic patients than with White patients. Some of the studies reviewed by Hall et al. contained evidence that the implicit attitudes were related to different health outcomes, although this was much less common.

Differences among messages directed to different audiences can also be used to investigate theoretical issues. Levin and Spates (1970), for example, used content analysis to investigate Parsons's (1951) propositions about the importance to subcultures of instrumental and expressive values. According to Levin and Spates, what had been labeled the "hippie" movement of the 1960s should be a prime example of an **expressive subculture**—*one characterized by an emphasis on feelings over accomplishment.*

They compared the content of various publications of the 1960s underground press to that of *Reader's Digest*, a much more traditional publication. They found that 46% of the content in underground publications included expressive themes, whereas only 10% of the content included instrumental themes. On the other hand, *Reader's Digest* included 23% expressive themes and 42% instrumental themes. Clearly, the communications directed toward hippies emphasized expressive themes, whereas the more traditional press emphasized instrumental themes. The communication of different messages to different audiences, although nothing new in and of itself, did provide supporting evidence for Parsons's (1951) theory.

How—Communication Techniques in Messages

Investigating the *how* of communication is a relatively rare application of content analysis, although the few investigations into this matter have been highly informative. Holsti's (1968) work, for example, provides an excellent starting point for research on propaganda, as does that of Crano and Brewer (1973). Another example is the work of McHugo, Lanzetta, Sullivan, Masters, and Englis (1985), which involved an analysis of Ronald Reagan's communication techniques. More recently, Liu and Khine (2016) examined the use of diagrams in science textbooks used for first through fifth grades.

Liu and Khine (2016) used a sample of science textbooks to assess the extent to which science textbooks used in Bahrain were consistent with existing theories of knowledge development. They focused on the diagrams contained in textbooks and categorized the diagrams as iconic (simple depiction, such as a picture of an animal), schematic (presentation of unseen phenomena, such as magnetic waves), charts and graphs (numeric presentation, such as a pie chart), and augmented reality (virtual reality images, such as images of the body with see-through skin). They categorized all 3,125 of the images contained in almost 1,500 pages in 20 different texts. An important part of their article includes reporting a reliability check on a random sample of the categorized images; we know that their categorization process was objective. Aside from the obvious fact that the texts averaged more than two images per page, they found that the majority (>80%) of the images were iconic. The prevalence of iconic images decreased with advancing grades; that is, more complex images were included in textbooks for higher grades. Clearly, images are an important part of the *how* of communicating science to young readers.

With What Effect—The Effect of Messages

Assessing effects through content analysis can be approached in one of two ways. One way involves examining the effects of some phenomenon by analyzing the content of documents related to the phenomenon. A content analysis of interviews with first-grade children (Kounin & Gump, 1961), for example, provided evidence that the attitudes of the children's teachers affected the children's perceptions of inappropriate behaviors. The other way to assess effects is to examine the effects produced by the content of the documents themselves. An example of this approach is Levin and Spates's (1970) previously mentioned analysis of the impact of the 1960s underground press on traditional publications.

Kounin and Gump (1961) studied the effects of teachers' styles through their pupils' beliefs about misbehavior. Using consensus among raters, they categorized teachers as either punitive or nonpunitive. The children were then asked to answer two questions: *What's the worst thing a child can do at school? Why is that so bad?* The results clearly demonstrated that children who had punitive teachers were much more likely to consider fighting and other physical behaviors to be misconduct, whereas children with nonpunitive teachers were more likely to consider behaviors such as lying to be misconduct.

Of greater relevance to our educational system, children with punitive teachers were much less likely to consider poor academic performance to be misconduct. The authors concluded that a punitive teaching style is less likely than a nonpunitive style to produce high levels of academic performance. You may be thinking to yourself, "So what else is new?" but you should realize that the research was completed in 1961, when punitive teaching styles were considered the norm. This content analysis was influential in leading others to conduct research that has since made this conclusion old hat (see, for example, Ferlazzo, 2011, 2012).

Why—The Reasons for Communication

Attempting to discover why various archives were created deals with one of the most difficult questions to answer using content analysis. Most research dealing with *why* has to do with biographical material and investigations of individuals' motivations for various actions. Using content analysis for such purposes has been variously labeled *life history analysis*, *case study methodology*, *psychobiography*, and *psychohistory*. Proponents of these different labels vary a little in their specific methods and purposes but, for the most part, are highly similar (Runyan, 1982).

One use for investigating the *why* of archives is gaining an understanding of the social and political motives of biographers. Runyan (1982), for example, provided an insightful look at the motives of the Nixon administration through his analysis of two different archives concerning biographical material on Daniel Ellsberg. (Ellsberg leaked the Pentagon Papers to the U.S. press; these were classified documents that provided evidence of the deceitful and otherwise unethical activity of the Nixon administration during the Vietnam War.) More recently, Prentice, Taylor, Rayson, Hoskins, and O'Loughlin (2011) used both quantitative and qualitative content analyses to begin to understand the intent of authors of extremist literature calling for violent attacks upon enemies. Prentice et al. (2011) included descriptions of the multiple ways in which they assessed the reliability of their coding schemes. They also reported that **outgroup derogation**, *discrimination against individuals who do not share the same social membership,* was present in about one fourth of the messages and was the predominant mechanism used to justify a call to violence. Outgroup derogation may be an effective tactic in that it seems to increase the stress associated with a perceived threat to one's own group (Sampasivam, Collins, Bielajew, & Clément, 2016).

In summary, content analysis can be rather effectively used to answer a variety of questions. Understanding the variability of applications, however, is not the same thing as understanding the technique itself. For this reason, we turn next to procedural issues concerning content analysis.

METHODOLOGICAL ISSUES IN CONTENT ANALYSIS

The first step in any content analysis research is deciding what part of the "Who says what to whom, how, with what effect, and why?" question is to be addressed. That decision, of course, depends on the researcher's interests, the theory with which he or she is working, and the research hypotheses developed from the theory. Making that decision, however, is only the beginning of content analysis. A researcher must also make a series of decisions concerning units of analysis, units of observation, sampling techniques, and coding before he or she can begin to collect data. Your understanding of these decisions should provide considerable insight into how to interpret the results of content analysis.

Suppose, for example, that a researcher decides to investigate the degree of sexism displayed on television, as did Ellis (1988). The next decision would concern *the objects about which a researcher would like to answer a research question*—the **units of analysis**. One could not, for example, analyze everything on television. Even if one chose to select a relatively small period of time—say, a day or two—one would still have a great deal of programming, given the number of sources of television content across the country (or the world, for that matter). One would have to choose a sample of programming that included network broadcasts; independent, cable, and streaming channels; time-of-day programming for broadcast and cable; children's programs; news shows; commercials; and so forth to limit the research observations.

Deciding on units of analysis then enables one to choose the **units of observation**—*the specific material, objects, or people to be measured in a research project.* After deciding to use television commercials, for example, the researcher must refine the choice by deciding which of the myriad commercials will actually be examined for sexist content. Will the researcher deal only with a specific type of commercial, such as cleaning products? Or commercials presented at specific times of the day—say, during prime time? Or commercials aired during specific programs, such as during the news? The researcher must refine the choice until he or she has a concrete description of the archives to be examined.

Seider (1974), for example, decided to use speeches as units of observation in his study of corporate ideologies. He wanted to obtain a cross section of business leaders, and he decided that *Vital Speeches* sufficiently represented the range of material of interest to him. Were someone to replicate Seider's research today, the researcher might decide that the annual reports of the various corporations would have served equally well as units of observation. The point is not that there may be better units of observation, only different units; of course, different units of observation can also lead to different results, so the issue is not moot. As the consumer of research, you also need to be aware of other potential units of observation as well as understand the biases that might exist in the units selected by the researcher.

Deciding on the units of observation, in turn, leads to a series of decisions about sampling, about how to select representative units. If, for example, a researcher decided to examine commercials presented during network news programs, he or she could probably look at every commercial during every newscast on every network for some specified period of time, but it would be unnecessary to do so. The researcher could instead, for example, plan a procedure that involved sequentially and randomly choosing a day of the week, a time period, a network, and a newscast to be observed for any given data collection session. The researcher could record the newscasts he or she randomly selected and then view the commercials at a convenient time.

The reason for establishing a systematic sampling procedure is to avoid having to observe everything included in the units of observation. A systematic sampling procedure provides the researcher a representative sample from which he or she can generalize to the entire set of observational units. The researcher doesn't have to watch every television commercial to be able to draw conclusions about television commercials in general. Chapter 4 contains more detail about specific sampling procedures.

Having defined the sample, a researcher must then decide how to measure the variables contained in the research hypothesis. This, of course, involves determining the operational definitions the researcher will include in the research. One might, for example, simply decide to categorize commercials as either sexist or nonsexist, but even such a simple measure requires an operational definition. What makes a commercial sexist? Is there more than one way to define *sexist*? If there are different types of sexism, is the researcher going to consider all types or only some of them? How many examples of sexism must a commercial contain in order to categorize it as sexist? To know how to apply the research results to your practice, you need to understand the operational definition(s) used by the researcher(s). When dealing with content analysis, the researcher must decide between two different levels of content: manifest and latent.

Manifest content—*the physical or noninferential material that makes up an archive*—is usually coded in terms of words or letters in written material, words and pauses in audio material, concrete actions in visual material, and so forth. Kounin and Gump (1961), for example, used manifest content in their study of children's impressions of misconduct. Such words as *hitting*, *pushing*, and *kicking* were coded as assaultive behaviors; such phrases as *talking out of turn*, *yelling at someone*, or *lying to someone* were coded as nonassaultive. Manifest content is usually relatively easy to code reliably; few people would disagree about the presence or absence of a word or an action in an observation.

Latent content refers to *inferred, underlying, or hidden meaning in material that makes up an archive*. It may be coded in terms of words or actions, and it usually involves inferences from sentences, paragraphs, facial expressions, and tone of voice as well as other indications of meaning. When someone says that my research (or my drumming) is "interesting," for example, it may be a compliment or a sarcastic appraisal of my relative incompetence. Contextual information is required to interpret "interesting," and we as consumers should read the researchers' description of how they inferred latent content.

Because coding latent content involves making inferences about the manifest content of an archive, latent content is generally less reliable than manifest content. On the other hand, latent content may be the only way to operationalize some concepts. Advertisers are not likely, for example, to come out and straightforwardly say, "Women are inferior decision makers" in their commercials. They may, however, show women deciding to buy a car because of its color and show men basing their decisions on gas mileage or investment value. Coding manifest content and coding latent content are not mutually exclusive practices. The same archive, *The Federalist*, was coded for manifest content by Mosteller and Wallace (1964) and for latent content by Rokeach et al. (1970); both research teams arrived at the same conclusions but used different coding practices in the process.

To summarize, we as consumers need to track a number of different but related decisions made by researchers to ensure our ability to use the research to engage in evidence-based practice. We need to know which archives were analyzed and which specific documents among those archives were actually observed or measured. We need to know how the researchers obtained a representative sample of the archives and how they operationally defined the measured variables. As consumers of research, it's our job to consider each of those decisions critically to determine whether or not the decisions are consistent with the issue we wish to inform empirically.

Quantification in Content Analysis

Virtually anything is quantifiable, provided the principles and procedures of measurement are followed correctly. Measurement in general is covered in Chapter 5, but some measurement issues are specific to content analysis. It is these specific issues to which we turn our attention in this section. The type of quantification procedure selected for a content analysis project depends on the units of observation and the coding procedures the researcher has selected. One or more of the procedures outlined below will be appropriate for a content analysis study. As the procedures are discussed, we'll consider an example from my own research to illustrate the differences among the procedures.

The most common method of quantifying variables in content analysis involves measuring frequency—counting the number of times a given variable appears in the observational unit. In a study of simulated jury deliberations, for example, I counted the number of times jurors mentioned an item of evidence, a personal experience, the judge's instructions, and a few other variables in an effort to examine the relationship between the content of deliberations and the final verdict. By tallying the frequency with which each topic was discussed, I was able to determine that jurors made more remarks about evidence than about any other topic. I also discovered a relationship between the amount of evidence-related discussion and the verdict: More talk about evidence was associated with a greater likelihood of conviction.

One common difficulty associated with the frequency method of quantification, however, is deciding what to do with repetitions. One juror may say, "We have to remember that he had a knife," and another juror may echo that with, "Yeah, a knife." Do both statements count? Or only the first? Or should there be a separate category for repetitions? If a researcher wants to measure the number of times a certain word occurs, as did Mosteller and Wallace (1964), then repetitions are no problem. But if a researcher wants to measure the number of times an idea is presented, repetition becomes a question that must be resolved. There is no single solution, for the decision depends on the hypotheses and other considerations. I decided not to count repetitions, partly because I was interested in counting how many times evidence was discussed, not simply how many times someone referred to any particular piece of evidence. As consumers, however, we need to pay attention to the decision made by the researcher and decide whether or not it is consistent with our purposes.

An alternative to frequency counts—one that also overcomes the potential problem of repetitions—involves measuring the amount of space (for written material) or time (for audio and visual material) appropriated to the variable. Using the same deliberations, I compared the amount of time jurors spent discussing evidence and other topics. With the temporal measure, however, I discovered that less time was devoted to discussion of the evidence, despite the fact that the frequency measure indicated that evidence statements were most frequent. That is, the jurors mentioned evidence more often than any other topic, but the amount of time spent discussing evidence was relatively brief. More to the point, using temporal coding resulted in no apparent relationship between discussion of evidence and verdict.

Different operational definitions of the variable produced different results, which is not unusual. One reason for the difference was that my unit of analysis was the sentence. There were more sentences about evidence than about any other topic, but the evidence-related sentences were also shorter than sentences about any other topic.

To avoid the problem introduced by differential sentence (or other unit) length, some researchers use a technique first developed by Osgood and his colleagues (Osgood, 1959; Osgood, Sporta, & Nunnally, 1956). The technique, called evaluative assertion analysis (EAA), involves breaking down statements into one of two structural forms: subject–connector–descriptor or subject–connector–object. Using EAA, the sentence "There are people who are unbalanced and pick up a knife" can be separated into two statements: Some people–are–unbalanced and unbalanced people–pick up–a knife. The first statement, according to my coding scheme, was categorized as general knowledge; the second was categorized as a remark about the defendant's character.

Of course, when one uses EAA, one cannot measure the amount of time devoted to a topic. When I used EAA on jury deliberations, I obtained essentially the same results as when I used simple frequency counts. Evidence was the most frequently discussed topic and was related to verdicts.

Perhaps the most difficult quantification method to use is the intensity method. Whenever the units of analysis might vary in intensity—some statements have more meaning or more relevance than others—it is often the case that simple frequency or space/time enumeration is insufficient. A number of different techniques can be used for intensity analysis, all of which involve using some sort of rating scale. For example, one of the coding categories I used in the content analysis of jury deliberations was verdict preference, an indication of the juror's intention to vote guilty, not guilty, or undecided. There are different ways, however, to indicate a preference. One juror might say, "He might be guilty," whereas another might say, "He's definitely guilty." Clearly, these two jurors are expressing the same belief with different intensities.

Although there are a number of different ways to scale intensity (see, e.g., Chapter 5), I decided to ask several individuals to rate each statement on a scale from 1 to 10; the more intense the statement, the higher the rating. The first statement quoted above received an average rating of 5, and the second received an average rating of 8. I discovered that intensity ratings of statements about the incriminating nature of evidence—"No matter what his reasons, he still stabbed someone"—was the variable most strongly related to final verdicts, even more strongly related than were initial statements about verdict preferences.

Different quantification methods may lead to different results, although that does not mean that one method is necessarily better than another. In the above examples, the research question addressed by each method was slightly different. With frequency analysis, the analysis dealt with the relationship between frequency of occurrence and verdict; for the space/time analysis, the relationship examined was between verdicts and time spent discussing topics; the intensity method assessed the relationship between verdicts and strength of opinion. Once again, the questions asked have a great deal to do with the answers obtained. When reading research, you need to consider the decisions made by the researcher. Ask yourself whether or not the method enabled the researcher to answer the question(s) identified in the introduction and whether or not the method is relevant to your questions about improving your practice.

EXISTING DATA ANALYSIS

Up to now, our discussion has dealt with creating data from existing archives, typically archives not created for the purpose of research. In this section, we consider research in which the data already exist. **Existing data** are *the archived results of research accomplished by someone else.* They are typically found in one of three formats: raw data, aggregate or summary data, and the results of completed data analyses (statistical results).

The raw data format generally contains measurements in the original units of observation. Thus, using existing raw data is analogous to hiring someone else to collect the researcher's data, except that the researcher doesn't have the latitude to determine which data are collected. The records stored by the registrar's office at your university, for example, contain raw data. The registrar collected the data and, if a researcher can obtain access to them, they may be analyzed however the researcher sees fit. Archived raw data are the most flexible of the forms of existing data.

Aggregate or summary data are not nearly as flexible as raw data. They typically are archived as one or more combinations of the original measures. For example, if the registrar will release only grade point averages (GPAs) instead of grades for every course, those average or mean scores would be considered aggregate data. The original units of observation were the individual course grades, but they have been combined into a higher-order unit of analysis, the mean. Because the researcher doesn't have access to the original units of observation for aggregate data, his or her use of them is somewhat limited. The researcher cannot, for example, use GPA to investigate an individual's improvement during a given semester, although the researcher could use it to determine the extent to which the individual improved across semesters.

The third format for existing data, statistical results, is the format with which you are probably most familiar. The statistical results included in research reports are a form of existing data, although this format has the most restrictions. Consistent with the previous examples, the statistical result format would be analogous to the registrar releasing only correlations between semesters, not the GPA itself for each semester.

Raw Data

Regardless of their complexity or the format in which they are stored, all existing data, including raw data, have one thing in common: Someone else was responsible for their collection; all of the decisions about measurement have already been made by the time the researcher gets the data. If those decisions match the researcher's purposes, then he or she can use the data as they are. At other times, however, the researcher may need to build upon the decisions made by the original researcher. In this section, you will learn how to evaluate existing data studies by reading about examples.

Ali et al. (2016) were able to use existing data from a clinical trial of a cholera vaccine to test their hypothesis regarding ring vaccination to establish a form of **herd immunity**, which is *a form of indirect immunity for non-vaccinated members of a population result-ing from reduced likelihood of contact with infected individuals because immunized individuals prevent the spread of the disease* (also known as **community immunity**). **Ring vaccination**, in turn, refers to *vaccinating individuals within a geographic cir-cumference around index cases.* Ring vaccination is of particular interest when there is a shortage of vaccine and not everyone can be vaccinated, which is the case for cholera. The idea is that, like putting an extra layer of clothing between your skin and cold air, the ring reduces the likelihood of transmission from the index cases to those residing outside the ring. Ali et al. were able to demonstrate that a 25-meter ring provided indirect vaccination effectiveness of 93% and 72% at two- and three-year periods, respectively, after adjusting for age and sex.

The rings in their analyses, however, were not part of the original data-collection procedure. The original vaccination researchers did not administer vaccinations on the basis of spatial orientation to target cases. Instead, Ali et al. used residential and other information about individuals in the existing data to determine the proportion of vacci-nated people within a specific geographic distance from the target cases. Then they com-pared cholera rates within rings that had a high vaccination proportion with rates in rings that had a low vaccination proportion. They made these comparisons for rings of various sizes. When deciding on how this research might inform your practice, you then have to consider the extent to which this indirect test of ring vaccination is sufficient for your purposes. That is, you have to read their method section carefully to decide how their decisions about the existing data match your purposes.

In a very different use of existing data, Guthrie, Declercq, Finne-Soveri, Fries, and Hirdes (2016) examined the prevalence and outcomes of dual sensory impairment (DSI), a combi-nation of hearing and vision deficits or loss that prevents the individual from using one of the senses to overcome deficits in the other, such as using sign language to overcome hear-ing loss. Using data already collected in the United States, Canada, Belgium, and Finland, the researchers were able to demonstrate that individuals with DSI exhibited relative impairment on almost every measure, including cognition, independence, gait, falls, self-rated health, and depression. Some of outcome differences were more or less pronounced when comparing individuals living at home with those living in a long-term care facility.

Guthrie et al. (2016) noted a number of limitations for their study, limitations that are not at all unusual for studies involving existing data. The original data set, for example, did not include a measure of when the individual began to experience DSI so they could not determine the extent to which the outcomes are short- or long-term. The existing data also did not have a variable specific to diagnosis of DSI, so the researchers had to con-struct the measure from two items about vision and hearing impairment. Because some of the countries had rules about individual-level data leaving the country, the authors were not able to make comparisons among the countries. All of these limitations were included in the article, but there are sure to be other aspects of the study that require critical consideration before you apply the findings to your practice.

Although the raw data format is the most flexible of the formats for existing data, existing data are rarely as flexible as those one collects for oneself—for one's own purposes and for testing one's own hypotheses. Thus, when consuming this type of archival research, we need to be a little more forgiving when researchers don't have certain types of data. By *forgiving*, I mean that we don't necessarily fault the researchers for the limits of the data collection, as we would, say, if a researcher collecting his or her own data forgot to collect what obviously should have been an important variable. On the other hand, just because a researcher dealt with archival data does not excuse him or her for overgeneralizing from the data or from conducting inappropriate analyses.

Aggregate Data

Aggregate data refers to *measurements that have been combined at a level higher than the unit of observation*. A report that *X*% of the people in a given region voted for a particular candidate is an aggregate report; we don't know, and can't find out, how each person in the region voted (raw data). Similarly, the average GPA of first-year students at a particular institution is aggregate data; we don't know an individual student's GPA.

The classic illustration of the use of aggregate data is Durkheim's (1951/1897) research on environmental correlates of suicide. In an effort to address the question of why people take their own lives, Durkheim obtained and analyzed suicide rates and other demographic statistics from a number of different European countries. Although he identified a number of patterns in the suicide rates—including information that refuted the then-accepted explanation of uncomfortably hot weather—the most intriguing aspects of the data were the associations of suicide rates with both political activity and religious affiliations. Durkheim noted, for example, a dramatic increase in suicides during 1848, a particularly tumultuous year politically for many European countries. He also noted that countries with larger proportions of Catholic residents exhibited consistently lower suicide rates.

But Durkheim did not have access to information on the religious denominations of individuals who committed suicide. Instead, he investigated the religious connection by using the relative number of Catholics and Protestants within various countries. For example, predominantly Catholic Bavaria exhibited one third fewer suicides than predominantly Protestant provinces. Generally, the greater the proportion of Catholics in a given region, the lower the suicide rate in that region.

Taken together, the associations of suicide rates with both religious affiliation and political turmoil led Durkheim to conclude that **anomie**—*a feeling that stems from a lack of integration into a social network; a general sense of instability or disintegration*—was an important contributory factor in suicide. Political changes led to instability in everyday life, which in turn produced anomie. Fewer suicides among Catholics may have been due to the fact that Catholicism in the 1800s was more structured and more authoritarian than Protestant denominations, and the structure available to Catholics may have provided stability and prevented anomie.

Somewhat more recently, Adsera and Menendez (2011) used aggregate data from 18 countries in Latin America to determine that the number of children is correlated with economic conditions such that more births occur when the economy is better. The data covered the period from 1953 to 2000, during which birthrate generally declined in all of the countries, but they were able to pinpoint unemployment as the primary predictor. Unlike Durkheim (1951/1897) and many other researchers using aggregate data, Adsera and Menendez (2011) also were able to collect individual data, through which they were able to show that the individual-level results were consistent with the aggregate-level results. At the individual level, they found that unemployment was the most important predictor of the timing of having one's first child (measured as elapsed time from age 12). Their article includes a detailed description of the sources of the data and the assumptions made in using those data, which, of course, is necessary and useful information for anyone who intends to include their results in evidence-based practice.

In Chapter 3, you learned how to review existing literature, a process analogous to a qualitative content analysis. Researchers who write **narrative reviews** provide *a verbal, as opposed to numerical, description of the state of the literature.* Often, the search strategy is not detailed in a narrative review; that is, the exact key words are usually not specified, nor usually are the search engines identified. For these reasons, narrative reviews might be considered to be an introduction to the literature regarding a particular area of research. They are useful for learning about one or more important issues in the literature but should not be considered to be a comprehensive description of all research on a given topic. Pace and Shulman (2016), for example, completed a narrative review of research regarding breast cancer in low- and middle-income countries in sub-Saharan Africa. Through their description of the research they chose to include in their review, we can learn that the much higher death rate in sub-Saharan Africa appears to result from a combination of delay in seeking treatment and a delay in diagnosis or treatment initiation after treatment is sought. The authors provide sufficient information about the research included in the article to enable one to decide whether the research is relevant to one's practice, which is one of the purposes of a review. As with all review articles, reading their descriptions of the research is not a replacement for reading the original publications.

In contrast to a narrative review, a **systematic review** is one *in which the search process, including search terms and sources, is specified. It can be a verbal or numeric review.* The goal is to include all research on the topic, and the specification of the search process enables the reader to judge how well that goal was achieved. Systematic reviews can be verbal or numerical; the latter is also called a *meta-analysis*, which is discussed in more detail below. Strang and Baia (2016), for example, conducted a systematic review of resident- and faculty-development programs regarding teaching in pharmacy. They provided information about the key words that were used as well as the search engines involved in their search, which produced 19 publications about 21 different programs. The specificity of their search terms enables any reader to make decisions about the likelihood that the authors may have missed some topics that should have been included. Interestingly, only one program was offered to existing faculty; the rest were programs for residents who intended to become teaching faculty. The review contains considerable detail about the elements included in the development programs, which enables one also to decide whether or not research about programs in pharmacy may be relevant to teaching development in other professions. The authors also noted that only one publication included measures of actual teaching behavior, and none of the articles included measures of student learning as a result of changes in teaching behavior.

It is also possible to engage in a quantitative analysis of previous research using statistical results as data. When statistical results are the source of existing data, the research is called **meta-analysis**, *the collective name for the various quantitative techniques used to combine the results of empirical studies; integrating research findings by statistically analyzing the results from individual studies* (Glass, McGraw, & Smith, 1981). Meta-analysis, also described in Chapter 7, has become a means by which to determine how strong a particular empirical effect may be, which is particularly useful when some researchers find the effect and others do not. Of key interest in a meta-analysis is something called the **effect size**, *a statistical term for the estimate of the magnitude of the difference between groups or the relationship between variables*. Effect size is reported in many different ways (Cohen, 1988; McShane & Bockenholt, 2016), so it is important to understand how effect size was calculated in the article you are reading. For those reported as a ratio, usually a ratio of mean difference over standard deviation, effect sizes are larger as they exceed 1.00. For those reported as proportions (or percentages), larger effect sizes are those approaching 1.00 (or 100%).

For example, Hall et al. (2015) conducted a systematic review of studies of implicit racial bias among healthcare professionals. Their search process is described in considerable detail (almost an entire page) and includes a report of interrater reliability regarding judgments for inclusion and exclusion of studies. Among the 15 studies they reviewed, only one found no evidence of bias against people of color. The proportional effect size they calculated was 0.34, which indicates a moderate effect. Reports of meta-analyses also include a measure of **heterogeneity**, which is *a measure of the inconsistency of the results among individual studies in a meta-analysis*. Hall et al. (2015) reported little heterogeneity; there was a great deal of consistency among the studies they reviewed. Meta-analyses should be read as critically as any other publication; how a particular meta-analysis is done will affect its utility and relevance to your practice. A systematic review and meta-analysis by Uttl, White, and Gonzalez (2016), for example, contains a thorough critique of previous meta-analyses on the topic of student course evaluations and their relationship to student learning. Uttl et al. reanalyzed the existing literature and concluded that there is no relationship between liking a course and the amount learned during the course. It is unlikely, however, that theirs will be the last word on the topic; as I have noted often herein, research generates more knowledge, but there is always more research to be done.

METHODOLOGICAL ISSUES IN EXISTING DATA ANALYSIS

As with all research, critical reading of archival research requires that we make explicit decisions about the match between the units of analysis and the conclusions drawn. Durkheim (1951/1897), for example, analyzed regional suicide rates but drew conclusions about individual suicide rates. *A mismatch between units of analysis and the research hypothesis* is known as an **ecological fallacy**. A specific type of ecological fallacy is **reductionism**, *the logical fallacy of drawing conclusions about individuals' behaviors from units of analysis that do not deal with individuals.*

Durkheim's data dealt with groups, but his hypotheses were about individuals. Consider his conclusion regarding religious affiliation: Catholics committed fewer suicides because their religion reduced anomie. That hypothesis was tested by comparing the suicide rates in predominantly Catholic regions with the rates in predominantly Protestant regions. Babbie (1983) suggested that it may be that Catholics committed just as many suicides as Protestants but did so in predominantly Protestant areas. Certainly, Durkheim's explanation seems more plausible than the notion of Catholics (but not Protestants) traveling away from home to commit suicide. On the other hand, proponents of either hypothesis cannot claim to have clear empirical support from Durkheim's data.

Similarly, Uttl et al. (2016) argued that previous reviewers used study as the unit of analysis in their meta-analyses of student evaluations and learning and therefore incorporated sample size into their meta-analysis. Even so, *study* was still the unit of analysis for Uttl et al.; they adjusted the influence of each study based on its size, but they still used *study* as the unit of analysis. Our conclusions from reading archival research are subject to the same logic; aggregate data cannot be used to test hypotheses about the individual units that produced the aggregate.

Another threat to validity is the quality of the data. When reading archival research, we should look for explicit discussion of the quality of the archived data. Data collected for research purposes are generally going to be more reliable and valid than data collected for other purposes, but we should not assume that research data are always reliable and valid. When reading reviews, for example, we should look for a description of how the researchers assessed the quality of the individual studies included in the review.

Just as the researcher must rely on the original collectors of existing data for the data's validity, the researcher must also rely on them for the data's reliability. Again, consider Durkheim's (1951/1897) study. At the time the data were collected, suicide carried a much greater stigma for Catholics than for Protestants, and thus it is possible that some suicides in Catholic regions were mislabeled as accidental or due to some other cause. The suicide rates on which Durkheim depended for his research therefore may not have been reliable. Durkheim did not have direct experience with the data collection procedures, nor do most researchers who use existing data. Before drawing conclusions from research involving existing data, carefully examine the research procedures to ensure sufficient reliability and validity for your purposes.

SUMMARY

- Archival research includes any project in which existing documents or data are the units of observation. These may include novels, music, movies, and other reports as well as raw, aggregate, or statistical data collected by others.

- Content analysis may be used to answer questions of the general form "Who says what to whom, how, with what effect, and why?" Although any communication medium can be content analyzed, it is more appropriate to compare two or more messages than to draw conclusions about a single message.

- Coding in content analysis can involve either manifest content or latent content. Coding manifest content—concrete denotations—usually results in more reliable data because the coding is more objective. Although sometimes less reliable, coding latent content may be the only way to operationalize complex theoretical concepts.

- Quantifying data in content analysis can involve recording either the frequency of variables or the amount of time or space devoted to a topic in the message; either may be used for manifest content or latent content. Evaluative assertion analysis can also be used for messages that contain complex statements.

- Archival research involving existing data relies on data collected in the past, usually by other researchers. Analyzing raw data is the most flexible procedure, provided the operational definitions used to collect the data match those in the researcher's hypotheses. Aggregate data may be less flexible but may provide better operational definitions of complex concepts. Meta-analysis of statistical results limits the researcher to hypotheses about research studies but may be used to support conclusions drawn from narrative reviews.

- The analysis of existing data includes the potential problems of ecological fallacy and reductionism. The former occurs when there is a mismatch between the units of analysis and the research hypotheses, and the latter occurs when conclusions about individuals are drawn from aggregate data.

- When reading about research involving data collected by others, it is sometimes more difficult to determine their reliability and validity. Because you lack direct experience with the data collection procedures, a careful reading of the original procedures is the only way to determine whether the data fit your purposes.

EXERCISES

1. Find an article in which the authors report on content analysis research. Determine how many answers to the "Who says what to whom, how, with what effect, and why?" question were answered by the researchers.

2. Using the same or a different article, identify the unit(s) of observation employed in the research.

3. Find an article in which the researchers report on analyses of existing data. Identify the source of the data and what allowances the researchers had to make in order to use those data.

4. Find an article in which the researcher reports a meta-analysis. Identify the variables employed in the meta-analysis.

11

Survey Research

> *The latest research on polls has turned up some interesting variables.*
> *It turns out, for example, that people will tell you any*
> *old thing that pops into their heads.*
>
> —Caption from a cartoon by Charles David Saxon

OVERVIEW

The purpose of this chapter is to introduce the main issues regarding reading and using survey research. Survey research generally includes methods in which participants are asked questions directly. The questions may be part of an interview or a questionnaire and may be asked through one of several different procedures in a variety of media. It is extremely difficult to interpret the results of survey research if you know nothing about how those results are obtained, so you will learn about techniques for preparing survey instruments and which research purposes are most effectively accomplished via surveys. You will also learn interviewing, the way researchers administer a survey face-to-face or via a medium (telephone or computer), as well as learn about surveying, how researchers administer questionnaires through mail or other media. The relative merits of each technique will be discussed, and sampling issues specific to each technique will be examined.

INTRODUCTION

Survey methods are probably the oldest methods in the researcher's repertoire, and they are the methods with which the general public is most familiar. All of us have asked people for information, and all of us have been asked by others to provide information.

As humorously illustrated in the opening quote, however, there is more to survey research than simply asking people to provide information. How researchers conduct scientific surveys and how to evaluate such research is what this chapter is all about.

Survey research is a general label applied to a variety of different research methods that share a common purpose. **Survey research** involves *directly obtaining retrospective information from a group of individuals*. More often than not, it includes interviews or questionnaires, but it is important to keep in mind that the use of an interview or a questionnaire does not, by itself, define survey research methods; the procedure is not what defines the method but rather the method is defined by the manner in which the procedure is carried out.

Survey research methods involve obtaining information directly from the participants by posing questions. The questions may be presented orally, electronically, on paper, or in some combination, but the response comes from the person to whom the question is addressed at the time the question is asked; it is, so to speak, a live data collection technique. Thus, the researcher and the participant are working together to collect the data; the researcher asks and the participant answers. Even when questions are written on paper, you need to keep in mind the interactive aspect of survey research. Responses must be interpreted in terms of potential self-presentation effects and other effects related to recollection; thus, live does not refer to the researcher's being physically present while the questions are answered but instead refers to participants' awareness that someone (the researcher) is going to be learning about them through their responses.

Although interviewing and questionnaires may be part of any type of research project, the sample size helps to distinguish survey research from other methods. The sample size in survey research is generally large, although it is not possible to provide an exact range. A survey research project may include as few as 100 participants or as many as 300 million.

As you might expect, directly obtaining information from a group of participants is more efficient for some research purposes than others. Survey methods are most appropriate for description and prediction, although they may be used less efficiently for exploration and action. Even though surveys can sometimes be used for explanatory research, they typically are not used for explanatory research purposes because it is difficult to manipulate independent variables and assign participants randomly to conditions via survey techniques.

Description is perhaps the most frequent purpose for survey methods. The classic example is the U.S. Decennial Census, which includes a sample of hundreds of millions of participants. The relative frequency data obtained from the census are often used by other researchers as a basis for their sampling procedures, particularly those who want to obtain a sample representing a particular region of the country. On a smaller scale, the examinations you take in class can be considered a form of survey research. Your instructor, through a questionnaire called an *exam*, attempts to assess the relative amount of information you can correctly recall about the subject matter. Examinations, however, are missing at least one important ingredient of scientific research: The results are rarely reported to the scientific community.

The predictive survey research with which you may be most familiar is the use of college entrance examinations to predict first-year grades in college. The results of the research are reported, although their circulation is somewhat limited. A more traditional use of survey methods is the work of Hill, Rubin, and Peplau (1976), who attempted to determine the characteristics that predict the continuation or breakup of romantically involved couples. Although a number of variables were related to the status of the relationship, the predominant predictor was the general similarity of the two people. The more similar the two individuals in the relationship, the more likely they were to remain a couple during the two-year period of the study. Another traditional use of surveys is the Annual Time Use Survey conducted by the Bureau of Labor Statistics. Most recently, the Bureau surveyed almost 19,000 people regarding almost all aspects of their time use (Bureau of Labor Statistics, 2016). We will come back to examples of survey research, but first we'll briefly examine why survey research is inefficient for exploratory and action purposes.

Although survey research invariably involves either a questionnaire or an interview, you will soon learn that there is more to survey research than simply putting together a collection of questions. Surveys can be used for exploratory research, but not with any degree of efficiency. One of the first rules of survey research is to know what kind of information to collect. The survey instrument should be designed on the basis of a research hypothesis, a condition antithetical to exploratory research. More often than not, designing a good survey study involves too much time and effort for exploratory research purposes.

If the intended effect of action research is to change the opinions of a large group of people, survey methods are an appropriate means by which to accomplish such research. Back (1980), for example, described the important role of surveys in an extensive program of research concerning population control. The surveys were used to assess the effectiveness of information campaigns designed to change attitudes about population control in general and birth control as a specific means. Similarly, Strandberg et al. (2016) included survey research in their study designed to combat overprescription of antibiotics in primary healthcare centers. Survey research may help to pinpoint reasons for a behavior change, but surveys may not be the most efficient way to measure the change itself.

In general, any question that can be expressed in terms of the relative frequency of information can be addressed through survey research. Put another way, whenever a researcher wants to know what a lot of people are thinking but doesn't necessarily need to know why they are thinking that way, survey methods can be used.

SURVEY CONTENT

To be a critical consumer of survey research, it is important to understand that there are three different types of information that may be obtained from the participants in a survey research project: facts, opinions, and behaviors. Although most surveys include all three types of information, we will examine them separately. The words used to label the different types of information may be familiar, but they have very specific meanings in the context of survey research.

A **fact** is *an objectively verifiable phenomenon or characteristic available to anyone who knows how to observe it*. Often called *sociological* or *demographic characteristics*, facts include such variables as age, race, gender, income, and years of education. Facts are anything that can be verified independently. Hill et al. (1976) found that couples who were similar in age, education, and physical attractiveness were much more likely to remain in the relationship than were couples whose facts were not similar.

In most surveys, the word *fact* is somewhat misleading because respondents' self-reports are usually accepted without independent verification. That a survey fact can be verified doesn't necessarily mean that it will be verified, and respondents have been known to misrepresent themselves on a variety of different facts. Don't confuse the label as it is used in survey research with its use in everyday speech; just because someone says it's so doesn't make it so.

An **opinion** is *an expression of a respondent's preference, feeling, or behavioral intention*. Opinions can be objectively measured, but they cannot be verified independently. Suppose, for example, I declined a social invitation by telling my friends that I was going to stay home in order to finish writing this chapter. Thus, my stated intentions may have led my friends to believe that I intended to complete this chapter. But there is no way that those people could have verified that my intentions truly were to finish this chapter. I could have been going through the motions to make people think I worked hard, for example, while having no real intention of bringing the project to completion. As you read this now, however, you can verify the fact that I did complete this chapter, but at the time I wrote this, no one could have verified my intentions. Indeed, even though you know that I finished writing the chapter, you don't know that I did that work the same afternoon I declined that social invitation.

Therefore, the major difference between facts and opinions lies in agreement about the ways in which the two can be operationally defined. A researcher can operationally define my age in terms of the date of birth on my birth certificate, for example, and encounter little or no disagreement about that operational definition; it has inherent face validity as well as inherent reliability (anyone who can read my birth certificate and subtract two numbers can calculate my age). However, there may be considerable disagreement about the face validity of defining my intention to complete this chapter in terms of my sitting in front of the computer; that I'm sitting here with the file open doesn't necessarily mean that I intend to finish the chapter (all writers know that there are times when one is looking at a document with no intent to finish it). That differential consensus about operational definitions exists does not necessarily mean that facts are necessarily more valid than opinions. It does mean that the validity of facts is easier to establish than the validity of opinions.

Using agreed-upon operational definitions of opinions concerning closeness, love, traditional sex roles, and religiosity, Hill et al. (1976) found that all these variables were related to a successful relationship. In general, the more similar were the couple's opinions on these topics, the more likely the couple was to remain in their relationship. Also using agreed-upon operational definitions, Strandberg et al. (2016) found that there were few patient differences between clinics with a higher-than-average antibiotic prescription rate versus those with lower-than-average prescription rates. Patients in clinics with higher prescription rates were more likely to report that it was easy to get an appointment and were less likely to report that their purpose in visiting the clinic was to obtain a prescription for antibiotics.

The third type of survey content, **behavior**, refers to *an action or actions completed by a respondent*. A typical behavior question may be worded something like, "How many times did you attend your research methods class this week?" Like facts, behaviors can be verified but only if a witness or indirect evidence can be obtained. Hill et al. (1976), for example, included questions about such behaviors as frequency of sexual intercourse and cohabitation. Clearly, the former is more difficult to verify than the latter. Interestingly, respondents' self-reports of these behaviors were not related to the success of their relationships. Strandberg et al. (2016) obtained actual prescription data as well as observed patient interactions with nurses, physicians, and others in the clinics.

One difference between behavior and opinion is that behavior involves observed or reported completion of action (How many times did you attend class?), whereas opinion includes intention to engage in an action (How many times will you attend your class next week?). Like facts, behaviors can either be verified through observation or measured through self-report. You must keep in mind that self-reports are not the same as verified independent evidence; information from the two sources doesn't always agree.

Within any categorization system, there always seem to be things that do not fit cleanly. Knowledge is one of these things. Because most of their respondents were college students, Hill et al. (1976) attempted to assess knowledge through SAT math and verbal scores. Strandberg et al. (2016) attempted to measure knowledge through questions such as whether or not antibiotics help against viruses (they don't) or help against a cold (they don't). Other researchers may measure knowledge in other subject areas, but the problem involves determining whether or not, for the purposes of analysis, knowledge should be considered a fact (an SAT score is verifiable) or a behavior (an attempt to remember information) or an opinion (a belief that the knowledge area is important). The resolution to the problem depends on the research purposes: If the researcher is using knowledge as an operational definition of a behavior, then treating the variable as a behavior measure is a solution.

Because most surveys include all three types of content, there is a tendency to disregard distinctions among them. Do not fall prey to this tendency. As you will learn later in this chapter, some types of content are best given precedence over other types of content. If you don't pay attention to the type of content in a survey, you may introduce considerable error into your interpretation of the results and thereby introduce error into your practice. The nature of self-report information already introduces some error into survey research (Mingnan, Sunghee, & Conrad, 2015; Newell, Logan, Guo, Marks, & Shepperd, 2015; Phillips, 1971), and there is no point to adding more error through careless interpretation of survey results.

SURVEY INSTRUMENTS

Just as the dials, gauges, and lights on the instrument panel of an automobile provide the means by which a driver obtains information about the car, the items on a survey instrument provide the means by which a researcher obtains information about respondents. The item topics, instructions, item formats, and arrangement of the items can all have an effect on the information the researcher obtains. In this section, you will learn enough about these issues to evaluate the quality of survey research in order to interpret results more accurately. The discussion is equally appropriate for interviews and questionnaires, with the exceptions that interviewers can be trained to overcome some instrument shortcomings while questionnaires cannot be altered once given to respondents. The discussion is also relevant to any data collected through a questionnaire, even if the research is technically not survey research. Some of what you read below will not apply to your critical analysis if you are not able to see the actual instrument as it was presented to the respondents, but the general considerations can be used to evaluate instruments even when you are privy only to a summary of the instrument. As you read articles involving survey research, look for information about these issues in the method section.

Survey Topics

Every survey instrument should have a topic—a central issue to which most of the items are related. Which topic is addressed, of course, depends on the researcher's interests and research hypotheses. The items included on a survey should be at least partially derived from theoretical interests. Although this may seem obvious and unnecessary, it is too often the case that researchers include items, and sometimes even create entire questionnaires, without giving enough thought to what questions are to be answered by the data. Such shotgun approaches to data collection rarely provide the wealth of informative data expected by those who use them, but that does not necessarily stop researchers from using a shotgun approach and, subsequently, reporting the results of the survey.

Some topics will be perceived as sensitive by the respondents, and questions dealing with these topics are likely candidates for responses based on self-presentation instead of accuracy. Data from such questions may be incomplete or reflect beliefs about what is appropriate. Respondents are generally unwilling to admit to illegal or socially deviant activities, for example, but they may also be unwilling to report even what seems to be innocuous information. In one survey (Dane, 1988a), for instance, respondents were unwilling to identify their employer. They had no reservations about revealing what they did for a living but did not want to tell us for whom they did it. Thus, survey results may often not contain information that you think should have been obvious for the researcher to include. The researcher may have included the questions but may not have obtained enough responses to enable the data to be analyzed and reported.

That certain topics or items may be sensitive, however, does not automatically mean that a researcher will not be able to obtain information. **Anonymity**, which *exists when no one knows the identity of the person who provides the information*, or **confidentiality**, which *exists when only the researchers are aware of the participants' identities and have promised not to reveal those identities to others*, can facilitate respondents' willingness to reveal such information. Years ago, Kinsey and his colleagues (Kinsey, Pomeroy, & Martin, 1948; Kinsey, Pomeroy, Martin, & Gebhard, 1953) were able to obtain interview responses on a topic as sensitive as sexual practices, and Hunt (1974) was able to obtain questionnaire responses on the same topic. More recently, Murdoch et al. (2014) demonstrated that incentives may play a larger role than perceived privacy regarding response rates, while Malavige, Wijesekara, Seneviratne Epa, Ranasinghe, and Levy (2015) found that relevance of the topic to the respondent is related to response rates. If survey research involving sensitive information may be relevant to your practice, you should have little difficulty in finding publications.

Survey Instructions

The instructions for completing the survey instrument can be used to eliminate some of the response biases mentioned above through assurances of anonymity or confidentiality. Of course, one must be careful to be sure that one can guarantee anonymity or confidentiality if one promises to do so (Stone, 2002). False claims are unethical and usually cannot be justified simply in order to produce better response rates or more accurate responses. As a consumer of survey research, you may not have access to the specific instructions used by the researcher(s), but there is usually a summary of the instructions included in survey research articles. You need to consider those instructions critically to understand the way in which the instructions may have affected the responses obtained in the survey.

The first part of any set of instructions should be a brief introduction to the study. When using a questionnaire, the instructions are usually placed on a cover sheet or in an accompanying cover letter. When conducting an interview, the introduction of the study is usually the first statement made to the respondents. The instructions should explain what the survey is about, how the results will be used, why the individual respondent's data are important to the study, and the level of anonymity or confidentiality with which the data will be treated. Ideally, the instructions will also include some mention of how respondents were selected to be included in the survey. The instructions don't need to contain great detail about the sampling procedures, but most respondents are interested in finding out how they came to be respondents and may become suspicious if they are not so informed.

More specific instructions about how to complete survey items are usually included throughout the instrument. Inclusion of sample items that illustrate the type of response or the length of responses for open-ended items tends to increase the amount of usable data (Dillman, 1978, 2007; Dillman, Gallegos, & Frey, 1976; Smyth, Dillman, Christian, & McBride, 2009). If more than one topic is covered by the survey, the items for each topic are usually separated by brief explanations about the kind of information desired. Something as simple as "In this section, you are being asked to provide your opinion about several political issues" would be an adequate transitional explanation. In general, any point at which the topic or response format changes is a good point to include transitional instructions. Such instructions need not be extensive; they should provide a transition to avoid surprising respondents and to inform them about how to provide the information desired. While reading publications of survey research, look for information about instructions in the method section. You probably will not find detailed instructions, but you should find mention of them. Malavige et al. (2015), for example, wrote only "The invitation pack contained a personalized invitation letter, information sheet and the consent form" (p. 2), followed by information about the languages into which the materials were translated. Although we cannot evaluate the specific instructions they used, their mention of instructions gives us an idea that instructions were important to them.

Survey Formats

The general layout of any survey instrument is not something to which you will be privy as a consumer, but understanding the variety of survey formats will enable you to evaluate survey results more critically. A great deal of information about the format can be gleaned from the more general description of the procedures that are included in comprehensive research reports. The format should, of course, be neat. One characteristic that contributes to neatness is space between items. Spacing prevents a cluttered appearance and makes it less likely that a respondent or interviewer will skip an item. Researchers who are tempted to make the instrument appear shorter than it is by crunching the items together generally have problems with inaccurate or missing responses. The respondent who begins to tire before turning the first page (or before noticing the interviewer turning the first page) is probably going to decide that the remainder of the instrument will require too much time and effort. Short is not necessarily better; what is better is anything that helps the respondent to understand.

Response formats for specific items were discussed in detail in Chapter 5. However, some general considerations need to be addressed here. Regardless of the format selected, the researcher should be sure the respondents and interviewers understand how to use the format. If a researcher asks an open-ended question—the kind of question asked on essay exams—the researcher should be sure to allow sufficient space to write a response (Smyth et al., 2009) or, in an interview, pause long enough to allow the respondent to answer the question fully. If the respondent is to choose from among multiple choices, the choices should represent the range of possible responses and be mutually exclusive. If the response involves choosing a point on a continuum, then clear labels for the endpoints of the continuum should be included. If you have an opportunity to see actual survey items, think critically about them. Your ability to understand the labels used by the researcher is an indication of the likelihood that the respondents also understood the labels.

Arrangement of Survey Items

Items within the instrument are often arranged to reduce response bias or other forms of unusable data. Within a section dealing with a particular topic, for example, the more sensitive items are generally placed toward the end of the section. Respondents should be gently led toward more sensitive items, not hit over the head with them.

For questionnaires, the first set of items should deal with the most interesting but least threatening topic and should be directly related to the overall purpose of the survey. At the beginning, the researcher is trying to get the respondent interested in completing the instrument, and one way to do this is to create the impression that the instrument actually does accomplish the purpose outlined in the cover letter. Factual items—age, race, and so forth—should be placed toward the end of the questionnaire.

For interviews, nonthreatening factual items—length of time at current address, age, and so on, but not income—are best placed first. They allow the interviewer to establish rapport without having to challenge the participant. Factual items help the interviewer to appear genuine and increase the likelihood that the respondent will indeed begin to respond; once begun, an interview is likely to be completed. As with a questionnaire, threatening items, even if they are factual, should be placed near the end of the interview. Thus, the same set of items would best be presented in somewhat different order for a questionnaire than for an interview.

In many survey instruments, some form of contingency item is necessary. A **contingency item** is *an item on a survey that is relevant only if a certain response was provided for a previous item.* A loan application, which is essentially a survey of your credit history, often requests a previous address if you have been at your current address for less than three years. Similarly, an item for which the respondent indicates that he or she is a registered voter might be followed by a contingency item such as "In what year, then, did you last vote in a national election?"

When only one or two contingency items follow a particular item, researchers usually offset them simply by using different margins. Different margins indicate that the item is special in some way, much the same way that different margins for extensive quotes in a manuscript indicate that the material is from a different author. If a series of contingency items is appropriate—say, 10 items for registered voters and 10 different ones for those not registered to vote—the researcher will usually instruct the respondent to skip to the appropriate section.

The order of items is important when leading respondents into sensitive topics and when dealing with contingency items. Order, however, can both create and eliminate response bias. People have a tendency to want to appear consistent (Muste, 2014), and a series of items on the same topic may lead respondents to alter their responses to later items just to be consistent with their earlier responses. Not many people are willing to admit that they haven't voted in the last 10 years, for example, after they've indicated that voting is an important responsibility of every good citizen. Similarly, a series of items on one topic may influence responses to items on a different topic. Responding to 20 items about the threat of terrorism, for example, is likely to alter responses to a subsequent series of items dealing with budget allocations. Response bias can occur as a result of the order of the items, even if the items themselves are not biased.

Unfortunately, there is little a researcher can do to prevent response bias due to the order of items. Randomizing the order of items may reduce the bias, but it is also likely to confuse respondents. Few people enjoy being questioned when the topic of inquiry is constantly changing. What can be done, however, is to estimate the extent to which order bias exists. If there is reason to suspect order bias, researchers might prepare different versions of the instrument and compare the responses, much the same way that researchers using a repeated-measures design in an experiment (Chapter 6) will test **order effects** (*changes in participant responses resulting from the sequence in which they experience multiple levels of an independent variable*). This procedure is best done when pretesting an instrument, but different versions of the final instrument may be required under some circumstances. If you don't read anything about dealing with response biases in an article, then you need to consider carefully the possibility that some of the survey results may be biased and adjust your interpretation accordingly. As with other threats to internal validity, it is not sufficient merely to suspect that bias might have occurred; a critical interpretation includes understanding explicitly how the bias may have occurred and how the bias may have affected the results of the research.

Pretesting Survey Instruments

I'll go out on the proverbial limb and state that pretesting is the most important phase of survey research. It's a sturdy limb; no survey data can be trusted fully unless the researcher can be sure the respondents understood the instrument and provided appropriate responses. In addition to editing the instrument to avoid various forms of bias, pretesting is required to ensure that assumptions made while editing were reasonable. If you read nothing about the researcher's having pretested a survey instrument or there are no references to previous research in which the instrument was pretested, then you should become very suspicious indeed of the results.

Pretesting—*administering research measures or procedures under special conditions in order to evaluate the validity or reliability of the measures or procedures*—involves giving a draft of the instrument to a relatively small group of people. Pretesting allows the researcher to fine-tune the instrument in much the same way that a bench check allows a technician to evaluate a part before installing it. Pretesting is not exactly the same as a pilot test, however, because the researcher is not trying to make a test run of the entire research procedure; only the measures are tested. When reading about survey research, check carefully to make sure that the researcher(s) used pretesting to check on the reliability and validity of the measures. It was during pretesting (fortunately) that I discovered that respondents were unwilling to identify their employers, even though they were willing to provide their job titles. I had to rewrite that part of the survey instrument, but rewriting was better than getting no data at all.

Some researchers also conduct a **pilot study**—*a small-scale version of a research project in which the researcher practices or tests the procedures to be used in the full-scale project*. Normally, however, survey procedures are planned well enough to make a pilot study unnecessary (cf. Logan, Wolfaardt, Boulanger, Hodgetts, & Seikaly, 2013). Unless the procedure involves some sort of manipulation to create different groups—an experiment using survey procedures to measure the dependent variables—there is usually no need to conduct a pilot study in addition to pretesting, and you should not be concerned if the research article contains no mention of a pilot study.

ADMINISTERING SURVEYS

Every method for administering surveys has advantages and disadvantages, regardless of the amount of pretesting completed to facilitate proper administration. It is impossible to declare categorically that one method is better than any other. Research purposes, intended respondents, report audience, instrument length, and staff availability all enter into decisions about administrative procedures. Before interpreting any survey research results, carefully weigh the relevant aspects of the procedures used to collect the data.

Face-to-Face Interviews

In what was probably the first instructional volume on face-to-face interviews, Bingham and Moore (1924) described an interview as a conversation with a purpose. For our purposes, we can define an **interview** as *a structured conversation used to complete a survey*. The survey instrument provides the structure for the conversation, and collecting the data is the purpose. Face-to-face administration includes electronic surveys as well as in-person surveys; the method is characterized by one-on-one presence, although it can be used for focus groups, too.

The amount of structure in an interview depends on the amount of structure in the survey instrument. *Survey instruments that are essentially orally administered questionnaires* are called **schedules**, and they impose a high degree of structure on the interview. In some cases, schedules may consist of cards given to respondents; all the interviewer does is establish rapport, provide instructions, record responses, and answer the respondents' occasional questions (Gorden, 1969). Of course, establishing rapport, providing instructions, and answering questions are probably the most important things an interviewer does. Given the increased mistrust of strangers, however, a highly structured interview will probably produce a better response rate if administered through a mailed (paper or electronic) questionnaire or a telephone interview (Nederhof, 1981). Finch et al. (2015) increased their response rate by 40% by texting respondents to expect a telephone call through which they would be surveyed.

When items are likely to engender questions from respondents or the sequence of items is complicated, a structured interview is the most effective means for ensuring responses based on an accurate understanding of the questions. Structured interviews are also very effective when particular members of a household, such as the oldest person or employed individuals only, comprise the sample. In such cases, the interviewer will be able to ascertain the propriety of a potential respondent. Foldes-Busque et al. (2016), for example, used a structured interview in their study of the relationship between noncardiac chest pain and heart-focused fear among patients who experienced panic disorder.

In a partially structured, semi-structured, or **focused interview**, the *interviewer poses a few predetermined questions but has considerable flexibility concerning follow-up questions* (Merton, Fiske, & Kendall, 1956). Focused interviews are typically used when respondents consist of a specific group chosen for their familiarity with the research topic. A focused interview might be used to survey graduating seniors as part of an evaluation of the quality of a major program or for some other type of exit interview. As you might expect, it is also important that the interviewer be somewhat familiar with the topic; otherwise, the interviewer will be at a loss when the time comes to generate follow-up questions. The primary emphasis of a focused interview is gaining information about the subjective perceptions of respondents.

The major advantage of a focused interview is its flexibility, but that is also its major disadvantage. The flexibility enables the interviewer to explore more fully the opinions and behaviors of respondents; thus, the total collection of responses should contain more and more varied detail than would the data from a structured interview. On the other hand, because not every respondent will be asked exactly the same questions, it is more difficult to interpret differences obtained when responses are compared. Thus, because some questions (and therefore some responses) will be unique to a given respondent, comparisons across respondents are best limited to the predetermined questions to which everyone responds unless the researchers have conducted a content analysis (see Chapter 10) of the responses.

Consider an exit interview, for example, in which everyone is asked why they are leaving their jobs (Johns & Gorrick, 2016). Some might say they were dissatisfied with their position, which would naturally lead to a follow-up question about specific aspects of the position. Others may say they are leaving to take advantage of a better offer, which would lead to questions comparing the new offer with the current position. Still others may be leaving to make a career change, which leads to entirely different follow-up questions. Although everyone has been asked why they are leaving, it would make no sense to compare the three groups' responses to follow-up questions. The entire set of responses from each participant, however, may be subjected to a content analysis in order to determine the main themes underlying the responses. Comparisons may then be made across respondents on the basis of the themes rather than on the exact responses. When the *wording* of responses cannot be compared, the issues addressed by the responses may be comparable. Through content analysis, Johns and Gorrick (2016) were able to identify three themes—communication, promotion, and pay—as the primary reasons why individuals in their study chose to leave their current job.

The least structured kind of interview is the unfocused or **nondirective interview**, *in which the interviewer encourages the respondent to discuss a topic but provides little or no guidance and very few direct questions.* I've included nondirective interviews here to provide the full range of structures available for interviews, but they are often not used to conduct a survey. With little or no guidance from the interviewer, responses are likely to be so idiosyncratic as to make analysis quite difficult. Nondirective interviews are, however, often used in qualitative research (see Chapter 8) to obtain the respondent's point of view. Nondirective interviews were among the procedures used by Ball and Nicolle (2015) in their study of the mobility concerns among visually impaired individuals.

It is certainly reasonable to use a combination of interview structures within a single study. A combination of structures both ensures that at least a portion of the responses are based on the same questions and provides an opportunity to pursue a promising line of questioning with less structured probes. A **probe** is *a phrase or question used by the interviewer to prompt the respondent to elaborate on a particular response.* Indeed, all of the survey research cited above (Ball & Nicolle, 2015; Finch et al., 2015; Foldes-Busque et al., 2016; Johns & Gorrick, 2016) included combinations of interview structures,

If a researcher were conducting a survey of psychology majors about the relationship between satisfaction with research methods courses and intended career plans, one item on the schedule might involve having respondents rate (say, on a 10-point scale) the overall utility of their most recently completed methods course. If a respondent rated the course toward the "useful" end of the continuum, the researcher might follow up with a focused question, such as "What about the course did you find useful?" Such nondirective probes as "What else?" or "Can you tell me more?" could be used to obtain more comprehensive information. Often, however, the most useful nondirective probe involves simply keeping the pen on the paper and waiting for the respondent to continue talking. Should a respondent begin to drift off the topic, a probe such as "That reminds me, I wanted to ask you about . . ." will usually get the interview back on track.

Telephone Interviews

The telephone interview is an alternative to face-to-face interviews that had a justifiably bad reputation for many years. At one time, the primary problem with telephone interviews was, very simply, that not enough people had telephones. The size of the potential sample was relatively small, which introduced a fair amount of error into results obtained through telephone surveys. Today, however, the proportion of homes with telephones is sufficiently large to obviate the problem. According to the United States Bureau of the Census (1979), about 97% of homes in the United States had at least one telephone, and that was back in the 1970s. At about the same time, Klecka and Tuchfarber (1978) used a telephone survey to replicate a survey done via face-to-face interviews and found no appreciable differences between the results of their survey and those of the original interviews. Current estimates continue to be around 97% to 98%, estimated from the number of telephone numbers. Now, however, the same number can be accessed by more than one device. The bad reputation of telephone interviews is no longer justifiable.

The technique used to obtain respondents in Klecka and Tuchfarber's survey, and indeed in most telephone surveys, is known as *random digit dialing*. **Random digit dialing** is *a sampling procedure in which a valid telephone exchange is sampled from a region and the telephone number is completed with four randomly selected numbers.* For national surveys, area codes are randomly selected, then valid exchanges within each area code are randomly selected, and then the final four digits are randomly selected from a random number table or generated by a computer program. Nonworking or invalid numbers (such as a business instead of a residence) are removed from the list of generated numbers as soon as their invalid status is determined.

Random digit dialing can be entirely automated. Indeed, we all have received calls—usually attempts to sell us something—that even include a computer-generated message. One of the disadvantages to random digit dialing is that it is extremely difficult to obtain a specific sample, such as members of a particular economic, religious, or political group. The researcher may have to make many phone calls before he or she reaches enough of the right type of respondents. On the other hand, random digit dialing does overcome the problem of unlisted phone numbers. Siahpush et al. (2016) used random digit dialing in their study of the perceived influence of point-of-sale advertising on smokers. Apparently, displays, advertising, and promotions in stores all brought about cravings, which increased unplanned cigarette purchases.

Telephone interviews can overcome one of the major disadvantages of face-to-face interviews—generally low response rates. Steeh (1981), for example, observed a trend of declining response rates for face-to-face interviews. Since the 1950s, willingness to be interviewed in person has steadily decreased, making it more difficult to complete a sample. Hawkins (1977) studied face-to-face interview response rates in the Detroit area and noted a decline from an 85% response rate in the 1950s to a 70% response rate in the early 1970s. Similarly, Goyder (1985) found a distinct advantage of telephone over face-to-face administration methods.

Another major disadvantage of face-to-face interviews is their cost (Dillman, 1978, 2007). Nederhof (1981) noted that some face-to-face interviews can cost as much as $100 per respondent. Hawkins (1977) pointed out that interviews can require as many as 17 repeated attempts to locate and talk to a given respondent. Of course, using the telephone won't necessarily reduce the number of attempts to locate a respondent, but a phone call is certainly less expensive than a drive to the respondent's home.

There are other advantages to telephone interviews. Although not necessarily a major advantage, telephone interviewers do not have to concern themselves with their physical appearance. Also, calls made from a central office allow the interviewer to consult with a supervisor if a problem develops or a question arises that the interviewer cannot handle. An interviewer in the field must deal with such matters without supervision, which makes it more difficult to implement a consistent strategy for such occurrences.

Telephone interviews, however, are not a miracle cure for problems encountered with face-to-face interviews. Indeed, if the interview schedule is very long or complex, a face-to-face interview is more appropriate than a telephone interview. It is generally accepted that telephone interviews ought not to exceed 15 minutes, which is not much time to complete a lengthy instrument. Similarly, focused and nondirective interviews are more difficult over the phone.

Another disadvantage to telephone interviews is the relative ease with which the respondent can break off the interview (Amaya, Leclere, Carris, & Youlian, 2015). It is considerably easier to refuse to begin or continue an interview when not facing the interviewer. Furthermore, the telephone interviewer must obtain all information through direct questions. One cannot unobtrusively measure such variables as race, age, or relative economic status over the telephone.

Mail Surveys

Distributing survey instruments through the mail (paper or electronic) to a predetermined sample is an example of a **self-administered survey**—*an instrument the respondent completes without intervention by the researcher*. Self-administered surveys provide greater privacy for the respondent, but they also increase the likelihood of misunderstood items or incomplete responses. There is no opportunity to follow up a seemingly inconsistent response, which makes instructions for a self-administered survey more important than those for an interview.

As a means by which to *reach* a specific sample, a mailed survey is the least expensive, least time-consuming, and most effective administration method; indeed, most survey research about which you read will have been done through the mail or direct administration. However, mailed surveys also rank lowest among administration methods with respect to response rates for reasons we'll discuss next. E-mail–based surveys, however, tend to have a lower response rate than on-paper surveys (Paolo, Bonaminio, Gibson, Partridge, & Kallail, 2000), but Amaya et al. (2015) have demonstrated that a combination of telephone and mail produce higher response rates.

Surveys administered through the mail lack one very important ingredient—an interviewer. No one is there to answer questions about the items or explain instructions. It's also a great deal easier to throw a survey in the trash than to say no to an interviewer. Essentially, the more distant—physically and psychologically—the maker of a request, the more likely it is that the request will be refused (Latané & Liu, 1996). A survey researcher at the other end of a mailed questionnaire is about as distant as one can be. For this reason, a variety of practices have been developed to increase response rates by making the instrument, which is not distant, as inviting as possible.

Dillman (1978, 2007) has provided the most comprehensive set of practices designed to increase response rates. Known collectively as the Total Design Method or the Tailored Design Method (or TDM for those who like acronyms), these practices have been supported by empirical research. Some of the individual practices may seem to be mere gimmicks, but they do enhance response rates. Dillman views the survey research process as a **social exchange**—*an interpersonal relationship in which an individual's willingness to enter or remain in the relationship depends on expectations of rewards and costs* (Dykema et al., 2015; Kelley & Thibault, 1978). From that viewpoint, a researcher must make completing and returning a questionnaire worthwhile for the prospective respondent. Dillman's TDM involves making the instrument well organized and easy to complete, and through it, the researcher attempts to reward respondents by offering them copies of the research results.

A variety of other specific recommendations are incorporated into the TDM, and I suggest you read one of Dillman's books if you are interested. As a consumer of research, however, you are not likely to have an opportunity to conduct the kind of full-scale mailed questionnaire survey to which Dillman is referring. Nevertheless, the ideas and intentions underlying TDM can be incorporated into any survey research project. Essentially, getting a good response rate boils down to making respondents feel as though they are doing something worthwhile that also happens to be enjoyable and making sure respondents know that the researcher appreciates the effort they made. Good response rates, as you learned in Chapter 4, make it more likely that the sample represents the population of interest.

DATA ANALYSES IN SURVEY RESEARCH

How a researcher analyzes data depends on the research hypotheses and the types of measurement scales used. There are three general types of analyses appropriate for survey data: description, association, and elaboration. Within each of these types, you may encounter either categorical or continuous data. We'll examine each type of analysis in this section with sufficient detail for you to be able to determine whether or not a particular researcher analyzed data acceptably. If you are unfamiliar with these analyses, read Chapter 9, which provides considerably more detail about data analyses. As a result of

WikiProject Statistics (https://en.wikipedia.org/wiki/Wikipedia:WikiProject_Statistics), information about statistical procedures on Wikipedia is quite useful and accurate, which makes it a convenient resource for a quick overview of statistical tests. Detailed information about a statistic is best obtained from a textbook or professional book, of which there are hundreds. If you are fortunate enough to know one or know how to contact one, a statistician is always a great resource for additional information.

Description

The analyses best suited for descriptive purposes are generally referred to as *summary* or *exploratory* statistics. They include frequency displays and measures of central tendency (mean, median, mode) and variability (standard deviation, interquartile range).

Nominal data yield categories rather than amounts, which is why they are also called *categorical data*. Gender, religious denomination, and voting preferences are some examples of nominal variables. Frequency distributions are a common way to describe such data. Frequency distributions may also be expressed as percentages, such as, "75% of the respondents responded 'yes.'" You may encounter reports of the modal response—the most frequently chosen response alternative—for variables with more than three categories.

If the researcher has obtained a representative sample, you may read inferences about the population from which the sample was selected in the form of inferential statistics appropriate for nominal data. The most common of these, chi-square, usually involves a goodness-of-fit test. A **goodness-of-fit** test is *one in which data values obtained from one sample are compared to theoretical values to determine whether the two sets of values are equivalent.* The ultimate outcome of a goodness-of-fit test is a probability value—the probability that the obtained data fit the theoretical data. Chi-square tests are particularly common for survey data in which comparisons to earlier data are to be made or when comparisons between subsamples are necessary.

One example of a chi-square goodness-of-fit analysis is when television network anchors declare the winner of an election based on only 2% or 3% of the election returns. They are really saying that the obtained returns do not fit distributions of returns that would enable any of the other candidates to win the election. The actual returns are the survey data; the predicted distributions are the theoretical values to which the actual data are fit. The probability associated with the obtained data (the declared winner) fitting the theoretical values (one of the other candidates winning) is so low that the network is willing to claim that the obtained data could never fit the theoretical data in which one of the other candidates is a winner. Of course, they don't say all of that when they report the projected winner; they just say so-and-so is projected to be the winner on the basis of scientific polls (surveys).

Frequency distributions and goodness-of-fit analyses are sometimes used to describe continuous data, but they are not the most efficient way to report such data. Continuous data reflect amounts—more or less of whatever is being measured—such as temperature, annual income, and so forth. For such data, a stem-and-leaf display is more informative and efficient than a simple frequency distribution. If you are unfamiliar with stem-and-leaf displays, you may want to consult Chapter 9. It would be common to include a stem-and-leaf display in a report to be read by other researchers but probably not in a report for the general public.

Again, for continuous data, researchers will most likely report the mean for each variable as well as describe the variability by calculating the standard deviation or variance. The mean and standard deviation are usually the most efficient way to describe continuous data distributions.

For inferential purposes, the standard error of the mean can be used to determine the probability that a theoretical population mean falls within a range about the sample mean. Also described in Chapter 9, the standard error provides an indication of what the population mean should be if the sample is a random sample from the population. When the sample mean is very different from the theoretical mean, the researcher may conclude that the data are not from the theoretical population. It is essentially the same concept as a goodness-of-fit test, except that it is based on sample means instead of categorical distributions.

When the U.S. Bureau of the Census reports that the population is getting older, for example, it is really indicating that the mean age of the latest sample is considerably higher than the mean age of the previous sample; that is, the probability that the two sample means came from the same population is very low, and the Bureau is confident that the two means could not have come from the same population. A probability smaller than .05—less than a 5 in 100 chance—is usually low enough to make such a decision. When several groups are being compared, it is common to use an analysis of variance test, which is also based on the standard error of the mean.

Whatever statistics you encounter in a report of group differences, you must keep in mind that the researcher is trying to describe the fact that the groups are different. Unless the researcher has met the condition of random assignment and a manipulated variable, he or she should not do much more than speculate about why the differences are there. Speculation is, of course, permitted so long as the researcher clearly labels it as such.

Association

Surveys for which association (or correlation) analyses are commonly reported are those for which the hypotheses involve relationships between variables. One of the appropriate association analyses for categorical data is, again, a chi-square statistic. The procedure for association analyses, however, is a contingency analysis. **Contingency analyses** are *used to determine the probability that the results for one variable are related to the results for another variable.* Recall the Hill et al. (1976) survey of romantically involved couples in the Boston area. They performed contingency analyses to determine whether remaining a couple was related to living together. If the two variables were associated, the researchers expected a greater proportion of one kind of couple to have lived together than another kind of couple. They did not find evidence for that association; the proportion of intact couples who had lived together was not sufficiently different from the proportion of unsuccessful couples who had lived together.

Another way to word the above conclusion is to report that the probability that an intact couple had lived together was the same as the probability that an unsuccessful couple had lived together. Similarly, a researcher might report that breaking up was not related to cohabitation. All three statements are different ways to convey the same idea—that remaining a couple and living together were not associated in their sample.

The most common association statistic for continuous data is the correlation coefficient, also covered in Chapter 9. Hill et al. (1976) calculated a number of correlations from their data. They found, for example, that the correlation between the age of one member of a couple and the age of the other member was positive, $r = .19$, meaning that couples tended to be composed of individuals of about the same age.

Reading the results of correlational analyses is fairly straightforward—you will see the correlation coefficient and the probability associated with it, along with the degrees of freedom for the sample size. Going beyond the results, however, can be very tempting but should be avoided. If a researcher reports that parents' income and children's income are related—$r(98) = .50$, for example—you might be tempted to conclude that wealthy parents tend to give their children more money than do poor parents. Although the conclusion might make sense, it is not appropriate to draw that conclusion from the results. Unless the researcher has somehow managed to assign parents randomly to different levels of wealth, the researcher has not met the necessary conditions to claim a causal relationship. You know that parental and child wealth are related, but the methodology is not adequate to allow you to know why they are related.

Elaboration

The difficulty of being able to draw conclusions about causal relationships from survey data is one of the reasons why Lazarsfeld and his colleagues at Columbia University developed the elaboration model for analyzing survey data (Merton & Lazarsfeld, 1950). **Elaboration** is *a process in which data analyses are used to explore and interpret relationships among variables*. The logic of elaboration enables one to dissect a relationship by examining how it changes when additional variables are included in the analysis. The original outline of the method makes interesting reading, but you are better off reading about hierarchical chi-square, multiple regression, path analysis, and related statistics that are currently used as a form of elaboration.

The starting point in elaboration is an observed relationship between two variables. For illustration, let's assume a researcher has conducted a survey and found a relationship between parents' and children's wealth; at age 22, wealthy respondents are more likely to have wealthy parents. The researcher doesn't believe this relationship exists merely because parents are giving money to their children but would like to examine that and other hypotheses in order to more fully understand what's going on:

Why?

Parents' wealth $\leftrightarrow$ Children's wealth

Luckily, the researcher has some data with which to test some of the hypotheses suspected to explain the relationship:

Education?

Employment?

Direct support?

Parents' wealth $\leftrightarrow$ Children's wealth

Using the logic of elaboration, the researcher might first determine whether respondents with college degrees exhibit the same relationship between parental and respondent wealth as those who do not have college degrees. That is, could the relationship exist because wealthy parents can better afford to provide a college education for their children? If the relationship remains unchanged after separating the sample into those with and those without college degrees, then the researcher can rule out education as one of the explanatory variables. If the relationship is different for the two subsamples, then education becomes part of the underlying mechanism:

Parents' wealth $\rightarrow$ Education $\rightarrow$ Children's wealth

Essentially, elaboration enables one to control variables statistically that may contribute to (elaborate on) the basic relationship identified in the initial data analyses. Again, keep in mind that statistical control is not the same as actual control through manipulation. Just as matching is only a second-best alternative for random assignment, statistical control is only a second-best alternative for manipulating the independent variable in a true experiment.

Despite the remaining inability to draw fully supportable causal explanations from survey data, elaboration has a decided advantage over simply guessing about underlying mechanisms. The hypotheses that remain viable after elaboration are more likely to be supported by additional research; that is, the data already collected are consistent with the hypotheses, and it makes sense that additional data will likely be equally consistent.

When reading about elaboration (which may not be called *elaboration* in the article) or about any analysis dealing with association, you should avoid falling into the trap of ex post facto explanations. **Ex post facto explanations** are *untested causal statements applied to observed relationships*. (The phrase is Latin for "after the fact.") Suppose, for example, that a researcher determined through elaboration that parental wealth was related to respondent wealth more strongly for males than for females. If you proceeded to interpret this elaboration by concluding that males are more likely to inherent the family fortune, you would be guilty of an ex post facto explanation. The difference between genders is real, but the underlying mechanism (inheritance) is not something that has been tested with the data.

Elaboration and ex post facto explanation are often mistaken for the same process, but there is one very important difference between them: Applying the logic of elaboration provides a test of the proposed hypotheses; ex post facto explanation is nothing more than speculation. Granted, the test of a proposed hypothesis through elaboration is not as rigorous a test as would be obtained through an experiment or quasi-experiment, but it is a test.

There exists a chi-square analysis known as *hierarchical chi-square*, which can be used for elaboration when variables are categorical. As a consumer of research, however, you may only need to know that hierarchical chi-square analyses enable the researcher to employ elaboration in order to follow the researcher's presentation of results.

Elaboration can be accomplished using correlation coefficients for continuous data in much the same way as described in the example concerning parental and child wealth: Separate the samples and recalculate the coefficient. For continuous data, however, multiple regression analyses are more efficient and more statistically correct. **Multiple regression** is *a statistical technique for estimating simultaneous correlations among any number of predictor variables and a single, continuous response variable.* When multiple regression is used, the coefficients are called *regression coefficients*, and they can be interpreted in much the same way as correlation coefficients.

SUMMARY

- Survey research methods are used to obtain self-report information from research participants, mainly in order to accomplish descriptive or predictive goals. Although less efficient for such purposes, survey methods can be used for exploratory and action goals but rarely for explanation because it is usually too difficult to assign respondents randomly to different conditions produced by manipulating variables.

- The items contained in a survey instrument are used to measure facts, opinions, and behaviors. Facts are verifiable characteristics of respondents; opinions are preferences expressed by respondents; behaviors are reports of completed actions. Care must be taken to avoid response bias or incomplete responses to sensitive topics. Anonymity or confidentiality generally alleviates such bias.

- Instructions and formats should make it easy for respondents to complete the instrument. Pretesting should be used extensively to accomplish this goal.

- The face-to-face interview is the preferred method for administering relatively unstructured instruments, although it is also the most expensive method. Probes may be used more effectively with this than with any other method.

- Telephone interviews are less expensive than face-to-face interviews, but the acceptable length of a telephone interview is considerably shorter. The onetime problem of limited availability of samples because potential respondents lacked telephones is no longer relevant, but random digit dialing is necessary to reach respondents with unlisted numbers.

- Mail surveys can be used for relatively structured instruments, but care must be taken to ensure that the items and instructions can be understood by respondents. Mail surveys also produce lower response rates than interviews do.

- The Total Design Method (TDM) has been successfully used to increase response rates for mail surveys, and it has been demonstrated to be more successful than merely offering incentives. The TDM involves a collection of procedures that make the instrument pleasant to complete as well as worth the respondent's investment of time and effort.

- As the need arises, various administration methods can be mixed to obtain the best combination of advantages.

- Data analyses used for surveys depend on the purpose of the research and the type of data collected. Summary statistics are most appropriate for descriptive purposes. Association statistics are used for data analyses when predictive goals are to be met. Care must be taken, however, to avoid unsupportable cause–effect conclusions from association analyses.

- Elaboration is a logical process for analyzing data that enables one to test tentative hypotheses about relationships among variables, but it is not as rigorous a form of causal analysis as a true experiment. Ex post facto explanations are untested assumptions about association data. Although similar to elaboration analyses in the final outcome, elaboration involves a statistical test of the hypothesis whereas ex post facto explanations are nothing more than speculation.

EXERCISES

1. Find an article in which the authors report on survey research. For each variable, determine whether it can be considered fact, opinion, or behavior.

2. Using the same or a different article, determine whether or not the investigators pretested their survey instrument and identify the administration method employed.

3. Find an article in which the investigators employed a survey or interview for a descriptive purpose and explain to someone who did not read the article why the purpose is descriptive.

4. Find an article in which the investigators employed a survey or interview for some purpose other than description. Identify the researchers' purpose and explain to someone who has not read the article why they decided upon that purpose.

Epilogue

We have come to the end of our exploration of evaluating research. You have a solid understanding of a framework for evaluating almost any research project you encounter, and I hope you have a better appreciation for both the utility of research and the limitations of research. Along the way, you learned that the phrase *research proves* is meaningless, at least when taken literally. Researchers can demonstrate phenomena, predict outcomes, and test explanations to determine which is more probable, but they cannot prove that a particular explanation is true or that a particular phenomenon will happen in the future. You are able to distinguish among a priori logic, appeals to authority, tradition, and science, and you know the differences among the purposes of research—description, prediction, exploration, explanation, and action. You also know to ask, and answer, the important questions about research—who, what, where, when, how, and why. In short, you have a way "to counteract and eliminate as much intellectual error as possible" (Bartley, 1962, p. 140).

You have learned about sampling and how the sampling process affects the conclusions you may draw from the research, and you have learned about research design. Indeed, you probably learned more about research design than you thought you ever wanted to know, but now you can identify the flaws in most research projects. More importantly, you know that there always are flaws, that more research is always needed, but that need does not prevent you from forming tentative conclusions about a phenomenon, an explanation, or the implementation of a policy.

That is, you know how to use research to engage in evidence-based practice.

So, now what? The short answer is, "Use it!" Whatever you may be doing, whatever your profession may be, you are able to engage in evidence-based practice. You no longer have to assume—you can read and understand the relevant research. Also, make sure those who need to know about the research actually know about it. Help them to understand how the results can be applied to improve their practice. As well, make sure that you know about unreliable and invalid research and can correct the errors of those who are using less-than-worthy research to inform their practice. Help those who know less than you about evaluating research to distinguish between good research and not-so-good research and between relevant and irrelevant research. In short, promote evidence-based practice at every opportunity. Like it or not, you are now something of an expert on research—share that expertise!

Admittedly, the task may seem daunting at first, in part because it is much easier to rely on authority or tradition. In the middle of another long meeting, when someone says, "So-and-so did a study, so we know this will work," it can be difficult to ask who, what, where, when, how, and why; everyone just wants to make a decision and get on with the real work of figuring out what to do next. You know that the real work might never get done if the evidence on which it is based makes little empirical sense, if there is no evidence that the proposed protocol can produce the intended effects. Indeed, without critical evaluation of research applied to practice, the resulting protocols might have unintended effects and make real work even more difficult or do real damage.

Even though the task is somewhat daunting, you are well prepared to help bring about an evidence-based approach to practice. You know a great deal about research design and methodology and how to apply that knowledge. You also have many resources, in the form of the references for this book, to consult when you need additional information. You also have my e-mail address: Feel free to send your questions about research to me, including how to apply research. You may not have a great deal of confidence, but you are a knowledgeable person. Go use that knowledge; make the world a better place.

Glossary

a priori method (of knowing): in epistemology, this method defines knowledge as anything that appears to make sense, to be reasonable.

abscissa: the horizontal axis of a graph.

action research: refers to research conducted to solve a social problem.

activity: the extent to which the concept is associated with action or motion in a semantic differential scale.

aggregate data: measurements that have been combined at a level higher than the unit of observation.

alternate-forms reliability: comparing two different but equivalent versions of the same measure.

alternative explanation: any of a number of defined reasons why an independent variable is not the only suspected cause of changes in a dependent variable.

analysis of variance: *see* **ANOVA**.

anomie: a feeling that stems from a lack of integration into a social network; a general sense of instability or disintegration.

anonymity: exists when no one, including the researcher, can relate an individual's identity to any information pertaining to the project; when no one knows the identity of the person who provides the information.

ANOVA: analysis of variance; a statistic in which the variance among the means is compared to the variance among the observations to determine whether or not the groups represented by the means are too different to be considered samples from the same population.

archival research: any research in which a public record is the unit of analysis.

attrition effect: changes in the dependent variables caused by a loss of participants during a research project.

auditability: in qualitative research, refers to the use of memos to maintain an audit trail of the research process.

authority: in epistemology, believing something because the source of the knowledge is accepted as inherently truthful.

autonomy: the ability to direct oneself, particularly through the exercise of independent processing of information.

baseline design: pre-independent variable measures are compared with post-independent measures for a single participant.

behavior: an action or actions completed by a respondent.

beneficent subject effect: occurs when participants are aware of the research hypothesis and attempt to respond so as to support it.

blind rater: someone who is unaware of either the research hypothesis or the experimental group from which the responses came.

bracketing: in qualitative research, the processes whereby the researcher identifies his or her own experiences, assumptions, and other beliefs relevant to the participant's and sets them aside temporarily during the research.

case series: a study of several (usually similar) participants.

case study: intensive study of a single participant over an extended period of time.

categorical data: values presenting discreet qualities that cannot be meaningfully subdivided, typically measured as counts of things.

categorical measurement: *see* **nominal measurement**.

causal analysis: the logical process through which we attempt to explain why an event occurs.

chi-square analyses: statistical techniques used to determine whether the frequencies of scores in the categories defined by the variable match the frequencies one would expect on the basis of chance or on the basis of predictions from a theory.

cluster sampling: randomly selecting hierarchical groups from the sampling frame.

coding: attaching some sort of meaning to the observation.

community immunity: *see* **herd immunity**.

comparative format: a response format in which direct comparisons among various positions are provided to respondents.

concept: abstract word that is used to represent concrete phenomena.

concurrent validity: comparing a new measure to an existing, valid measure.

confidence interval: the inclusive, probabilistic range of values around any calculated statistic.

confidence level: the probability associated with the accuracy of an inferential statistic.

confidentiality: exists when only the researchers are aware of the participants' identities and have promised not to reveal those identities to others.

construct validity: the extent to which a measure represents concepts it should represent and does not represent concepts it should not represent.

content analysis: a research method used to make objective and systematic inferences about theoretically relevant messages.

content validity: *see* **face validity**.

contingency analyses: statistical procedures used to determine the probability that the results for one variable are related to the results for another variable.

contingency item: an item on a survey that is relevant only if a certain response was provided for a previous item.

continuous data: values representing placement along an ordered range; values representing positions on some interval.

control condition: the level of an independent variable that represents the absence of manipulation; *see also* **control group**.

control group: the group in a study composed of individuals who received the original treatment or no treatment at all; the group to which the treatment group is compared.

convenience sample or convenience sampling: selection based on the availability of participants or ease of inclusion.

convergent validity: extent to which a measure correlates with existing measures of the same concept.

correlation: a statistical procedure that estimates the extent to which changes in one variable are associated with changes in another.

correlational research: empirical studies in which the relationship between two (or more) quantitative variables is examined.

counterbalancing: a methodological tactic in which all orders of levels of an independent variable are employed in a within-subjects design to assess the impact that order may have on the dependent variable.

credibility: in qualitative research, the extent to which the research enables the consumer to understand (and perhaps visualize) the research participants.

criteria for growth: standards that can be used to decide whether one explanation or theory is better than another.

criterion validity: the process in which the validity of one measure is compared against another measure of known validity.

cross-sectional design: one measurement of different groups that represents different time periods.

cumulative scale: *see* **Guttman scale**.

deception: providing false information about the research project.

definitional operationism: failure to recognize the difference between a theoretical concept and its operational definition.

definitive study: a research project that completely answers a question; such a study does not exist.

dependent variable: the effect under investigation in an experiment.

descriptive research: a research goal that involves examining a phenomenon to characterize it more fully or to differentiate it from other phenomena.

descriptive statistics: used to summarize or represent some aggregate value from a set of data and are not used to make inferences about a larger data set or population.

design: the number and arrangement of independent variable levels in a research project.

determinism: the philosophical assumption that every event has at least one discoverable cause.

dimensionality: the number of different qualities inherent in a theoretical concept.

divergent validity: the extent to which a measure does not correlate with measures of a different concept.

double-barreled item: a single item that contains two or more questions or statements.

double-blind procedure: the raters (or investigators) and participants are unaware of the research hypothesis or of group memberships related to that hypothesis.

ecological fallacy: a mismatch between units of analysis and the research hypothesis.

effect size: a statistical term for the estimate of the magnitude of the difference between groups or the relationship between variables.

elaboration: a process in which data analyses are used to explore and interpret relationships among variables.

element: *see* **sampling element**.

epistemic correlation: the theoretical relationship between the true component of a measure and the concept it represents.

epistemology: the study of the nature of knowledge, of how we know what we know.

equal-appearing interval technique: a scaling technique that produces a series of items, each of which represents a particular point value on the continuum being measured; also known as a **Thurstone scale**.

ethnography: a research method involving lengthy observation of and interaction with members of a group to understand their culture.

evaluation: the overall positive or negative meaning attached to the concept in a semantic differential scale.

evaluation apprehension: concern about being observed.

ex post facto explanations: untested causal statements applied to observed relationships.

existing data: the archived results of research accomplished by someone else.

experimental research: the general label applied to methods developed for the specific purpose of testing causal relationships.

experimenter bias: the researcher's differential treatment of experimental groups.

expert validity: *see* **face validity**.

explanatory research: a research goal that involves testing a cause–effect relationship between two or more phenomena.

exploratory research: a research goal that involves an attempt to determine whether or not a phenomenon exists.

expressive subculture: one characterized by an emphasis on feelings over accomplishment.

external validity: the relationship between the research experience and everyday experience; the similarity between the physical and social aspects of the research environment and the target environment; the extent to which the data may be generalized beyond the research project.

face validity: consensus that a measure represents a particular concept.

fact: an objectively verifiable phenomenon or characteristic available to anyone who knows how to observe it.

factor analysis: a statistical technique used to separate continuous variables into groups of variables that can be interpreted as single dimensions of a multidimensional concept.

factorial design: a research design that includes more than one independent variable.

focused interview: technique in which an interviewer poses a few predetermined questions but has considerable flexibility concerning follow-up questions.

forced-choice format: a response format in which the respondents must choose between discrete and mutually exclusive options.

found experiment: *see* **quasi-experiment**.

generalize: to relate the findings gathered from the research situation to other situations.

goodness-of-fit test: one in which data values obtained from one sample are compared to theoretical values to determine whether the two sets of values are equivalent.

graphic format: an item on which responses are presented along a graded continuum and the respondent chooses one of the options.

grounded theory: in qualitative research, a method that involves an inductive process of developing explanations from data.

Guttman scale: a scale on which it is possible to order both the items and the respondents on a single, identifiable continuum of measurement.

herd immunity: a form of indirect immunity for non-vaccinated members of a population resulting from reduced likelihood of contact with infected individuals because immunized individuals prevent the spread of the disease.

heterogeneity: a measure of the inconsistency of the results among individual studies in a meta-analysis.

heuristic value: the quality associated with stimulating a great deal of additional research activity.

historical research: the investigation of the past based on primary or secondary sources for the purpose of enhancing current knowledge.

history effect: a potential alternative explanation to the results of an experiment, produced whenever some uncontrolled event alters participants' responses.

hypothesis: a statement that describes a relationship between variables (plural is *hypotheses*).

implicit attitudes: evaluations of specific objects that occur without the individual's general awareness of the existence of the evaluation.

independent variable: the suspected cause under consideration in a research project.

inductive reasoning: a process of generalization; involves applying specific information to a general situation or future events.

inferential statistics: values calculated from a sample and used to estimate the same value for a population.

informant: usually in field research, anyone who is knowledgeable about the participants to be observed.

informed consent: the process by which potential research participants are provided with all of the information necessary to allow them to make a reasonable decision concerning their participation.

instrumentation effects: changes in the manner in which the dependent variable is measured.

intellectual honesty: the individual scientist's ability to justify the use of science itself.

interaction: a result that occurs when the effect of one variable depends upon which level of another variable is present; also called a **moderator effect.**

internal validity: the extent to which the independent variable is the only systematic difference among experimental groups; in nonexperimental research, the extent to which methods and procedures enable the stated purpose(s) of the research.

interpretation: the process whereby recorded observations are used to describe events, generate hypotheses, or test hypotheses.

interquartile range: a measure of variability or degree of dispersion calculated by the difference between the values representing the 75th and 25th percentiles in a distribution of scores.

interrater reliability: the consistency with which raters or observers make judgments.

interrupted time-series design: a design in which the implementation of the independent variable is experienced as a change in the normal stream of events in participants' lives.

interval measurement: a level of measurement that involves a continuum divided into equally spaced or equally valued parts.

intervention: *see* **manipulation**.

interview: a structured conversation used to complete a survey.

item bias: the extent to which the wording or placement of an item (question, rating, etc.) affects someone's response to the item.

item-total reliability: an estimate of the consistency of one item with respect to other items on a measure.

itemized format: any response format that involves presenting a continuum of statements representing various choice options.

key-informant sampling: *see* **snowball sampling**.

latent content: inferred, underlying, or hidden meaning in material that makes up an archive.

Likert scale: a unidimensional measure containing items reflecting extreme positions on a continuum, items with which people are likely either to agree or to disagree.

literature: the generic term used to refer to the collection of articles, chapters, and books that contain research results relevant to a particular topic.

logical positivism: a philosophy of science that asserted that theories could be demonstrated to be correct, or at least confirmed, through sufficient collection of quantifiable data.

longitudinal designs: designs in which the same participants are repeatedly measured over time.

main effect: occurs when different levels of one independent variable evidence different results in the dependent variable.

maleficent subject effect: occurs when participants are aware of the research hypothesis and attempt to respond in a way that will undermine it.

manifest content: the physical or noninferential material that makes up an archive.

manipulation: procedures employed by researchers to create differences between groups of participants or to change participants over time.

MANOVA: multivariate analysis of variance; one of the more complicated forms of ANOVA; employed whenever two or more dependent variables are analyzed simultaneously, usually because there is reason to believe that the multiple dependent variables are related in some way.

matching: an attempt to equalize scores across groups on any relevant variable(s).

maturation: any process that involves systematic change over time, regardless of specific events.

mean: the arithmetical average of a set of scores.

measurement: a process through which the kind or intensity of something is determined.

median: the 50th percentile score, which separates the lower and upper halves of a distribution of scores.

mediation analysis: a technique in which the importance of a given variable is examined as part of a suspected chain of variables in an existing relationship.

meta-analysis: the collective name for the various quantitative techniques used to combine the results of empirical studies, integrating research findings by statistically analyzing the results from individual studies.

microaggressions: insults or other type of denigration directed toward individuals or groups.

mixed method study: one in which both quantitative and qualitative research is included in a single project.

mode: the most frequent score in a set of scores.

moderator effect: a result that occurs when the effect of one variable depends upon which level of another variable is present; also called an **interaction effect.**

mortality effects: a type of attrition caused by the death of participants during the project.

multiple regression: a statistical technique for estimating simultaneous correlations among any number of predictor variables and a single, continuous response variable.

multivariate analysis: *see* **MANOVA.**

mundane realism: the extent to which the experience of research participants is similar to the experiences of everyday life.

narrative review: a verbal, as opposed to numerical, description of the state of the literature.

natural event: an event that is not created, sustained, or discontinued solely for research purposes.

natural experiment: *see* **quasi-experiment.**

nominal measurement: determining the presence or absence of a characteristic; it is naming a quality.

nonconscious ideology: a prejudice that has lost its label as prejudice and has become an implicit assumption that strongly affects the roles of certain members of a society.

nondirective interview: a technique in which the interviewer encourages the respondent to discuss a topic but provides little or no guidance and very few direct questions.

nonjustificationism: a philosophy of science in which the major premise is that we cannot logically prove that the way we go about doing research is correct in any absolute sense.

nonparametric group comparisons: statistics that compare groups based on medians or other distributional characteristics than means.

nonprobability sampling: any procedure in which elements have unequal chances for being included in the sample.

null hypothesis: a proposed result indicating that there are no differences between groups or no relationship between variables.

objectivity: an observation that can be replicated (observed by more than one person under a variety of different conditions).

operational definitions: concrete representations of abstract theoretical concepts.

opinion: an expression of a respondent's preference, feeling, or behavioral intention.

order effects: changes in participant responses resulting from the sequence in which they experience multiple levels of an independent variable.

ordinal measurement: a level of measurement in which scores are ranked or otherwise placed in order with respect to the intensity for a quality.

outgroup derogation: discrimination against individuals who do not share the same social membership.

overgeneralization: drawing conclusions too far beyond the scope of immediate observation.

paradigm: a logical system that encompasses theories, concepts, models, procedures, and techniques.

parameter: a value associated with a population.

participant bias: any intentional effort on the part of participants to alter responses for the purpose of self-presentation.

participant characteristics: variables that differentiate participants but cannot be manipulated and are not subject to random assignment.

phenomenology: the philosophical position that there are individual differences with respect to the experience of reality.

philosophy of science: any set of rules that defines what is acceptable, empirical knowledge.

pilot study: a small-scale version of a research project in which the researcher practices or tests the procedures to be used in the full-scale project.

placebo: a treatment that appears to be real but is not effective.

population: all possible units or elements that theoretically could be included in research.

potency: the overall strength or importance of the concept in a semantic differential scale.

power: in statistics, the probability of correctly rejecting the null hypothesis or the probability of finding an effect that really is there.

pragmatic action: determining how we should go about putting a scientific approach into practice.

predestination: the philosophical assumption that events are unalterable and that, once initiated, events cannot be changed.

prediction: a research goal that involves identifying relationships that enable us to speculate about one thing by knowing about some other thing.

predictive research: involves any study in which the purpose is to determine whether a relationship between variables exists such that one can use one of the variables in place of another.

predictive validity: established by comparing a measure with the future occurrence of another, highly valid measure.

predictor variable: the measure one hopes will predict the response or outcome variable in predictive research.

pretest: a measure of the dependent variable that is administered before intervention or treatment so that change can be determined.

pretesting: administering research measures or procedures under special conditions in order to evaluate the validity or reliability of the measures or procedures.

primary sources: period artifacts that may include an original, direct account created at the time being considered.

probability sampling: any technique that ensures a random sample.

probe: a phrase or question used by the interviewer to prompt the respondent to elaborate on a particular response.

propensity scoring: statistically matching participants on a variety of variables or measures to rule out those variables as alternative explanations.

publication bias: in meta-analysis, an estimate of the influence produced by the tendency of journal editors to be more likely to publish manuscripts in which statistically significant effects are included.

purposive sampling: procedures directed toward obtaining a certain type of element.

Q-sort: a scale used to measure an individual's relative positioning or ranking of a variety of different concepts.

qualitative research: the general label applied to a collection of methods used to obtain information about lived experience.

quasi-experimental designs: research designs that approximate experimental designs but do not include random assignment to conditions.

quota sampling: selecting sampling elements on the basis of categories assumed to exist within the population.

random assignment: any procedure that provides all participants with an equal opportunity to experience any given level of the independent variable.

random digit dialing: a sampling procedure in which a valid telephone exchange is sampled from a region and the telephone number is completed with four randomly selected numbers.

random sampling or random selection: any technique that provides each population element an equal probability of being included in the sample.

randomized controlled trial: another label for an experiment, usually used in health-related disciplines; *see* **experimental research**.

range: in statistics, the mathematical difference between the highest and lowest score in a set of scores.

ratio measurement: a level of measurement that involves a continuum that includes an absolute zero, a value of zero that represents the complete absence of a quality.

rational inference: a philosophical problem concerning the difficulty inherent in supporting any claim about the existence of a universal truth.

recording: making a permanent copy of the observation, usually in field research but relevant to all research.

reductionism: the logical fallacy of drawing conclusions about individuals' behaviors from units of analysis that do not deal with individuals.

regression equation: a formula for predicting a score on the response variable from the score on the predictor variable.

repeated measures design: a design in which the dependent variable is measured more than once for each participant.

replication: any repetition of a study.

representative sample: a sample that resembles the population within an acceptable margin of error.

research: a critical process for asking and attempting to answer questions about the world.

response variable: the measure one would like to predict in predictive research, the outcome variable.

ring vaccination: vaccinating individuals within a geographic circumference around index cases.

sample: a portion of the elements in a population.

sampling: the process of selecting participants for a research project.

sampling distribution: a distribution (or collection) of statistics theoretically created by repeatedly selecting random samples from a population.

sampling element: the single thing selected for inclusion in a research project.

sampling error: the extent to which a sample statistic incorrectly estimates a population parameter.

sampling frame: a concrete listing of the elements in a population.

sampling unit: *see* **sampling element**.

scale: a measurement instrument that contains a number of slightly different operational definitions of the same concept.

scalogram analysis: a determination of the extent to which the pattern of actual responses fits the ideal pattern of a Guttman scale.

scalogram scale: *see* **Guttman scale**.

scatterplot: a graph in which corresponding codes from two variables are displayed on two axes.

schedules: survey instruments that are essentially orally administered questionnaires.

science: the process of using systematic, empirical observation to improve theories about phenomena based on a set of rules that defines what is acceptable knowledge.

secondary source: any material that is not contemporary with the time in question and not produced by those who were present.

selection effect: an alternative explanation produced by the manner in which the participants were recruited or recruited themselves.

self-administered survey: an instrument the respondent completes without intervention by the researcher.

self-presentation: concern for the impression one makes upon others.

self-selection: any circumstances in which the participants are already at different levels of an independent variable.

semantic differential scale: designed to measure the psychological meaning of concepts along three different dimensions: evaluation, potency, and activity.

semi-interquartile range: a measure of variability or degree of dispersion calculated by halving the difference between the values representing the 75th and 25th percentiles in a distribution of scores.

simple random sampling: techniques that involve an unsystematic random selection process.

single-participant design: a design specifically tailored to include only one participant in the study; *see also* **case study**.

snowball sampling: a form of random sampling in which researchers obtain suggestions for other participants from those they have already observed.

social action: research conducted to solve a social problem.

social constructionist: a research philosophy that holds that all knowledge is changing and must be situated within a particular community.

social exchange: an interpersonal relationship in which an individual's willingness to enter or remain in the relationship depends on expectations of rewards and costs.

sociometric scale: a scale designed specifically for measuring relationships among individuals within a group.

split-half reliability: consistency measured by creating two scores for each participant by dividing the measure into equivalent halves and correlating the halves.

SQ3R: survey, query, read, recite, and review; a technique designed to enhance understanding while reading.

standard deviation: the square root of the value produced by dividing the sum of squared deviation from the mean by one less than the sample size.

standard error: the standard deviation of the sampling distribution of a statistic.

statistic: any numerical value calculated from a sample (as opposed to a **parameter**).

statistical regression effect: an artifact of measurement that occurs when extreme scores are obtained and the participant is tested again at a later time. The more extreme a score the first time a measurement is taken, the more likely that the second measure will produce a more average score.

stem-and-leaf display: allows a view of the entire data set as a distribution of scores without having to lose information about what the specific scores are; it also enables informal examination of differences among groups.

stratified random sampling: employing random selection separately for each subgroup in the sampling frame.

subject variables: *see* **participant characteristics**.

summative scale: any measurement scale for which scores are calculated by summing responses to individual items.

survey research: directly obtaining retrospective information from a group of individuals.

systematic random sampling: choosing elements from a randomly arranged sampling frame according to ordered criteria.

systematic review: a review of literature in which the search process, including search terms and sources, is specified. It can be a verbal or numeric review; *see also* **meta-analysis**.

t **test:** a parametric statistical analysis used to determine the probability that two group means are different.

temporal priority: the requirement that causes precede their effects.

testing effects: changes in responses caused by measuring the dependent variable.

testing–treatment interaction: participants experiencing one level of the independent variable may be more sensitive to testing effects than participants experiencing a different level of the independent variable.

test–retest reliability: measurement consistency estimated by comparing two or more repeated administrations of the same measurement.

Thurstone scale: *see* **equal-appearing interval technique**.

time-series design: a type of extended repeated measures design in which the dependent variable is measured several times before and after the introduction of the independent variable.

tradition: in epistemology, believing something because of historical precedent or because it has always been believed.

transferability: in qualitative research, refers to the extent to which the research is relevant to the consumers' interests; sometimes called *fittingness*.

units of analysis: the objects about which a researcher would like to answer a research question.

units of observation: the specific material, objects, or people to be measured in a research project.

vaccine hesitancy: the parental desire to delay or refuse vaccinations for their children.

validation by consensus: *see* **face validity**.

validity: the extent to which a claim or conclusion is based on sound logic; in measurement, the extent to which a variable measures the theoretical concept it is supposed to measure.

variable: a measurable entity that exhibits more than one level or value and serves as an operational definition of a theoretical concept.

visual analog scale: a type of response item with a continuous graphic display.

withdrawal design: the treatment (independent variable) is presented and removed several times for a single participant.

within subjects design: a design in which the same participants are exposed to more than one level of an independent variable.

worldview: the basic set of untestable assumptions underlying all theory and research.

References

Abu-Zidan, F. M., Abbas, A. K., & Hefny, A. F. (2012). Clinical "case series": A concept analysis. *African Health Sciences, 12*(4), 557–562.

Adams, G. R. (1977). Physical attractiveness research: Toward a developmental social psychology of beauty. *Human Development, 20*(4), 217–239.

Adams, G. S. (1964). *Measurement and evaluation in education, psychology, and guidance.* New York, NY: Holt, Rinehart & Winston.

Adams, P. J. (2007). Assessing whether to receive funding support from tobacco, alcohol, gambling and other dangerous consumption industries. *Addiction, 102*(7), 1027–1033.

Adams, S., Carryer, J., & Wilkinson, J. (2015). Institutional ethnography: An emerging approach for health and nursing research. *Nursing Praxis in New Zealand, 31*(1), 18–26.

Adsera, A., & Menendez, A. (2011). Fertility changes in Latin America in periods of economic uncertainty. *Population Studies, 65*(1), 37–56. doi: http://www.tandfonline.com/loi/rpst20

Ali, M., Debes, A. K., Luquero, F. J., Kim, D. R., Park, J. Y., Digilio, L., . . . Sack, D. A. (2016). Potential for controlling cholera using a ring vaccination strategy: Re-analysis of data from a cluster-randomized clinical trial. *PLoS Medicine, 13*(9), e1002120–e1002120. doi: 10.1371/journal.pmed.1002120

Allen, M. J., & Yen, W. M. (1979). *Introduction to measurement theory.* Belmont, CA: Wadsworth.

Amaya, A., Leclere, F., Carris, K., & Youlian, L. (2015). Where to start. *Public Opinion Quarterly, 79*(2), 420–442. doi: 10.1093/poq/nfv012

American Heart Association. (2006). 2005 American Heart Association (AHA) guidelines for cardiopulmonary resuscitation (CPR) and emergency cardiovascular care (ECC) of pediatric and neonatal patients: Pediatric basic life support. *Pediatrics, 117*(5), e989–1004.

American Psychological Association. (2010). *Publication manual of the American Psychological Association* (6th ed.). Washington, DC: Author.

APA Presidential Task Force on Evidence-Based Practice. (2006). Evidence-based practice in psychology. *American Psychologist, 61*(4), 271–285. doi: 10.1037/0003-066X.61.4.271

Archibald, M. M., Radil, A. I., Xiaozhou, Z., & Hanson, W. E. (2015). Current mixed methods practices in qualitative research: A content analysis of leading journals. *International Journal of Qualitative Methods, 14*(2), 5–33.

Arons, A. M. M., Krabbe, P. F. M., Schölzel-Dorenbos, C. J. M., van der Wilt, G. J., & Olde Rikkert, M. G. M. (2012). Thurstone scaling revealed systematic health-state valuation differences between patients with dementia and proxies. *Journal of Clinical Epidemiology, 65*(8), 897–905. doi: 10.1016/j.jclinepi.2012.01.018

Aronson, E. (1980). Persuasion via self-justification: Large commitments for small rewards. In L. Festinger (Ed.), *Retrospections on social psychology* (pp. 3–21). New York, NY: Oxford University Press.

Axelrod, M. I., Tornehl, C., & Fontanini-Axelrod, A. (2014). Enhanced response using a multicomponent urine alarm treatment for nocturnal enuresis. *Journal for Specialists in Pediatric Nursing, 19*(2), 172–182. doi: 10.1111/jspn.12066

Babbie, E. R. (1983). *The practice of social research.* Belmont, CA: Wadsworth.

Bachrach, A. J. (1981). *Psychological research: An introduction.* New York, NY: Random House.

Back, K. W. (1980). The role of social psychology in population control. In L. Festinger (Ed.), *Retrospections on social psychology* (pp. 22–45). New York, NY: Oxford University Press.

Bain, J., James, D., & Harrison, M. (2015). Supporting communication development in the early years: A practitioner's perspective. *Child Language Teaching & Therapy, 31*(3), 325–336. doi: 10.1177/0265659015596795

Ball, E. M., & Nicolle, C. A. (2015). Changing what it means to be 'normal': A grounded theory study of the mobility choices of people who are blind or have low vision. *Journal of Visual Impairment & Blindness, 109*(4), 291–301, 211p.

Bang, K.-S., Chae, S.-M., Hyun, M.-S., Nam, H. K., Kim, J.-S., & Park, K.-H. (2012). The mediating effects of perceived parental teasing on relations of body mass index to depression and self-perception of physical appearance and global self-worth in children. *Journal of Advanced Nursing, 68*(12), 2646–2653, 2648p. doi: 10.1111/j.1365-2648.2012.05963.x

Baron, R. M., & Kenny, D. A. (1986). The moderator–mediator variable distinction in social psychological research: Conceptual, strategic, and statistical considerations. *Journal of Personality and Social Psychology, 51*(6), 1173–1182.

Bartley, W. W., III. (1962). *The retreat to commitment.* New York, NY: Knopf.

Becker, L. J., & Seligman, C. (1978). Reducing air conditioning waste by signaling it is cool outside. *Personality & Social Psychology Bulletin, 4*(3), 412–415.

Bell, S., McCallum, R., Ziegler, M., Davis, C., & Coleman, M. (2013). Development and validation of an assessment of adult educators' reading instructional knowledge. *Annals of Dyslexia, 63*(3), 187–200. doi: 10.1007/s11881-012-0079-z

Bem, S. L., & Bem, D. J. (1970). Case study of a nonconscious ideology: Training the woman to know her place. In D. J. Bem (Ed.), *Beliefs, attitudes, and human affairs* (pp. 89–99). Belmont, CA: Brooks/Cole.

Berkman, D. (1963). Advertising in *Ebony* and *Life*: Negro aspirations vs. reality. *Journalism Quarterly, 40*, 53–64.

Betancourt, T. S., Frounfelker, R., Mishra, T., Hussein, A., & Falzarano, R. (2015). Addressing health disparities in the mental health of refugee children and adolescents through community-based participatory research: A study in 2 communities. *American Journal of Public Health, 105*, S475–S482. doi: 10.2105/ajph.2014.302504

Bingham, W. V. D., & Moore, B. V. (1924). *How to interview.* New York, NY: Harper and Row.

Bland, J. M., & Altman, D. G. (1986). Statistical methods for assessing agreement between two methods of clinical measurement. *The Lancet, 29*, 307–309.

Brookes, R. L., Hollocks, M. J., Khan, U., Morris, R. G., & Markus, H. S. (2015). The Brief Memory and Executive Test (BMET) for detecting vascular cognitive impairment in small vessel disease: A validation study. *BMC Medicine, 13*(1), 1–8. doi: 10.1186/s12916-015-0290-y

Browne, K. (2005). Snowball sampling: Using social networks to research non-heterosexual women. *International Journal of Social Research Methodology, 8*(1), 47–60. doi: 10.1080/1364557032000081663

Bureau of Labor Statistics. (2016). *American Time Use Survey: 2015 results.* (USDL-16-1250). Washington, DC: PressOffice@bls.gov.

Cain, D. M., Loewenstein, G., & Moore, D. A. (2005). Coming clean but playing dirtier: The shortcomings of disclosure as a solution to conflicts of interest. In D. A. Moore, D. M. Cain, G. Loewenstein, & M. H. Bazerman (Eds.), *Conflicts of interest: Challenges and solutions in business, law, medicine, and public policy* (pp. 104–125). New York, NY: Cambridge University Press.

Calati, R., Laglaoui Bakhiyi, C., Artero, S., Ilgen, M., & Courtet, P. (2015). The impact of physical pain on suicidal thoughts and behaviors: Meta-analyses. *Journal of Psychiatric Research, 71*, 16–32. doi: 10.1016/j.jpsychires.2015.09.004

Camara, W. J., & Kimmel, E. W. (Eds.). (2005). *Choosing students: Higher education admissions tools for the 21st century.* Mahwah, NJ: Lawrence Erlbaum.

Campbell, D. T. (1969). Reforms as experiments. *American Psychologist, 24*, 409–429.

Campbell, D. T. (1971, September). *Methods for the experimenting society.* Paper presented at the American Psychological Association, Washington, DC.

Campbell, D. T., & Fiske, D. W. (1959). Convergent and divergent validation by the multitrait–multimethod matrix. *Psychological Bulletin, 56*, 81–105.

Campbell, D. T., & Stanley, J. C. (1963). *Experimental and quasi-experimental designs for research.* Chicago, IL: Rand McNally.

Carlston, D. L. (2011). Benefits of student-generated note packets: A preliminary investigation of SQ3R implementation. *Teaching of Psychology, 38*(3), 142–146. doi: 10.1177/0098628311411786

Carroll, R. T. (2005). Alien abduction. In *The skeptics dictionary.* Retrieved December 2005 from http://www.skepdic.com/aliens.html

Cerdá, M., Morenoff, J. D., Hansen, B. B., Tessari Hicks, K. J., Duque, L. F., Restrepo, A., & Diez-Roux, A. V. (2012). Reducing violence by transforming neighborhoods: A natural experiment in Medellín, Colombia. *American Journal of Epidemiology, 175*(10), 1045–1053.

Chaplin, W. F., Phillips, J. B., Brown, J. D., Cianton, N. R., & Stein, J. L. (2000). Handshaking, gender, personality, and first impressions. *Journal of Personality and Social Psychology, 79*(1), 110–117.

Chase, S. E. (2011). Narrative inquiry: Still a field in the making. In N. K. Denzin & Y. S. Lincoln (Eds.), *The SAGE handbook of qualitative research* (pp. 421–434). Los Angeles, CA: SAGE.

Christ, T. W. (2013). The worldview matrix as a strategy when designing mixed methods research. *International Journal of Multiple Research Approaches, 7*(1), 110–118. doi: 10.5172/mra.2013.7.1.110

Cicchetti, D. (2014). On scales of measurement in autism spectrum disorders (ASD) and beyond: Where Smitty went wrong. *Journal of Autism & Developmental Disorders, 44*(2), 303–309. doi: 10.1007/s10803-012-1486-z

Cohen, J. (1988). *Statistical power analysis for the behavioral sciences* (2nd ed.). Hillsdale, NJ: Lawrence Erlbaum Associates.

Collins, K. M. T. (2012). Epilogue: Is mixed research science? Empirical evidence from the field of educational research. *International Journal of Multiple Research Approaches, 6*(3), 332–342. doi: 10.5172/mra.2012.6.3.332

Committee on Assessing Integrity in Research Environments. (2002). *Integrity in scientific research: Creating an environment that promotes responsible conduct.* Washington, DC: National Academies Press.

Cook, S. (1981). Ethical implications. In L. H. Kidder (Ed.), *Selltiz, Wrightsman and Cook's Research methods in social relations.* New York, NY: Holt, Rinehart & Winston.

Cooper, T. L. (1998). *The responsible administrator: An approach to ethics for the administrative role* (4th ed.). San Francisco, CA: Jossey-Bass.

Corrigan, P. W., Bink, A. B., Fokuo, J. K., & Schmidt, A. (2015). The public stigma of mental illness means a difference between you and me. *Psychiatry Research, 226*(1), 186–191. doi: 10.1016/j.psychres.2014.12.047

Costa, F., Adamo, M., Ariotti, S., Navarese, E. P., Biondi-Zoccai, G., & Valgimigli, M. (2015). Impact of greater than 12-month dual antiplatelet therapy duration on mortality: Drug-specific or a class-effect? A meta-analysis. *International Journal of Cardiology, 201*, 179–181. doi: 10.1016/j.ijcard.2015.08.058

Cox, J., Clark, J. C., Edens, J. F., Smith, S. T., & Magyar, M. S. (2013). Jury panel member perceptions of interpersonal-affective traits of psychopathy predict support for execution in a capital murder trial simulation. *Behavioral Sciences & The Law, 31*(4), 411–428. doi: 10.1002/bsl.2073

Cox, J., & Roche, S. (2015). Vasopressors and development of pressure ulcers in adult critical care patients. *American Journal of Critical Care, 24*(6), 501–511. doi: 10.4037/ajcc2015123

Crano, W. D., & Brewer, M. B. (1973). *Principles of research in social psychology.* New York, NY: McGraw-Hill.

Cronbach, L. J. (1951). Coefficient alpha and the internal structure of tests. *Psychometrika, 16*(3), 297–334.

Dalsgaard, S., & Morten, N. (2013). Introduction: Time and the field. *Social Analysis, 57*(1), 1–19. doi: 10.3167/sa.2013.570101

Dane, F. C. (1988a). *Community reactions to field testing genetically altered organisms.* Grant proposal submitted to Environmental Protection Agency, Clemson, SC.

Dane, F. C. (1988b). *The common and uncommon sense of social behavior.* Pacific Grove, CA: Brooks/Cole.

Dane, F. C. (1990). *Research methods.* Pacific Grove, CA: Brooks/Cole.

Dane, F. C. (2006). Ethical issues in statistical analyses: An argument for collective moral responsibility. *C-Stat News, 2*(3), 1, 3, 4.

Dane, F. C. (2007a). Ethics of stem-cell research: A framework for ethical dialogue regarding sources of conflict. [Electronic Version]. *Forum on Public Policy Online, Spring 2007.* Retrieved from http://www.forumonpublicpolicy.com/archivespring07/dane.pdf

Dane, F. C. (2007b, March). *Ethics of stem cell research: Sources of conflict.* Paper presented at the Oxford Roundtable Conference—Science and Religion: Is There Common Ground? Oxford, England.

Dane, F. C., & Parish, D. C. (2006). Ethical issues in registry research: In-hospital resuscitation as a case study. *Journal of Empirical Research on Human Research Ethics, 1*(4), 69–75.

Dane, F. C., Russell-Lindgren, K. S., Parish, D. C., Durham, M. D., & Brown, T. D., Jr. (2000). In-hospital resuscitation: Association between ACLS training and survival to discharge. *Resuscitation, 47*, 83–87.

Deaux, K., & Major, B. (1987). Putting gender into context: An interactive model of gender-related behavior. *Psychological Review, 94*, 369–389.

Dermer, M. L., & Hoch, T. A. (1999). Improving descriptions of single-subject experiments in research texts written for undergraduates. *Psychological Record, 49*, 49–66.

Descartes, R. (1637/1993). *Discourse on the method of rightly conducting the reason in the search for truth in the sciences.* Salt Lake City, UT: Project Gutenberg.

Devine, D. J., Clayton, L. D., Dunford, B. B., Seying, R., & Pryce, J. (2001). Jury decision making: 45 years of empirical research on deliberating groups. *Psychology, Public Policy, and Law, 7*(3), 622–727.

Dewey, J. (1929). *The quest for certainty: A study of the relation of knowledge and action.* New York, NY: Minton, Balch.

DiBennardo, R., & Gates, G. (2014). Research note: U.S. Census same-sex couple data: Adjustments to reduce measurement error and empirical implications. *Population Research & Policy Review, 33*(4), 603–614. doi: 10.1007/s11113-013-9289-2

Dillman, D. A. (1978). *Mail and telephone surveys: The total design method.* New York, NY: John Wiley & Sons.

Dillman, D. A. (2007). *Mail and Internet surveys: The tailored design method* (2nd ed.). New York, NY: John Wiley & Sons.

Dillman, D. A., Gallegos, J. G., & Frey, J. H. (1976). Reducing refusal rates for telephone surveys. *Public Opinion Quarterly, 40*, 360–369.

Doabler, C. T., Clarke, B., Fien, H., Baker, S. K., Kosty, D. B., & Cary, M. S. (2015). The science behind curriculum development and evaluation: Taking a design science approach in the production of a Tier 2 mathematics curriculum. *Learning Disability Quarterly, 38*(2), 97–111. doi: 10.1177/0731948713520555

Doniger, A. S., Riley, J. S., Utter, C. A., & Adams, E. (2001). Impact evaluation of the "Not Me, Not Now" abstinence-oriented, adolescent pregnancy prevention communications program, Monroe County, NY. *Journal of Health Communication, 6*(1), 45–60.

Duckworth, A. L., Kirby, T. A., Tsukayama, E., Berstein, H., & Ericsson, K. A. (2010). Deliberate practice spells success: Why grittier competitors triumph at the National Spelling Bee. *Social Psychological and Personality Science*, 1–8. doi: 10.1177/1948550610385872

Duckworth, A. L., Peterson, C., Matthews, M. D., & Kelly, D. R. (2007). Grit: Perseverance and passion for long-term goals. *Journal of Personality and Social Psychology, 92*(6), 1087–1101. doi: 10.1037/0022-3514.92.6.1087

Duckworth, A. L., & Quinn, P. D. (2009). Development and validation of the short grit scale (Grit–S). *Journal of Personality Assessment, 91*(2), 166–174. doi: 10.1080/00223890802634290

Duckworth, A. L., Quinn, P. D., & Seligman, M. E. P. (2009). Positive predictors of teacher effectiveness. *The Journal of Positive Psychology, 4*(6), 540–547. doi: 10.1080/17439760903157232

Duckworth, A. L., Weir, D., Tsukayama, E., & Kwok, D. (2012). Who does well in life? Conscientious adults excel in both objective and subjective success. *Frontiers in Psychology, 3*(356), 1–8. doi: 10.3389/fpsyg.2012.00356

Durkheim, E. (1951/1897). *Suicide.* Glencoe, IL: Free Press.

Dykema, J., Jaques, K., Cyffka, K., Assad, N., Hammers, R. G., Elver, K., . . . Stevenson, J. (2015). Effects of sequential prepaid incentives and envelope messaging in mail surveys. *Public Opinion Quarterly, 79*(4), 906–931. doi: 10.1093/poq/nfv041

Ellis, L. (1988, April). *The influence of feminist values on television viewing habits.* Paper presented at the Southeastern Psychological Association, New Orleans, Louisiana.

Ellison, J. W. (1965). Computers and testaments. In J. W. Ellison (Ed.), *Computers for the humanities* (pp. 72–74). New Haven, CT: Yale University Press.

Ellison, K. W., & Buckhout, R. (1981). *Psychology and criminal justice.* New York, NY: Harper & Row.

Elmer, J., Lee, S., Rittenberger, J. C., Dargin, J., Winger, D., & Emlet, L. (2015). Reintubation in critically ill patients: Procedural complications and implications for care. *Critical Care, 19*(12), 1–7. doi: 10.1186/s13054-014-0730-7

Eskreis-Winkler, L., Shulman, E. P., Beal, S. A., & Duckworth, A. L. (2014). The grit effect: Predicting retention in the military, the workplace, school and marriage. *Frontiers in Psychology, 5*(36), 1–12. doi: 10.3389/fpsyg.2014.00036

Ewy, G. A. (2014). Another step towards the acceptance of chest compression only CPR for primary cardiac arrest. *Evidence Based Nursing, 17*(1), 21–21. doi: 10.1136/eb-2013-101289

Fan, Y., Zhou, Y., Gong, D., & Zou, C. (2015). No evidence for increased prostate cancer risk among calcium channel blockers user. *International Journal of Cardiology, 201*, 255–257. doi: 10.1016/j.ijcard.2015.08.046

Farmer, J. L., Allsopp, D. H., & Ferron, J. M. (2015). Impact of the Personal Strengths Program on self-determination levels of college students with LD and/or ADHD. *Learning Disability Quarterly, 38*(3), 145–159. doi: 10.1177/0731948714526998

Feigl, A. B., Salomon, J. A., Danaei, G., Ding, E. L., & Calvo, E. (2015). Teenage smoking behaviour following a high-school smoking ban in Chile: Interrupted time-series analysis. *Bulletin of the World Health Organization, 93*(7), 468–475 468p. doi: 10.2471/blt.14.146092

Feilzer, M. Y. (2007). Criminologists making news? Providing factual information on crime and criminal justice through a weekly newspaper column. *Crime Media Culture, 3*(3), 285–304. doi: 10.1177/1741659007082467

Feilzer, M. Y. (2010). Doing mixed methods research pragmatically: Implications for the rediscovery of pragmatism as a research paradigm. *Journal of Mixed Methods Research, 4*(1), 6–16. doi: 10.1177/1558689809349691

Feldt, R. C., & Hensley, R. (2009). Recommendations for use of SQ3R in introductory psychology textbooks. *Education, 129*(4), 584–588.

Ferlazzo, L. (2011). Involvement or engagement? *Educational Leadership, 68*(8), 10–14.

Ferlazzo, L. (2012). Get organized around assets. *Educational Leadership, 69*(6), 44–48.

Final regulations amending basic HHS policy for the protection of human research subjects, 45 CFR, Pub. L. No. 16 § 46 8366-8392 (1981).

Finch, S. A., Wasserman, R., Nabi-Burza, E., Hipple, B., Oldendick, R., & Winickoff, J. P. (2015). Overcoming challenges in the changing environment of practice-based research. *Annals of Family Medicine, 13*(5), 475–479. doi: 10.1370/afm.1809

Fischer, C. T. (2009). Bracketing in qualitative research: Conceptual and practical matters. *Psychotherapy Research, 19*(4/5), 583–590. doi: 10.1080/10503300902798375

Fisher, R. A. (1921). On the "probable error" of a coefficient of correlation deduced from a small sample. *Metron, 1*, 3–32.

Fleck, L. (1979). *Genesis and development of a scientific fact* (F. Bradley & T. J. Trenn, Trans.). Chicago, IL: University of Chicago Press.

Fogerty, J. C. (1970). Who'll stop the rain? On *Cosmo's Factory*. San Francisco, CA: Fantasy Records.

Foldes-Busque, G., Hamel, S., Belleville, G., Fleet, R., Poitras, J., Chauny, J.-M., . . . Marchand, A. (2016). Factors associated with pain level in noncardiac chest pain patients with comorbid panic disorder. *BioPsychoSocial Medicine, 10*, 1–8. doi: 10.1186/s13030-016-0081-5

Frank, J. (1981). Social psychology and the prevention of nuclear war: What is our responsibility? *SASP Newsletter, 7*(2), 8.

Friedman, M. (1937). The use of ranks to avoid the assumption of normality implicit in the analysis of variance. *Journal of the American Statistical Association, 32* (200), 675–701. doi: 10.2307/2279372

Frost, M. H., Reeve, B. B., Liepa, A. M., Stauffer, J. W., & Hays, R. D. (2007). What is sufficient evidence for the reliability and validity of patient-reported outcome measures? *Value Health, 10*(Supplement 2), S94–S105. doi: 10.1111/j.1524-4733.2007.00272.x

Galton, F. (1886). Regression towards mediocrity in hereditary stature. *The Journal of the Anthropological Institute of Great Britain and Ireland, 15*, 246–263.

Geertz, C. (1973). *Interpretation of cultures.* New York, NY: Basic Books.

Gejman, P. V., & Weilbaecher, A. (2002). History of the eugenic movement. *Israel Journal of Psychiatry and Related Sciences, 39*(4), 217–232.

Gergen, K. J., Josselson, R., & Freeman, M. (2015). The promises of qualitative inquiry. *American Psychologist, 70*(1), 1–9. doi: http://dx.doi.org/10.1037

Gille, F., Smith, S., & Mays, N. (2015). Why public trust in health care systems matters and deserves greater research attention. *Journal of Health Services Research & Policy, 20*(1), 62–64. doi: 10.1177/1355819 614543161

Gilligan, P., Bhatarcharjee, C., Knight, G., Smith, M., Hegarty, D., Shenton, A., Todd, F., & Bradley, P. (2005). To lead or not to lead? Prospective controlled study of emergency nurses' provision of advanced life support team leadership. *Emergency Medicine Journal, 22*(9), 628–632.

Glaser, B. G., & Strauss, A. L. (1967). *The discovery of grounded theory: Strategies for qualitative research.* Chicago, IL: Aldine Publishing Company.

Glass, G. V. (1976). Primary, secondary, and meta-analysis of research. *Educational Researcher, 5,* 3–8.

Glass, G. V., McGraw, B., & Smith, M. L. (1981). *Meta-analysis in social research.* Beverly Hills, CA: SAGE.

Gnoth, J., & Zins, A. H. (2013). Developing a tourism cultural contact scale. *Journal of Business Research, 66*(6), 738–744. doi: 10.1016/j.jbucsres.2011.09.012

Gone, J. P. (2015). Reconciling evidence-based practice and cultural competence in mental health services: Introduction to a special issue. *Transcultural Psychiatry, 52*(2), 139–149. doi: 10.1177/1363461514 568239

Goodman, L. A. (1961). Snowball sampling. *Annals of Mathematical Statistics, 32*(1), 148–170. doi: 10.1214/aoms/1177705148

Gorden, R. L. (1969). *Interviewing: Strategy, techniques, and tactics.* Homewood, IL: Dorsey.

Gorman, H. M., & Dane, F. C. (1994). Balancing methodological rigour and ethical treatment: The necessity of voluntary, informed consent. In P. P. DeDeyn (Ed.), *Animal and human experimentation* (pp. 35–41). London, England: John Libbey.

Goyder, J. (1985). Face-to-Face interviews and mailed questionnaires: The net difference in response rate. *Public Opinion Quarterly, 49*(2), 234.

Guerra, F., Stringhini, S., Vollenweider, P., Waeber, G., & Marques-Vidal, P. (2015). Socio-demographic and behavioural determinants of weight gain in the Swiss population. *BMC Public Health, 15,* 73–73, 71p. doi: 10.1186/s12889-015-1451-9

Guthrie, D. M., Declercq, A., Finne-Soveri, H., Fries, B. E., & Hirdes, J. P. (2016). The health and well-being of older adults with dual sensory impairment (DSI) in four countries. *PLoS ONE, 11*(5), e0155073. doi: 10.1371/journal.pone.0155073

Guttman, L. L. (1944). A basis for scaling qualitative data. *American Sociological Review, 9,* 139–150.

Hagger, M. S., Wong, G. G., & Davey, S. R. (2015). A theory-based behavior-change intervention to reduce alcohol consumption in undergraduate students: Trial protocol. *BMC Public Health, 15*(1), 1–13. doi: 10.1186/s12889-015-1648-y

Hakel, K. (2015). Oscillating between conservation and investment: A grounded theory of students' strategies for optimizing personal resources. *Grounded Theory Review, 14*(1), 11–25.

Hall, W. J., Chapman, M. V., Lee, K. M., Merino, Y. M., Thomas, T. W., Payne, B. K., . . . Coyne-Beasley, T. (2015). Implicit racial/ethnic bias among health care professionals and its influence on health care outcomes: A systematic review. *American Journal of Public Health, 105*(12), e60–e76. doi: 10.2105/ajph.2015.302903

Hamdani, M. R., Valcea, S., & Buckley, M. R. (2014). The relentless pursuit of construct validity in the design of employment interviews. *Human Resource Management Review, 24*(2), 160–176. doi: 10.1016/j.hrmr.2013.07.002

Hampshire, K., Iqbal, N., Blell, M., & Simpson, B. (2014). The interview as narrative ethnography: Seeking and shaping connections in qualitative research. *International Journal of Social Research Methodology, 17*(3), 215–231. doi: 10.1080/13645579.2012.729405

Hansen, D. L., Holstein, B. E., & Hansen, E. H. (2009). "I'd rather not take it, but . . . ": Young women's perceptions of medicines. *Qualitative Health Research, 19*(6), 829–839. doi: 10.1177/1049732309335447

Harris, R., Bennett, J., & Ross, F. (2014). Leadership and innovation in nursing seen through a historical lens. *Journal of Advanced Nursing, 70*(7), 1629–1638. doi: 10.1111/jan.12325

Hatsumi, Y., Nozomu, M., Hidemitsu, S., & Kouhei, A. (2015). Reliability and validity of the workplace social distance scale. *Global Journal of Health Science, 7*(3), 46–51. doi: 10.5539/gjhs.v7n3p46

Hawkins, D. F. (1977). *Nonresponse in Detroit area study surveys: A ten-year analysis.* Chapel Hill, NC: Institute for Research in Social Sciences.

Hearnshaw, C. S. (1979). *Cyril Burt: Psychologist.* Ithaca, NY: Cornell University Press.

Helton, W. S., Funke, G. J., & Knott, B. A. (2014). Measuring workload in collaborative contexts: Trait versus state perspectives. *Human Factors, 56*(2), 322–332.

Higginbottom, G., & Lauridsen, E. I. (2014). The roots and development of constructivist grounded theory. *Nurse Researcher, 21*(5), 8–13, 16. doi: 10.7748/nr.21.5.8.e1208

Hill, C. T., Rubin, A., & Peplau, L. A. (1976). Breakups before marriage: The end of 103 affairs. *Journal of Social Issues, 32*(1), 147–168.

Holsti, O. R. (1968). Content analysis. In G. Lindzey & E. Aronson (Eds.), *The handbook of social psychology* (pp. 596–692). Menlo Park, CA: Addison-Wesley.

Howe, K. R. (1988). Against the quantitative–qualitative incomparability thesis, or, dogmas die hard. *Educational Researcher, 17*, 10–16.

Huber, J. A. (2004). A closer look at SQ3R. *Reading Improvement, 41*(2), 108–112.

Hudgins, T. A. (2015). Resilience, job satisfaction and anticipated turnover in nurse leaders. *Journal of Nursing Management, 24*(1), E62–E69. doi: 10.1111/jonm.12289

Hunt, M. (1974). *Sexual behavior in the 1970s.* Chicago, IL: Playboy.

Hurwitz, M., & Howell, J. (2014). Estimating causal impacts of school counselors with regression discontinuity designs. *Journal of Counseling & Development, 92*(3), 316–327. doi: 10.1002/j.1556-6676.2014.00159.x

Illingworth, P., & Parmet, W. E. (2015). Solidarity and health: A public goods justification. *Diametros: An Online Journal of Philosophy, 43*, 65–71. doi: 10.13153/diam.43.2015.715

Iqbal, M. R., Younis, M. U., & Saeed, H. (2015). Amyand's hernia: A case report. *The Professional Medical Journal, 22*(8), 1101–1103.

Jacobs, J. (1967). A phenomenological study of suicide notes. *Social Problems, 15*, 60–72.

Jairam, D., & Kiewra, K. A. (2009). An investigation of the SOAR study method. *Journal of Advanced Academics, 20*(4), 602–629.

Jairam, D., Kiewra, K. A., Rogers-Kasson, S., Patterson-Hazley, M., & Marxhausen, K. (2014). SOAR versus SQ3R: A test of two study systems. *Instructional Science, 42*(3), 409–420. doi: 10.1007/s11251-013-9295-0

James, W. (1907). *Pragmatism: A new name for some old ways of thinking.* New York, NY: Longman Green and Co.

Jansson, B. S., Nyamathi, A., Duan, L., Kaplan, C., Heidemann, G., & Ananias, D. (2015). Validation of the patient advocacy engagement scale for health professionals. *Research in Nursing & Health, 38*(2), 162–172. doi: 10.1002/nur.21638

Jenkins, K. E. (2003). Intimate diversity: The presentation of multiculturalism and multiracialism in a high-boundary religious movement. *Journal for the Scientific Study of Religion, 42*(3), 393–409.

Jewkes, R., Gibbs, A., Jama-Shai, N., Willan, S., Misselhorn, A., Mushinga, M., . . . Skiweyiya, Y. (2014). Stepping stones and creating futures intervention: Shortened interrupted time series evaluation of a behavioural and structural health promotion and violence prevention intervention for young people in informal settlements in Durban, South Africa. *BMC Public Health, 14*(1), 1–19. doi: 10.1186/1471-2458-14-1325

Johns, R., & Gorrick, J. (2016). Exploring the behavioural options of exit and voice in the exit interview process. *International Journal of Employment Studies, 24*(1), 25–41.

Johnson, R. B., & Onwuegbuzie, A. J. (2004). Mixed methods research: A research paradigm whose time has come. *Educational Researcher, 33*(7), 14–26.

Johnston, M., Dixon, D., Hart, J., Glidewell, L., Schröder, C., & Pollard, B. (2014). Discriminant content validity: A quantitative methodology for assessing content of theory-based measures, with illustrative applications. *British Journal of Health Psychology, 19*(2), 240–257.

Jones, C. A., Hoffman, M. R., Zhixian, G., Abdelhalim, S. M., Jiang, J. J., & McCulloch, T. M. (2014). Reliability of an automated high-resolution manometry analysis program across expert users, novice users, and speech-language pathologists. *Journal of Speech, Language & Hearing Research, 57*(3), 831–836. doi: 10.1044/2014_jslhr-s-13-0101

Jones, J. H. (1993). *Bad blood: The Tuskegee syphilis experiment.* New York, NY: Free Press.

Joshi, Y., Tripathi, M., Jinnah, Z., Bisht, K., & Upreti, D. K. (2016). Host specificity of epiphytic macrolichens: A case study of Jageshwar forest (Uttarakhand) India. *Tropical Ecology, 57*(1), 1–8.

Kamin, L. J. (1974). *The science and politics of IQ.* Potomac, MD: Erlbaum.

Kant, I. (1788/1997). *Critique of practical reason* (M. Gregor, Trans.). Cambridge, UK: Cambridge University Press.

Kaplan, B. G., Connor, A., Ferranti, E. P., Holmes, L., & Spencer, L. (2012). Use of an emergency preparedness disaster simulation with undergraduate nursing students. *Public Health Nursing, 29*(1), 44–51. doi: 10.1111/j.1525-1446.2011.00960.x

Kelley, H. H., & Thibault, J. W. (1978). *Interpersonal relations: A theory of interdependence.* New York, NY: Wiley-Interscience.

Kerlinger, F. N. (1973). *Foundations of behavioral science research.* New York, NY: Holt, Rinehart & Winston.

Kerr, N. L. (1998). HARKing: Hypothesizing after the results are known. *Personality and Social Psychology Review, 2*(3), 196–217.

Khoiriyah, U., Roberts, C., Jorm, C., & Van der Vleuten, C. P. M. (2015). Enhancing students' learning in problem based learning: Validation of a self-assessment scale for active learning and critical thinking. *BMC Medical Education, 15*(140), 1–8. doi: 10.1186/s12909-015-0422-2

Kiewra, K. A. (2005). *Learn how to study and SOAR to success.* Upper Saddle River, NJ: Pearson.

Kim, J. E., Gordon, S. L., Ferruzzi, M. G., & Campbell, W. W. (2015). Effects of egg consumption on carotenoid absorption from co-consumed, raw vegetables. *American Journal of Clinical Nutrition, 102*(1), 75–83. doi: 10.3945/ajcn.115.111062

Kimmelman, J. (2007). Inventors as investigators: The ethics of patents in clinical trials. *Academic Medicine, 82*(1), 24–31.

Kinsey, A., Pomeroy, W. B., & Martin, C. E. (1948). *Sexual behavior in the human male.* Philadelphia, PA: W. B. Saunders.

Kinsey, A., Pomeroy, W. B., Martin, C. E., & Gebhard, P. H. (1953). *Sexual behavior in the human female.* Philadelphia, PA: W. B. Saunders.

Kisaalita, N., Staud, R., Hurley, R., & Robinson, M. (2014). Placebo use in pain management: The role of medical context, treatment efficacy, and deception in determining placebo acceptability. *Pain (03043959), 155*(12), 2638–2645. doi: 10.1016/j.pain.2014.09.029

Klecka, W. R., & Tuchfarber, A. J. (1978). Random digit dialing: A comparison to personal survey. *Public Opinion Quarterly, 42*, 105–114.

Kontou, E., Thomas, S. A., & Lincoln, N. B. (2012). Psychometric properties of a revised version of the visual analog mood scales. *Clinical Rehabilitation, 26*(12), 1133–1140. doi: 10.1177/0269215512442670

Kounin, J., & Gump, P. (1961). The comparative influence of punitive and nonpunitive teachers upon children's concepts of school misconduct. *Journal of Educational Psychology, 52*, 44–49.

Kruskal, W., & Wallis, W. A. (1952). Use of ranks in one-criterion variance analysis. *Journal of the American Statistical Association, 47* (260), 583–621. doi: 10.1080/01621459.1952.10483441

Kuder, G. F., & Richardson, M. W. (1937). The theory of estimation of test reliability. *Psychometrica, 2*, 151–160.

Kuhn, T. (1962). *The structure of scientific revolution.* Chicago, IL: University of Chicago Press.

Kuncel, N. R., Hezlett, S. A., & Ones, D. S. (2001). A comprehensive meta-analysis of the predictive validity of the graduate record examinations: Implications for graduate student selection and performance. *Psychological Bulletin, 127*(1), 162–181.

Landon, 1,293,669: Roosevelt, 972,897. (1936). *The Literary Digest,* 5–6.

Lasswell, H. D., Lerner, D., & Pool, I. d. S. (1952). *The comparative study of symbols.* Stanford, CA: Stanford University Press.

Latané, B., & Liu, J. H. (1996). The intersubjective geometry of social space *Journal of Communication, 46*(4), 26–34.

Lea, S. E. G., & Webley, P. (2006). Money: Motivation, metaphors, and mores. *Behavioral and Brain Sciences, 29*(2), 196–204.

Leahey, T. H. (1980). The myth of operationism. *Journal of Mind and Behavior, 1*(2), 126–143.

Levin, J., & Spates, J. (1970). Hippie values: An analysis of the underground press. *Youth and Society, 2*, 59–72.

Lewin, K. (1946). Action research and minority problems. *Journal of Social Issues, 2*, 34–46.

Likert, R. (1932). A technique for the measurement of attitudes. *Archives of Psychology, 22*(140), 55.

Lindeman, R. H., Merenda, P. F., & Gold, R. (1980). *Introduction to bivariate and multivariate analysis.* New York, NY: Scott, Foresman, & Co.

Liu, Y., & Khine, M. S. (2016). Content analysis of the diagrammatic representations of primary science textbooks. *Eurasia Journal of Mathematics, Science & Technology Education, 12*(8), 1937–1951. doi: 10.12973/eurasia.2016.1288a

Logan, H., Wolfaardt, J., Boulanger, P., Hodgetts, B., & Seikaly, H. (2013). Pilot study: Evaluation of the use of the convergent interview technique in understanding the perception of surgical design and simulation. *Journal of Otolaryngology—Head & Neck Surgery, 42*(1), 40–46. doi: 10.1186/1916-0216-42-40

Malavige, L. S., Wijesekara, P., Seneviratne Epa, D., Ranasinghe, P., & Levy, J. C. (2015). Ethnicity and neighbourhood deprivation determines the response rate in sexual dysfunction surveys. *BMC Research Notes, 8*(1), 1–9. doi: 10.1186/s13104-015-1387-2

Mann, H. B., & Whitney, D. R. (1947). On a test of whether one of two random variables is stochastically larger than the other. *Annals of Mathematical Statistics, 18*(1), 50–60. doi: 10.1214/aoms/1177730491

Markowitz, D. M., & Hancock, J. T. (2014). Linguistic traces of a scientific fraud: The case of Diederik Stapel. *PLoS ONE, 9*(8), 1–5. doi: 10.1371/journal.pone.0105937

Markowitz, D. M., & Hancock, J. T. (2016). Linguistic obfuscation in fraudulent science. *Journal of Language & Social Psychology, 35*(4), 435–445. doi: 10.1177/0261927x15614605

Mastroianni, A. C., Faden, R., & Federman, D. (Eds.). (1999). *Women and health research: Ethical and legal issues of including women in clinical studies: Vol. 2. Workshop and commissioned papers.* Washington, DC: National Academy Press.

Mazurenko, O., Zemke, D., Lefforge, N., Shoemaker, S., & Menachemi, N. (2015). What determines the surgical patient experience? Exploring the patient, clinical staff, and administration perspectives. *Journal of Healthcare Management, 60*(5), 332–346.

McDougall, W. (1908). *Introduction to social psychology.* London, England: Methuen.

McHugo, G. J., Lanzetta, J. T., Sullivan, D. G., Masters, R. D., & Englis, B. G. (1985). Emotional reactivity to a political leader's expressive displays. *Journal of Personality and Social Psychology, 49*, 1513–1529.

McShane, B. B., & Bockenholt, U. (2016). Planning sample sizes when effect sizes are uncertain: The power-calibrated effect size approach. *Psychological Methods, 21*(1), 47–60. doi: 10.1037/met0000036

Mead, M. (1969). Research with human beings: A model derived from anthropological field practice. *Daedalus*, 361–386.

Mertens, D. M. (2010). Philosophy in mixed methods teaching: The transformative paradigm as illustration. *International Journal of Multiple Research Approaches, 4*(1), 9–18. doi: 10.5172/mra.2010.4.1.009

Merton, R. K., Fiske, M., & Kendall, P. L. (1956). *The focused interview.* Glencoe, IL: Free Press.

Merton, R. K., & Lazarsfeld, P. F. (Eds.). (1950). *Continuities in social research: Studies in the scope and method of "The American soldier."* New York, NY: Free Press.

Mesel, T. (2013). The necessary distinction between methodology and philosophical assumptions in healthcare research. *Scandinavian Journal of Caring Sciences, 27*(3), 750–756. doi: 10.1111/j.1471-6712.2012.01070.x

Milgram, S. (1963). Behavioral study of obedience. *Journal of Abnormal and Social Psychology, 67*(4), 371–378.

Miliotis, M., & Watkins, W. (2005). Quantitative risk assessment on the public health impact of pathogenic *Vibrio parahaemolyticus* in raw oysters (Executive Summary). Washington, DC: Food and Drug Administration. Retrieved from http://www.fda.gov/Food/ScienceResearch/ResearchAreas/RiskAssessmentSafetyAssessment/ucm050421.htm

Milsom, A., & Coughlin, J. (2015). Satisfaction with college major: A grounded theory study. *NACADA Journal, 35*(2), 5–14. doi: 10.12930/nacada-14-026

Mindick, B. (1982). When we practice to deceive: The ethics of metascientific inquiry. *The Brain and Behavioral Sciences, 5*(2), 226–227.

Mingnan, L. I. U., Sunghee, L. E. E., & Conrad, F. G. (2015). Comparing extreme response styles between agree–disagree and item-specific scales. *Public Opinion Quarterly, 79*(4), 952–975. doi: 10.1093/poq/nfv034

Mitchell, R. R., Tingstrom, D. H., Dufrene, B. A., Ford, W. B., Sterling, H. E., & VanDerHeyden, A. (2015). The effects of the good behavior game with general-education high school students. *School Psychology Review, 44*(2), 191–207.

Moore, D. A., & Loewenstein, G. (2004). Self-interest, automaticity, and the psychology of conflict of interest. *Social Justice Research, 17*(2), 189–202.

Moran, M. B., Lucas, M., Everhart, K., Morgan, A., & Prickett, E. (2016). What makes anti-vaccine websites persuasive? A content analysis of techniques used by anti-vaccine websites to engender anti-vaccine sentiment. *Journal of Communication in Healthcare, 9*(3), 151–163. doi: 10.1080/17538068.2016.1235531

Morris, D. (1971). *Intimate behaviour*. London, England: Jonathan Cape.

Morton, A. Q. (1963, November 3). A computer challenges the church. *The Observer*, p. 21.

Mosteller, F., & Wallace, D. L. (1964). *Inference and disputed authorship: The Federalist*. Reading, MA: Addison-Wesley.

Motter, J. N., Pimontel, M. A., Rindskopf, D., Devanand, D. P., Doraiswamy, P. M., & Sneed, J. R. (2016). Computerized cognitive training and functional recovery in major depressive disorder: A meta-analysis. *Journal of Affective Disorders, 189*, 184–191. doi: 10.1016/j.jad.2015.09.022

Munn, Z., Lockwood, C., & Moola, S. (2015). The development and use of evidence summaries for point of care information systems: A streamlined rapid review approach. *Worldviews on Evidence-Based Nursing, 12*(3), 131–138. doi: 10.1111/wvn.12094

Munsterberg, H. (1913). *On the witness stand*. New York, NY: Doubleday.

Murdoch, M., Simon, A. B., Polusny, M. A., Bangerter, A. K., Grill, J. P., Noorbaloochi, S., & Partin, M. R. (2014). Impact of different privacy conditions and incentives on survey response rate, participant representativeness, and disclosure of sensitive information: a randomized controlled trial. *BMC Medical Research Methodology, 14*, 90. doi: 10.1186/1471-2288-14-90

Muste, C. P. (2014). The implications of survey modes and methods in measuring social-group closeness. *Public Opinion Quarterly, 78*(4), 859–888. doi: 10.1093/poq/nfu025

National Commission for the Protection of Human Subjects of Biomedical and Behavioral Research. (1979). *The Belmont report: Ethical principles and guidelines for the protection of human subjects of research*. Washington, DC: Author.

Nederhof, A. J. (1981). *Some sources of artifact in social science research: Nonresponse, volunteering and research experience of subjects*. [PhD Doctoral Dissertation]. Rijksuniversiteit te Leiden, Leiden, Netherlands.

Neubauer, A. C., & Opriessnig, S. (2014). The development of talent and excellence—do not dismiss psychometric intelligence, the (potentially) most powerful predictor. *Talent Development & Excellence, 6*(2), 1–15.

Newell, S. M., Logan, H. L., Guo, Y., Marks, J. G., & Shepperd, J. A. (2015). Evaluating tablet computers as a survey tool in rural communities. *The Journal of Rural Health: Official Journal of the American Rural Health Association and the National Rural Health Care Association, 31*(1), 108–117. doi: 10.1111/jrh.12095

Nortje, N., & Hoffmann, W. A. (2015). Ethical misconduct by registered psychologists in South Africa during the period 2007–2013. *South African Journal of Psychology, 45*(2), 260–270. doi: 10.1177/0081246315571194

Nuremberg Military Tribunal. (1949). *Trials of war criminals before the Nuremberg military tribunals under Control Council Law No. 10* (Vol. 2). Washington, DC: Government Printing Office.

O'Donnell, L., Wilson-Simmons, R., Dash, K., Jeanbaptiste, V., Myint-U, A., Moss, J., & Stueve, Ann. (2007). Saving sex for later: Developing a parent–child communication intervention to delay sexual initiation among young adolescents. *Sex Education, 7*(2), 107–125.

Oermann, M. H., Kardong-Edgren, S. E., & Odom-Maryon, T. (2011). Effects of monthly practice on nursing students' CPR psychomotor skill performance. *Resuscitation*. doi: 10.1016/j.resuscitation.2010.11.022

Office for Human Research Protections. (2007). *International compilation of human subject research protections*. Retrieved from http://www.hhs.gov/ohrp/international/HSPCompilation.pdf

Okpala, C. O. (1996). Gender-related differences in classroom interaction. *Journal of Instructional Psychology, 23*(4), 275–285.

Oliveira, P. L. E., Motta, A. F. J. d., Guerra, C. J., & Mucha, J. N. (2015). Comparison of two scales for evaluation of smile and dental attractiveness. *Dental Press Journal of Orthodontics, 20*(2), 42–48. doi: 10.1590/2176-9451.20.2.042-048.oar

Orenstein, D. G., & Yang, Y. T. (2015). From beginning to end: The importance of evidence-based policymaking in vaccination mandates. *Journal of Law, Medicine & Ethics, 43*(1), 99–102. doi: 10.1111/jlme.12228

Osgood, C. E. (1959). The representational model and relevant research methods. In I. d. S. Pool (Ed.), *Trends in content analysis* (pp. 33–88). Urbana University of Illinois Press.

Osgood, C. E., Sporta, S., & Nunnally, J. C. (1956). Evaluative assertion analysis. *Litera, 3*, 47–52.

Osgood, C. E., Suci, G., & Tannenbaum, P. (1957). *The measurement of meaning*. Urbana: University of Illinois Press.

Pace, L. E., & Shulman, L. N. (2016). Breast cancer in sub-Saharan Africa: Challenges and opportunities to reduce mortality. *The Oncologist, 21*(6), 739–744. doi: 10.1634/theoncologist.2015-0429

Pachter, W. S., Fox, R. E., Zimbardo, P., & Antonuccio, D. O. (2007). Corporate funding and conflicts of interest: A primer for psychologists. *American Psychologist, 62*(9), 1005–1015.

Paolo, A. M., Bonaminio, G. A., Gibson, C., Partridge, T., & Kallail, K. (2000). Response rate comparisons of e-mail and mail-distributed student evaluations. *Teaching and Learning in Medicine, 12*, 81–84.

Parish, D. C., Dane, F. C., Montgomery, M., Wynn, L. J., Durham, M. D., & Brown, T. D. (2000). Resuscitation in the hospital: Relationship of year and rhythm to outcome. *Resuscitation, 47*(3), 219–229.

Parsons, T. (1951). *The social system*. New York, NY: Macmillan.

Patel, D., Devereaux, R. S., Teaford, G., Dane, F. C., Parish, D. C., Waring, M. E., & Kiefe, C. I. (2015). Medication adherence improves shortly after acute coronary syndrome admission and then declines over one year: Findings from TRACE-CORE. *Circulation: Cardiovascular Quality and Outcomes, 8*, A159.

Peirce, C. S. (1877). The fixation of belief. *Popular Science Monthly, 12*(November), 1–15.

Peirce, C. S. (1905). What pragmatism is. *The Monist, 15*(2), 161–181.

Peräkylä, A., & Ruusuvuori, J. (2011). Analyzing talk and text. In N. K. Denzin & Y. S. Lincoln (Eds.), *The SAGE handbook of qualitative research* (pp. 529–543). Los Angeles, CA: SAGE.

Peter, L. J. (1980). *Peter's quotations: Ideas for our time*. New York, NY: Bantam.

Phillips, D. (1971). *Knowledge from what? Theories and methods in social research*. Chicago, IL: Rand McNally.

Piaget, J. (1984). Piaget's theory. In P. Mussen (Ed.), *Handbook of child psychology* (4th ed., Vol. 1). New York, NY: Wiley.

Plato. (2005). *Early Socratic dialogues* (T. J. Saunders, Trans.). New York, NY: Penguin Classic.

Posavac, E. J. (1994). Misusing program evaluation by asking the wrong question. *New Directions for Program Evaluation, 1994*(64), 69–78.

Prentice, S., Taylor, P. J., Rayson, P., Hoskins, A., & O'Loughlin, B. (2011). Analyzing the semantic content and persuasive composition of extremist media: A case study of texts produced during the Gaza conflict. *Information Systems Frontiers, 13*(1), 61–73. doi: 10.1007/s10796-010-9272-y

Proctor, C., & Loomis, C. (1951). Analysis of sociometric data. In M. Jahoda, M. Deutsch, & S. Cook (Eds.), *Research methods in social relations* (pp. 561–586). New York, NY: Holt, Rinehart & Winston.

Prosser, W. L. (1964). *Handbook of the law of torts*. St. Paul, MN: West.

Protection of Human Subjects, 45 CFR 46 (2005).

Rahn, N. L., Wilson, J., Egan, A., Brandes, D., Kunkel, A., Peterson, M., & McComas, J. (2015). Using incremental rehearsal to teach letter sounds to English language learners. *Education & Treatment of Children, 38*(1), 71–91.

Ralph, N., Birks, M., & Chapman, Y. (2015). The methodological dynamism of grounded theory.

International Journal of Qualitative Methods, 14(4), 1–6. doi: 10.1177/1609406915611576

Rector, R. (2002). The effectiveness of abstinence education programs in reducing sexual activity among youth. [Electronic Version]. *The Heritage Foundation Backgrounder.* Retrieved January 2, 2008, from http://www.heritage.org/Research/Abstinence/BG1533.cfm

Rhodes, G., Halberstadt, J., Jeffery, L., & Palermo, R. (2005). The attractiveness of average faces is not a generalized mere exposure effect. *Social Cognition, 23*(3), 205–217.

Robinson, F. P. (1970). *Effective study* (4th ed.). New York, NY: Harper & Row.

Robinson-Wood, T., Balogun-Mwangi, O., Fernandes, C., Popat-Jain, A., Boadi, N., Atsushi, M., & Xiaolu, Z. (2015). Worse than blatant racism: A phenomenological investigation of microaggressions among Black women. *Journal of Ethnographic & Qualitative Research, 9*(3), 221–236.

Roche, W. P., III, Scheetz, A. P., Dane, F. C., Parish, D. C., & O'Shea, J. T. (2003). Medical students' attitudes in a PBL curriculum: Trust, altruism, and cynicism. *Academic Medicine, 78*(4), 398–402.

Rokeach, M., Homant, R., & Penner, L. (1970). A value analysis of the disputed federalist papers. *Journal of Personality and Social Psychology, 16,* 245–250.

Rooney, A. (1982). *And more by Andy Rooney.* New York, NY: Athenium.

Rosenthal, R., & Fode, K. L. (1963). The effect of experimenter bias on the performance of the albino rat. *Behavioral Science, 8*(3), 183–189.

Rosenthal, R., & Jacobson, L. (1966). Teachers' expectancies: Determinants of pupils' IQ gains. *Psychological Reports, 19,* 115–118.

Rounding, K., Jacobson, J. A., & Lindsay, R. C. L. (2014). Examining the effects of changes in depressive symptomatology on eyewitness identification. *Journal of Social & Clinical Psychology, 33*(6), 495–511. doi: 10.1521/jscp.2014.33.6.495

Rubin, D. B. (2001). Using propensity scores to help design observational studies: Application to the tobacco litigation. *Health Services & Outcomes Research Methodology, 2,* 169–188.

Rudnick, A. (2014). A philosophical analysis of the general methodology of qualitative research: A critical rationalist perspective. *Health Care Analysis, 22*(3), 245–254. doi: 10.1007/s10728-012-0212-5

Runyan, W. M. (1982). *Life histories and psychobiography: Explorations in theory and method.* New York, NY: Oxford University Press.

Rupp, D. E. (2011). Ethical issues faced by editors and reviewers. *Management & Organization Review, 7*(3), 481–493. doi: 10.1111/j.1740-8784.2011.00227.x

Russell, J. B. (1991). *Inventing the flat Earth.* Westport, CT: Praeger.

Sackett, D. L., Straus, S. E., Richardson, W. S., Rosenberg, W., & Haynes, R. B. (2000). *Evidence-based medicine: How to practice and teach EBM* (2nd ed.). Edinburgh, Scotland: Churchill Livingstone.

Sagan, C. (1980). *Cosmos.* New York, NY: Random House.

Sales, S. M. (1972). Economic threat as a determinant of conversion rates in authoritarian and nonauthoritarian churches. *Journal of Personality and Social Psychology, 23,* 420–428.

Sallee, M. W., & Flood, J. T. (2012). Using qualitative research to bridge research, policy, and practice. *Theory into Practice, 51*(2), 137–144. doi: 10.1080/00405841.2012.662873

Salvo, J., & Lobo, A. (2013). Misclassifying New York's hidden units as vacant in 2010: Lessons gleaned for the 2020 Census. *Population Research & Policy Review, 32*(5), 729–751. doi: 10.1007/s11113-013-9298-1

Sampasivam, S., Collins, K. A., Bielajew, C., & Clément, R. (2016). The effects of outgroup threat and opportunity to derogate on salivary cortisol levels. *International Journal of Environmental Research and Public Health, 13*(6). doi: 10.3390/ijerph13060616

Savarese, G., De Ferrari, G. M., Rosano, G. M. C., & Perrone-Filardi, P. (2015). Safety and efficacy of ezetimibe: A meta-analysis. *International Journal of Cardiology, 201,* 247–252. doi: 10.1016/j.ijcard.2015.08.103

Schmidt, S., & Eisend, M. (2015). Advertising repetition: A meta-analysis on effective frequency in advertising. *Journal of Advertising, 44*(4), 415–428. doi: 10.1080/00913367.2015.1018460

Seider, M. S. (1974). American big business ideology: A content analysis of executive speeches. *American Sociological Review, 39,* 802–815.

Seiler, L. H., & Murtha, J. M. (1981). Victory at HHS: Final regulations for the protection of human subjects of research provide a balanced compromise. *SASP Newsletter, 7*(2), 6–7.

Shadish, W. R., Cook, T. D., & Campbell, D. T. (2002). *Experimental and quasi-experimental designs for generalized causal inference*. Boston, MA: Houghton Mifflin.

Sheuya, S. A. (2010). *Informal settlements and finance in Dar es Salaam, Tanzania*. Nairobi, Kenya: United Nations Human Settlements Programme.

Shopes, L. (2011). Oral history. In N. K. Denzin & Y. S. Lincoln (Eds.), *The SAGE handbook of qualitative research* (pp. 451–465). Los Angeles, CA: SAGE.

Siahpush, M., Shaikh, R. A., Robbins, R., Tibbits, M., Kessler, A. S., Soliman, G., . . . Singh, G. K. (2016). Point-of-sale cigarette marketing and smoking-induced deprivation in smokers: Results from a population-based survey. *BMC Public Health, 16*, 1–8. doi: 10.1186/s12889-016-2992-2

Simon, R. J. (Ed.). (1975). *The jury system in America: A critical overview*. Beverly Hills, CA: SAGE.

Smith, S. (2016). (Re)Counting meaningful learning experiences: Using student-created reflective videos to make invisible learning visible during PjBL experiences. *Interdisciplinary Journal of Problem-Based Learning, 10*(1), 2–16. doi: 10.7771/1541-5015.1541

Smyth, J. D., Dillman, D. A., Christian, L. M., & McBride, M. (2009). Open-ended questions in web surveys. *Public Opinion Quarterly, 73*(2), 325–337.

Snelgrove, S. R. (2014). Conducting qualitative longitudinal research using interpretative phenomenological analysis. *Nurse Researcher, 22*(1), 20–25.

Snyder, M. (1987). *Public appearances and private realities*. New York, NY: W. H. Freeman.

Solomon, R. L. (1949). An extension of control group design. *Psychological Bulletin, 46*, 137–150.

Spoorenberg, S. L. W., Wynia, K., Fokkens, A. S., Slotman, K., Kremer, H. P. H., & Reijneveld, S. A. (2015). Experiences of community-living older adults receiving integrated care based on the chronic care model: A qualitative study. *PLoS ONE, 10*(10), 1–21. doi: 10.1371/journal.pone.0137803

Stager, S. V., Freeman, F. J., & Brauna, A. (2015). Characteristics of fluency and speech in two families with high incidences of stuttering. *Journal of Speech,* *Language & Hearing Research, 58*, 1440–1451. doi: 10.1044/2015_jslhr-s-14-0080

Steeh, C. G. (1981). Trends in nonresponse rates, 1952–1979. *Public Opinion Quarterly, 45*, 40–57.

Stephenson, W. (1953). *The study of behavior*. Chicago, IL: University of Chicago Press.

Stevens, S. S. (1946). On the theory of scales of measurement. *Science, 103*(2684), 677–680.

Stone, G. R. (2002). Discussion: Above the law: Research methods, ethics, and the law of privilege. *Sociological Methodology, 32*, 19–27.

Stone, W. L., & LaGreca, A. M. (1991). Social standing and children with learning disabilities. *Adapted Physical Activity Quarterly, 8*(2), 103–103.

Strandberg, E. L., Brorsson, A., André, M., Gröndal, H., Mölstad, S., & Hedin, K. (2016). Interacting factors associated with low antibiotic prescribing for respiratory tract infections in primary health care—a mixed methods study in Sweden. *BMC Family Practice, 17*, 1–10. doi: 10.1186/s12875-016-0494-z

Strang, A. F., & Baia, P. (2016). An investigation of teaching and learning programs in pharmacy education. *American Journal of Pharmaceutical Education, 4*, 1–15.

Strauss, M. E., & Smith, G. T. (2009). Construct validity: Advances in theory and methodology. *Annual Review of Clinical Psychology, 5*, 1–25. doi: 10.1146/annurev.clinpsy.032408.153639

Student (William Sealy Gossett). (1908). The probable error of a mean. *Biometrika, 6*(1), 1–25.

Svara, J. (2007). *The ethics primer for public administrators in government and nonprofit organizations*. Sudbury, MA: Jones and Bartlett.

Talbot, E. P., & McMillin, J. A. (2014). The social work reinvestment initiative: Advocacy and social work practice. *Social Work, 59*(3), 201–210.

Taylor, R. W., Roy, M., Jospe, M. R., Osborne, H. R., Meredith-Jones, K. J., Williams, S. M., & Brown, R. C. (2015). Determining how best to support overweight adults to adhere to lifestyle change: Protocol for the SWIFT study. *BMC Public Health, 15*, 861–861 861p. doi: 10.1186/s12889-015-2205-4

Thistlethwaite, D. L., & Campbell, D. T. (1960). Regression–discontinuity analysis: An alternative to the ex post facto experiment. *Journal of Educational Psychology, 51*, 309–317. doi: 10.1037/h0044319

Thompson, W. T., Cupples, M. E., Sibbett, C. H., Skan, D. I., & Bradley, T. (2001). Challenge of culture, conscience, and contract to general practitioners' care of their own health: Qualitative study. *BMJ, 323*(7315), 728–731. doi: 10.1136/bmj.323.7315.728

Thurstone, L. L. (1929). Theory of attitude measurement. *Psychological Bulletin, 36*, 222–241.

Thurstone, L. L. (1931). The measurement of social attitudes. *Journal of Abnormal and Social Psychology, 26*, 249–269.

Thurstone, L. L., & Chave, E. J. (1929). *The measurement of attitudes.* Chicago, IL: University of Chicago Press.

Tong, A., Sainsbury, P., & Craig, J. (2007). Consolidated criteria for reporting qualitative research (COREQ): A 32-item checklist for interviews and focus groups. *International Journal for Quality in Health Care, 19*(6), 349–357. doi: 10.1093/intqhc/mzm042

Tukey, J. W. (1977). *Exploratory data analyses.* Reading, MA: Addison-Wesley.

Tunnell, G. B. (1977). Three dimensions of naturalness: An expanded definition of field research. *Psychological Bulletin, 84*, 426–437.

Union of Concerned Scientists. (2006). *Scientific knowledge on abstinence-only education distorted.* [Electronic Version]. Retrieved January 2, 2008, from http://www.ucsusa.org/scientific_integrity/interference/abstinenceonly-education.html? print=t

United States Bureau of the Census. (1979). *Statistical abstracts of the United States.* Washington, DC: Government Printing Office.

Uttl, B., White, C. A., & Gonzalez, D. W. (2016). Meta-analysis of faculty's teaching effectiveness: Student evaluation of teaching ratings and student learning are not related. *Studies in Educational Evaluation.* doi: http://dx.doi.org/10.1016/j.stueduc.2016.08.007

Vacca, R. T., & Vacca, J. A. L. (1999). *Content area reading: Literacy and learning across the curriculum.* New York, NY: Longman.

Veer, K., Ommundsen, R., Yakushko, O., Higler, L., Woelders, S., & Hagen, K. (2013). Psychometrically and qualitatively validating a cross-national cumulative measure of fear-based xenophobia. *Quality & Quantity, 47*(3), 1429–1444. doi: 10.1007/s11135-011-9599-6

Versi, E. (1992). "Gold standard" is an appropriate term. *British Medical Journal, 305*(6846), 187.

Voicu, M.-C., & Babonea, A.-M. (2011). Using the snowball method in marketing research on hidden populations. *Challenges of the Knowledge Society, 1*, 1341–1351.

Wachter, K. W., & Straf, M. L. (Eds.). (1990). *The future of meta-analysis.* New York, NY: Russell Sage Foundation.

Wallace, J. E., & Lemaire, J. (2009). Physician well-being and quality of patient care: An exploratory study of the missing link. *Psychology, Health & Medicine, 14*(5), 545–552. doi: 10.1080/1354850 0903012871

Wartofsky, M. W. (1968). *Conceptual foundations of scientific thought.* New York, NY: Macmillan.

Watson, R. I. (1967). Psychology: A prescriptive science. *American Psychologist, 22*, 435–443.

Weimer, W. B. (1979). *Notes on the methodology of scientific research.* Hillsdale, NJ: Erlbaum.

White, A. M. (2004). Lewin's action research model as a tool for theory building: A case study from South Africa. *Action Research, 2*(2), 127–144.

Wilcoxon, F. (1945). Individual comparisons by ranking methods. *Biometrics Bulletin, 1* (6), 80–83.

World Medical Association. (1964). Declaration of Helsinki. *British Medical Journal, 313*(7070), 1448–1449.

Yarborough, M. (2014). Openness in science is key to keeping public trust. *Nature, 515*(7527), 313–313. doi: 10.1038/515313a

Young, I., Waddell, L., Harding, S., Greig, J., Mascarenhas, M., Sivaramalingam, B., . . . Papadopoulos, A. (2015). A systematic review and meta-analysis of the effectiveness of food safety education interventions for consumers in developed countries. *BMC Public Health, 15*, 822–822 821p. doi: 10.1186/s12889-015-2171-x

Zimbardo, P. G., & Meadow, W. (1974, April). *Sexism springs eternal—in the Reader's Digest.* Paper presented at the Western Psychological Association, San Francisco, California.

Author Index

Subject Index

About the Author

Francis C. Dane received a BS in psychology from the University of Wisconsin–Milwaukee and a PhD in social psychology from the University of Kansas. His advisor was Larry Wrightsman, and he has certainly followed in Dr. Wrightsman's footsteps in terms of staying active in publishing and doing research. He started as assistant professor of psychology at State University of New York in Oswego, New York, from 1979 to 1983. He moved to Clemson University in South Carolina from 1983 to 1988, where he was promoted to associate professor of psychology, and then moved to Mercer University in Macon, Georgia, where he was associate professor and department chair of psychology. He stayed at Mercer as the William Heard Kilpatrick professor of psychology in the college of liberal arts and as professor of internal medicine at Mercer University School of Medicine until 2002. He then became the inaugural James V. Finkbeiner endowed chair of ethics and public policy in the college of arts and behavioral sciences at Saginaw Valley State University in University Center, Michigan, until 2010, after which he accepted his current position, chair of arts and sciences at Jefferson College of Health Sciences in Roanoke, Virginia. He can be reached via e-mail at fcdane@jchs.edu and followed on Twitter as @FrankDaneDoc.